Ramlin Rose

Ramlin Rose

THE BOATWOMAN'S STORY

SHEILA STEWART

Illustrated by
DAVID MILLER

OXFORD UNIVERSITY PRESS
1993

Oxford University Press, Walton Street, Oxford OX2 6DP

Oxford New York Toronto
Delhi Bombay Calcutta Madras Karachi
Kuala Lumpur Singapore Hong Kong Tokyo
Nairobi Dar es Salaam Cape Town
Melbourne Auckland Madrid
and associated companies in
Berlin Ibadan

Oxford is a trade mark of Oxford University Press

Text © Sheila Stewart 1993
Illustrations © Oxford University Press 1993

British Library Cataloguing in Publication Data
Data available

ISBN 0–19–212326–2

Typeset by Cambridge Composing (UK) Ltd
Printed in Great Britain
on acid-free paper by
Biddles Ltd.
Guildford and King's Lynn

For ADA
and Jenny and
all the other 'Roses'
who 'stroved' to be
Best-Mates to their husbands
Best-Mums to their families
and kept their cabins like castles

PREFACE

I WAS amazed when Old Mont, the Enstone farm labourer whose life-story I wrote in *Lifting the Latch* (OUP, 1987), told me that even in the late 1920s he was still trundling cross-country in a horse and cart to collect the coke for Spelsbury church brought to Enslow Wharf by canal boat. By then Spelsbury was well served by rail at Charlbury and by road through Enstone.

'Were there families living on those boats, Mont?'

'Yes, Mam, women bringing up their childern.'

However did a boat-mother cope? I wondered. Who helped her when she had her babies? Where did she put her children to sleep? Did she sing to them? Tell them stories? Which stories? How did she stop them falling in? How did she do her cooking? Washing? Shopping?

I knew nothing about canals. I knew the Washerwoman character in *Toad* because I loved *The Wind in the Willows* when I was a child but I had never been on a 'barge' or a canal. Mont was in his eighties; those boatwomen he used to see at work on the Oxford Canal must now be in their eighties and nineties. If nobody had captured a boatwoman's life-story it would soon be too late. I resolved to find a woman born and bred on a horse-drawn boat on the Oxford Canal and write her life-story.

It had to be 'the Oxford' because that was my nearest canal. I knew from my experience of writing Mont's story how expensive and time-consuming driving miles every week to gather material could be. My nearest canal town was Banbury. I put a letter in the *Banbury Guardian* stating my aim and asking if anybody knew of such a person or could give me any helpful information. Jenny Glynn (née Littlemore) was the first to reply.

'I was born on a narrow-boat at Tusses Bridge on the North Oxford Canal but we came off the boats when I was ten. My mother was born and bred on the boats and raised six of us on the boat. Both my grandmothers and great-grandmothers were boatwomen. I'm delighted that you are writing this book. For so long the boatwoman has been looked upon as being dirty and foul-mouthed. There were some like that but in the main the ones we knew were very different. I've long felt this story ought to be told. I will do all in my power to help you.'

It was Jenny who led me to her mother, Ada Littlemore (née Mellor).

Margaret Curtis (née Hartree) wrote: 'I was not born on a boat but my mother was. She is elderly and very tired at the moment because my father has had a stroke but she is willing to talk to you.'

Through Margaret I met Mary Hartree (née Humphries), and Mary led me to others. 'Just tell 'em that Mary *Humphries* sent yer, moy dear, and *you'll be all right!*'

I felt very honoured to be welcomed and trusted by them. There are very few of them left. Some were willing to talk but did not want to be identified, fearing that the stigma of their illiteracy and impoverished beginnings might still reflect upon their educated and more accomplished children. Some would look to their husband to answer my questions: it was traditional for a woman not to have a 'say-so', as they call it, if a man was present. Some were not willing for me to use 'that theer' (my tape recorder), fearing it might loose the supernatural into the room around us. Only one refused to talk to me. Nearly fifty years earlier she had been blamed in the distressing inquest on the death of her child and was afraid I had come to re-open the case.

I could tune in to their dialect but I knew nothing about canals or boats. I had to read a tremendous amount of background material to understand what they were talking about. Eventually I discovered that though many books had been written about canals they were nearly all by men and mostly extolled their history and engineering. The few written by women were mostly by cultured independent women who had bravely volunteered to work the boats in wartime. I started with a little book loaned by a friend, Joan Baylis. 'I bought it to read in the war, Sheila. It's on rather scruffy paper because of the paper-rationing, but you might find it helpful.' I did not *then* appreciate that I was reading a precious first edition of *Narrow Boat* by L. T. C. Rolt.

From *Narrow Boat* I progressed to *British Canals, An Illustrated History* by 'somebody' called Charles Hadfield. This copy, from our little local library at Shipston, was published in 1959. I wondered if the writer were still alive. I wrote to him via his publisher explaining my project and to ask where I might find the various

Victorian books and tracts on the social conditions of the boat-children mentioned in his excellent book. This famous expert, who has written books on nearly every canal system in the world, still found time to help an unknown ignoramus like me.

'I wish you every success in your project which should fill a serious gap in our knowledge of the canal people. I have contacted Dr Mark Baldwin who has all the works you need in his Antiquarian Bookshop at Cleobury Mortimer. He is willing for you to study them on the premises providing you make an appointment. His telephone number is . . .' Mark and his wife made me very welcome and Mark launched me on an intensive reading course.

How fortunate we are to be able to read.

Reading expands our knowledge of life far beyond the bounds of our own experience. It revives long-forgotten memories, gives us the words to express deep emotions, to describe scenes and characters, to joke and converse. The illiterate boatwoman has none of these riches, no picture of the shape of a word, no concept of the pattern of her patter upon the page, the lie of the land on a map. We say 'up' North because we visualize the North lying towards the top of the map, she says 'down the North' because of the drop in the level of the Cut. All her hard narrow life was lived at Cut level.—Hardly ever composes a complete sentence—speaks in phrases—which makes for very disjointed reading. In the end I had to give up my original aim, take writer's licence and weave the memories of several women into a complete story. I could not find a single one who could furnish me with enough memories to compose her biography, though each prided herself on belonging to a traditional boat family, remembered who was related to whom among the canal community, and never forgot a kindness. We must realize that whereas the illiterate woman 'on the bank' often remained all her life within the one community, constantly meeting and conversing with other friends and relations, seeing re-enactments of parish events and family photos which strengthened her memories of the past, the illiterate boatwoman (without a *pied-à-terre* on the bank) was nearly always on the move on the water and had little chance or cabin space to garner mementoes. She had very few points of reference outside of her own narrow existence on which to pin memories. She had only what L. T. C. Rolt calls 'the slender threads of folk memory' which were often cut at a tender age when she was sent away from Mum and Gran to work on another boat.

After all those scholarly and meticulously researched factual books I had read about the canals I felt a complete failure in 'opting-out' to fiction until I read Mark Baldwin's reassuring words in his *Canal Books*: '*Some of the more solemn collectors of canal books reject canal fiction, regarding it as unworthy of serious attention. This is narrow-minded; a novel may not contain facts upon which one would rely, but its very publication is a historical fact, and its portrayal of the waterway scene is an encapsulation of the feelings of the author towards his subject.*'

Rose Ramlin did not exist. She is a composite of several boat-women most of whom were born and bred on the Oxford Canal and worked on horse-drawn narrow-boats during the first half of the twentieth century. Conditions on the Oxford, with its more rural landscape and higher proportion of owner-boatmen, probably brought about a more caring type of woman than the harsher image usually conjured up on the barges or on the industrial Cuts of London and the North. Many of those 'Roses' must have been equally courageous in raising their families on the boats. Where I have used real boatwomen I have kept as closely as possible to the original recordings I was privileged to make with them, sometimes putting their words into Rose's mouth, and sometimes letting them speak for themselves. This story is intended as a tribute to them all.

ACKNOWLEDGEMENTS

I WOULD like to thank my husband for his unfailing patience and encouragement with my writing; David Miller, who has collaborated so well with his delightful illustrations; writers of all those well-known canal books, too numerous to mention, which have helped in my research, particularly Charles Hadfield, who kindly put me in touch with M. and M. Baldwin's excellent stock of antiquarian, out-of-print, and second-hand waterway books at Cleobury Mortimer; the Centre for Oxfordshire Studies; Banbury Museum; Nan Neal; Elizabeth Sleight of The Book Shop, Chipping Norton; all who have supplied photographs; all those 'on the bank' who have kindly allowed me to use them as true characters in my story; and the following boatwomen, all of whom are now off the boats: Ada Littlemore, her sister Harriet, and her daughter Jenny; the late Rose Beauchamp and her daughters Phyllis and Rose; Lizzie Hone and her daughter Rose; Mary Hartree (née Humphries); Rose Whitlock and Laura Carter. Ada has been my chief mentor, but the responsibility for what I have written is mine and mine alone.

Sheila Stewart, Brailes, 1992

CONTENTS

Jinny 185

Spare h'Admirals 195

On the Bank 208

APPENDIX

Jenny's Essay 219

Maps and Diagrams 223

LIST OF PLATES

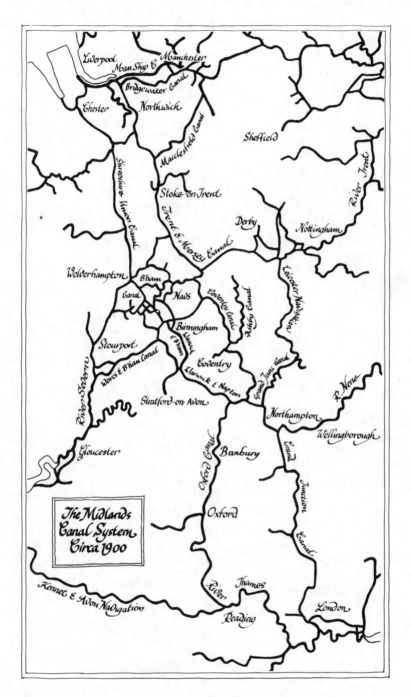

The Midlands
Canal System
Circa 1900

The boat people in the past had few friends and many enemies
. . . The owners of boats also complained of them for pilfering,
bartering coals from cargoes for food and drink, dumping coal
in rivers to lighten barges . . . and spending money in public
houses that had been given them to pay tolls, *while their good
service and hard laborious work remained unrecorded.*

Charles Hadfield, *British Canals, An Illustrated History*

It was the women who gave stability to this community . . .
*So much of the strivings of ordinary men and women escapes
the record* . . .

Mary Prior, *Fisher Row: Fishermen, Bargemen and
Canal Boatmen in Oxford, 1500–1800*

Ramlin Rose

Ilda 'Takes a Look'

THE day the mule fell in the Cut I knew I was born.

'Rose Mella,' Miss Sticks said to me, peerin her titchy wire specs over my tattered School Attendance Book, 'today is your birthday. Eight summers ago, on July 4th, nineteen hundred, you were born.'

It was the first *I'd* heard of it. I never knew I were borned. [*Rose never knew her name was Mellor neither, nor that 'Miss Sticks' was Miss Selina Dix. Rose was born on a horsedrawn narrow-boat on the Oxford Canal and couldn't read or write.*]

I know I miss-muddles words. It's a job to trim 'em oop when you ent never seed 'em. You missed out on a lot, livin on the boats, specially in them days before the grammerfone and the 'cumulated wireless sets. You missed out on birthdays, that's for sure! Too many mouths to feed to tally birthdays. Most of all you missed out on the schoolin, the power to read and rite, to *picture* words. That's the one thing I ankered after all me boatin life, the schoolin. Ooo! I would dearly love to of been proper-schooled.

I can't remember how old the mule was. Dad said she were borned in the haydays of Queen Victoria. And she was old cos she

kept her ears steady, didn't fidget 'em about like a young 'un, 'cept
when it were goin to rain. And she was a gal.

' 'Ow can yer tell she's a gal, Dad?'

'Cos 'er name's Ilda.'

Nobody never learned yer nothin about sex-n-birth in them days.
Just as well. A mule takes some explainin. A mule is a noffspring
tween a mare and a jack [*male donkey*] and can't usually have no
noffspring of its own. Years later I discovered our Ilda was called
after my Dad's Stowell Great Aunt Hilda 'who had the looks of a
donkey and the strength of a n'orse'. *She* never had no noffspring
neither.

The morning Ilda fell in the Cut we was on the Coventry [*Canal*].
We'd a load of grain from London docks bound for Robinson Powers
[*Robins and Power's granary in Coventry Basin*]. The night before
we'd tied-oop at Sutton Stop, where the h'Oxford joins the Coventry. They calls it 'Awkesbury Junction but we calls it Sutton Stop
after all the generations of Suttons wot kept the inn in the olden
times before the Beesleys and the Nelsons. We'd fetched her out
early that mornin from the stables and after her usual strainin and
stampin we was well away. That's always the hardest part of
draughtin for a mule or a n'orse, startin a fully-loaded boat, once
under way the water takes the weight. Dad would help by runnin
the tow round a moorin stump or bollard to help her take the
strain. Ilda would test the ground to get a good foothold, hang all
her weight into her collar, then stagger ahead until the boat began
to swim and she could ease into her steady gait along the towpath.
'Stubborn as a mule', folk say. It depends wot the mule has to put
oop with. When the hanimal's doin her level best to earn yer a livin
there ent no sense in knockin her about. Dad laid on the language
but seldom the whip. Ilda was the prime earner in our family.
Without Ilda we'd all be oop the crick.

I was on the steerin that mornin, standin on the stool Dad had
fixed for me in the slide-'ole so I could see over the roof of the cabin
and along the planks above the sheeted-oop wheat to the Cut
beyond. The hatch doors was fastened behind me to stop me fallin
into the starn [*stern*]. It's a tricky job for a child, steerin a cargo of
wheat, it can shift if yer not careful and capsize yer boat, specially
in wind.

All was plain sailin on that calm summer's morn, with no locks to work and Mum takin over at the bridge-'oles [*through the arch of each bridge*]. Time and again when I was a kiddy I recall people pointin from banks and bridges, 'Look at that little girl steering that great long boat!'

Most boat-children comed early to steerin. Steerin comed nat'ral, part of yer, like breathin. You was never really children, you was another pair of hands.

All along the Coventry there was big stones tellin' my Dad how many miles to the Basin and how many miles it was back the other way to the end of the canal. The church clocks told him the time.

Nigh past the stroke of eight we came oop agen Foze'll [*agen = against, i.e. close to Foleshill*]. In them days before the gasworks came Foze'll was only a little village, though the trams was creepin out from Coventry. The steam lorries was wrestin more and more traffic orf the canals but there was still a fair bit of horsedrawn traffic for Dad to meet and juggle the towrope. Though we had only the one boat in those days we had right of way cos we was goin *in* to Coventry and we was loaded. My Dad was a Number One [*owned his own boat*], Captain Dick Mella of the 'Percy Veruns', and my Mum, Rose Mella, was his Best-Mate [*wife*].

Mum was in the cabin with my two younger brothers, Albert and Ezme. I could just remember my two elder brothers, Eloy and Aymus [*Eli and Amos*], but they was away workin other boats. We always done it that way on the boats; when you was too many or too old to all sleep in the one cabin you was sent away to help other boat couples who was gettin too old to manage or had no children of their own. We was just the right squeeze in our cabin, me and Alby and Esme on the sidebed, and Mum and Dad on the crossbed.

I was their little right hand. I always got oop early, helped Dad to get Ilda from the stable and get the boat on the move while Mum packed away the crossbed into the bed-'ole cupboard and got the range goin.

I could tell by the stoked-oop factry chimneys and the trams hurryin to work over the bridges that we was gettin in to Coventry. There was a school I'd tended once or twice, I couldn't tell zackly where from the Cut because of the wharfs and ware'uses in between but I could sense we was gettin there and it would soon be marchin-in time.

'Can I go school today, Mum, ay? Take Alby, ay?'

'You know what yer Dad always says, Rose, *wait till we gets there.*'

'If we waits till we gets right to the Basin it'll be too late, they'll be all led in. If me and Alby gets orf at Priestley's Bridge, like we done afore, you and Dad can take the boat on round into the Basin and while yer unloadin me and Alby can snatch a mornin's schoolin. Can I, ay? Go on, Mum, ay?'

'Give over, Rose! Watch where yer steerin! Wait till we stops for the Basin, yer Dad's goin as fast as he can.'

Dad was keepin oop with Ilda's two miles-n-hour. Some boatmen drove their hanimal from the rear, Dad always walked beside the head. Ilda was havin her nostern [*feeding from her nose-tin*]. Dad believed in feedin her little and often. She didn't usually have it while she was walkin along, she had it while she was idle waitin for us to work the locks, but there's no locks along there and she couldn't come into the Basin. Dad had to take her orf to the stables and come back and shaft the boat under the bridge into the Basin. He wanted to make sure she had her feed but he didn't want to risk leavin the nostern at the stables. It was a metal bowl servin as a nosebag. Ourn was very old, pretty painted, with two metal rings hinged to the sides, and two straps to buckle over her head. It looped over her ears to another small strap on her gear [*harness*]. You had to buckle it just right, too long and she couldn't reach her breakfast, too short and she'd breathe it oop her—BANG!

Nobody seed where the cobble shied from. *Somebody* shied it, *that's* for sure! You was always a sittin target on the boats; airguns, chamberpots, street cobbles. This one grazed Dad's cap and hit Ilda BANG on the nostern. Poor Ilda! Thought her breakfast had exploded. One second, tuckin-in peaceful, the next,—in the Cut, thrashin for her life, drownin in her own nostern. Though Mum was just duckin down in the cabin she knew the second that tow 'went'. She snatched me down the steps—'STAY!'—and grabbed the tiller. I sat on the cabin floor starin oop the steps. I shall recall to my dyin day my Mum's face framed against the sky in her big black sunbonnet, the fear in her eyes, the set of her jaw, the powerful spread of her grasp on the tiller. It was takin all her strength and skill to steady the loaded craft and bring it alongside the bank without crushin Ilda.

A man's shout. Mum flung the rope. Somebody stayed us. Mum disappeared. I heard her boots makin their careful tread along the top planks, she didn't flit along as usual. She seemed to be gone ages. The littleones was cryin and I was longin to poke my head out the slide and see wot all the shoutin and rockin was about but Mum's 'STAY!' was still yellin in my ears. Just as well I didn't. Somebody pulled the starn in sharp, the rudder hit the bank, the big wooden tiller shot across. If I'd of been pokin my nose out of that slide it would of wopped my head orf. You learned young to do as you was told or get wopped on a boat.

Mum set-safe the tiller way-oop in its socket. A pair of boats had stopped astarn to help us. It was the Stathams' though I didn't know them well at that time. Ilda was standin sorry for herself on the towpath. It was the first time she'd ever 'taken a look' [fallen in the Cut]. Old Man Statham were chuckin water over her cleanin orf the weeds and muck. The nostern were hangin from one strap. Dad had struggled, lyin face down over the edge of the bank, to unbuckle the nostern. Ilda in her panic had kicked out, givin him a glancin blow on the nose. Luckily it was only a glancin blow and the rusty hinge of the can had broken else she'd of dragged Dad into the Cut and they could both of finished oop drownded. My poor Father was sittin slumped against a moorin stump holdin his neckerchif to his nose, blood all down the front of his weskut. Mum was sittin in the hatches holdin her stummick and rockin with shock. Alby and Ezme were howlin. I was tore which way to help.

'I'll make some tea, Mum, ay?'

'Get orf to school with Alby.' Mum's voice were very quiet.

I'd forgotten all about the schoolin. Suddenly I didn't want to go, didn't want to leave my Mum.

'Put on yer clean pinafore and take yer 'Tendance Books.' I knew when she spoke 'final' like that there were no answerin back. As soon as I opened the ticket-box to get the 'Tendance Books Alby's little face perked oop. He were just like a little puppy dog, go for a walk anytime.

'Come on, Alby.' I still didn't like leavin my Mum. 'Sure you'll manage without me, Mum, ay?'

'I'll manage.'

The Schoolin

ME and Alby scrambled oop the bank by Priestley's Bridge, through the little gate at the top, and clattered in our boots down the road to Arnle's Lane [*Harnall Lane*]. After the quiet tread of the towpath we always loved to clatter our boots on a real street; and we loved the lion's head drinkin fountain in Swansel Park [*Swanswell*]. When yer rationed to only so much water in a can on a boat a fountain can send yer excited. Us boat-children was always bein told orf for lettin water run and prancin round it. By the time I'd weaned Alby orf the fountain and away from the dooks [*ducks*] and clattered even louder along Wheatley Street they'd all led in.

'Rose Mella, why are you late?'

'Please, Miss Sticks, the mule took a look.'

Somebody giggled. We was always bein laughed at.

'*Took a look?*'

'Please, Miss Sticks, fell in the Cut.'

Somebody giggled again. SWISH! Her stick came down in warnin on her high desk. I don't know how many Girls-n-Infants was in that school, seemed to me oondreds. Miss Sticks ruled the lot. But she never caned us boat-children. For one thing we hardly dare open our mouths for fear of bein laughed at, and for another, she wanted us to come to school to be scholared.

She was a big woman in long black skirts, high stuffed bodice and big bustlin sleeves. In school she always weared a long black apron with a big pocket all across the bottom to hold her stick. Her hair was dark and screwed straight back into a bun. The boat families dreaded seein her bustlin along the warpath to where the boats was bein unloaded in Bishop Street basin, her little cape stiff, her big hat stabbed on with hatpins, to haul the children orf by lor to school. She never hauled me. I comed whenever I could, but as we had only the one boat we was never stopped for long. If I'd of 'ad the chance I'd of put me 'ole 'eart-n-sole into it.

She'd pore her titchy wire specs all over yer School 'Tendance

Book to see where else you'd picked oop a chance load o' learnin. It took some gettin; a few hours at the Brentford Mission Institute while we was bein loaded at the London end, a few hours at the Wyken Coalery or Wheatley Street Basin while we was loadin or unloadin at the Coventry end, was all the schoolin I got. They never catched yer at Banbury and h'Oxford. At Brentford they gived yer six pennorth of schoolin a week. If you couldn't manage to stop for a week's worth they let yer use it oop the next time. At the Wyken it were free. The school belonged to the coalery and they wanted us out of the way while the coal came tumblin dangerous out of their bogey-trucks into the hold. You was supposed by lor to take on board so many hours o' learnin each year. Nobody really gauged yer hours. We was more bother than we was worth to them h'Inspectors; moorin in their pound late at night and flittin on by next dawnin. The teachers had their regler hands full enough with forty to fifty kiddies at a sittin as it often was in those days. We was made to feel extra nuisance, croppin oop like mushrooms overnight and vanishin again before afternoon register. They'd hand yer a slate, 'Sit at the back and draw a boat'.

In the playground we was jeered at, 'Hee-haw! Hee-haw! The mule fell in the Cut!' 'Dirty boatees!' 'Lousy boatees!'

There *was* dirty boat families, we called 'em 'Rodneys' after them railroad rodneys, vagrans, wot rode rough on rail waggons. Like every other tribe in life we was some and some. Most of us was kept scrubbed regler with Wright's Coal Tar [*soap*] and Condey's Fluid [*disinfectant*]. Most busy wharfs, where they loaded or unloaded you, coverin you with dust, wouldn't allow yer to stop and have a wash. They wanted you out the way so the next boat could tie oop. It could be late by the time you had the chance to stop and have a good old clean oop. Coal carryin was the worst. Coaldust gets everywhere. You can taste it in yer mouth, breathe it in yer pores, smell it in yer chubes. No matter how well our Mum battened down the hatches with the clawths [*tarpaulins*] when we was loadin or unloadin coal it would sift into her clean cabin *somehow*.

Me and Alby was expectin to go back home to the boat for dinner that day at school but somebody gived us a slice of bread-n-lard and told us that as a special treat our Mum said we could stop till home time. By the end of the afternoon Alby was restin his head asleep on the desk. We was havin a story about a little chap, no bigger than yer thumb yet he could drive a great carthorse by sittin in its ear and whisperin. I was longin to hear how the little chap made out but we was hauled out of the class to Miss Sticks in the big hall before the finish. That's when she marked a WHOLE DAY somewhere in my 'Tendance Book and learned me I were borned.

Granny Statham's Girls was waitin for us outside. They wasn't truly girls they was growed-oop twins. They wasn't 'all there', they lacked somethin but it was a job to put yer finger on it. Where boats and locks was concerned they managed but where people was concerned they 'couldn't help it'. They giggled a lot and talked in high little-girl voices, and loombered rather than walked. Granny wasn't truly a granny but everybody called her 'Granny' on the h'Oxford Cut. She had no other children only her Girls and they'd come late in life.

'We've come to take you home,' they said, giggling in their high little-girl voices, 'you've got a new little lariat.'

I thought it was some sort of new tether for Ilda but it turned out to be my new little sister, Arryut [Harriet]. Mum always weared a long coverall white apron. It wasn't till I seed that apron lyin flat and empty on the sidebed and Mum's arms full of Arryut that I guessed where babies comed from. Mum knew she was 'comin to town' [nearing her confinement] but she hadn't planned to 'come' so soon, with all the weevil flies under Robinson Power's oyist [hoist] bein bumped about havin thirty ton of grain unloaded.

'Thank goodness we wasn't carryin coal,' Mum sez, 'else I don't know 'ow I'd of managed.'

That day, my 8 birthday, I left home and went to work for Granny Statham. It was the only full day of schoolin I ever had, the day the mule took a look, the day I learned that I were borned.

I've knowed I was borned ever since.

Granny's Little Runnerboat

'I'd give the world for one right leg', Granny Statham used to say.

She'd only got the one-left. She'd lost the one-right in Maffers Top Lock on the old Junction [*Marsworth, Grand Junction Canal*]. She tugged on a rope, not knowin it were frayed. It broke. She just saved herself from fallin backwards into the lock but her leg slipped and was wrecked between the boat and the wall. Maffers Top Lock was much narrower in them days. I reckon she must of been about forty when it happened cos she'd just had her precious twins.

'I was more worried about feedin *them*', she told me, 'than salvagin me *stoomp!*'

She never talked much about havin it orf, 'cept to boast, 'I were cloryfied at Lord Roofchild's' [*chloroformed at Lord Rothschild's*] as if she were nighted at Bookinum Palace. I believe Lord Roofchild gave the 'orspital where a passin farmer carted her in his waggon.

'*Three weeks* they wanted me to stop in that 'orspital! *Oo's* goin to suckle my babes? I sez.'

'Your husband will have to put them to the bottle, Mrs Statham.'

'*Oo's* going to pay for the milk? I sez. Every day I'm laid oop and

[10]

that boat's stop-moored my Mate's losin a whole day's travellin. *That* don't put no milk in no bottle!'

She and Old Man Statham had gotten in tow [*paired-up, i.e. married*] when they was only sixteen. They'd taken twenty-five years to begotten them twins and she wasn't goin to lose 'em for a sawed orf leg. In them days on the boats bottle-fed babies hadn't much chance. You had to foster 'em out on the bank. The boat always comed first. You had to keep that boat on the move, 'gettin 'em ahead' as we called it, you couldn't keep stoppin to use two hands to boil bottles and feed a babe. Them glass titty-bottles was dangerous, they'd shatter all over the cabin when you scalded 'em. The rubber chubes never had the 'oles just right, nothin would suck out so you used a needle to make the 'oles just a teeny bit bigger, and nearly drownded the poor little mite. It comed much more safer and nat'ral to suckle yer babe and steer at the same time. You reckoned to bring 'em oop on the breast for as long as you could till the next one come along. For Granny there were never to be a next one, twins was miracle enough.

After Granny's h'accident Old Man Statham moored along at a handy quay opposite the canal maintenance yard at Booburn [*Bulbourne*]. He seed a marster carpenter soakin a new lock gate in the canal.

'If that chap can make a gate for a lock', he says to himself, 'he can make a leg for my Missis.'

And he did. But not of oak, oak's too heavy to lug around as a spare leg. He whittled it of willa [*willow*], and he fashioned the bottom end into a ploomp [*platform, foot*]. Granny got Smiths the Bootmakers of Bedderth [*Bedworth*] to upholster the top into a padded holster for her stump with a leather harness to fasten round her waist, and a little lookerlite [*look-alike*] workin boot for every-day and another little button boot to go with her Sunday best. She had the poshest wooden leg on the Cut.

How she survived all them years, tottin orf and boardin on, crossin the locks and walkin the planks, I shall never know. In them dangerous days before the pertection [*protection*] for workers and the miracles of the National 'Ealth there was a 'bundance of limbless folk, peg-legs, 'ooky-arms, on the boats, on the wharfs, in the ware'ouses. Pain to be born without succa [*succour*] only a n'old winluss [*windlass*] to clinch or bite on when you was driven to rack-n-rave with pain. Until h'aspirin came in for the poor only the rich could afford to kill pain. In them days on the boats it was castor oil for yer insides; and for yer outsides, if yer couldn't poultice it, yer put oop with it. The boat comed first. You had to keep goin. The boat was yer livin, yer 'ome. It was the boat or the work'us. You never gived in. If yer gived in yer went under.

Granny never gived in. All those years she tottered on, Best-Mate to her husband, Best-Mum to her twins, trainin 'em, over and over, until at last between 'em they was workin their own butty-boat and makin all the locks. She must of been gettin on for seventy then. She stowed her willa-leg away in the best-box under the crossbed, and managed on her one-left, hotchin herself to rest her stoomp on the stool, the side, the step, or wotever came in handy, shufflin her bottom oop the steps of the 'Victoria' to sit, queenin it over the tiller, barkin orders in her deep gruff voice. By the time I boarded the 'Victoria' on my 8 birthday Granny was as broad as a butty and never left the boat but she were gettin weary of shuntin her bulk from bench to stool, cabin to hatch. She needed a little 'runnerboat' [run-about] as she called it in her broad h'Oxfordsheer, a little skivvy to fetch and carry. I was Granny's little runnerboat.

The Stathams had the two boats, the 'orseboat 'Victoria' and the butty the 'Princess May', drawed by the one 'orse, Troy. Troy were in his prime, strong enough for the job yet small enough to fit his omes [hames] under the low sides of the arched bridges. Troy was as black as a fun'ral 'orse and just as smart. Mr Statham did everything for Troy, led him, fed him, groomed and stabled, and polished his brightwork [brasses]. Granny Statham was dressed as black as a fun'ral 'orse too, decked over all in the deep mournin she'd donned when the old Queen died; long black skirts, full yoked black blouse with high balloon sleeves, and a coal scuttle bonnet with 'curtains' down the back. She kept to that fashion till her own dyin day. Deep as a covered waggon was the poke-brim of that black sunbonnet with her old brown weatherwore face nestlin beady-eyed in the back. Granny's brightwork needed no polishin. Her oops [hoop ear-rings], rings, and chunky rope-knot brooch were all of solid gold. If Granny had sunked they'd of rose her for buried treasure.

I was terrified of her at first. Those beady eyes never missed nothin. She kept me on the run with her deep man's voice, fetchin, cleanin, cookin, mendin, moppin. To me, skinny and undersized as I were in them days she were YOOGE [*huge*]. My Mum were big-made but Granny was bigger, specially across the chest and the upper arms. They say if one limb no longer functions the others make oop for it. Granny's arms had took the strain. I'd of made me a whole frock from one of her balloon sleeves.

The twins were broad-made too. They took turns steerin the butty and makin the locks. Each loombered along the towpath zackly alike, head butted into the weather, arms swingin across the front of her apron so's not to catch on her winluss tucked into her belt at the side. Granny made each of us wear a wide leather belt with another narrer belt on the top. We done it that way on the h'Oxford. The narrer belt to hold yer winluss, the wide to stop it rubbin and to act as a n'extra stay to yer stummick when shiftin heavy paddles. To me the twins was middle-aged. They treated me like their doll, askin Granny if they could play with me in their cabin, dressin me oop in their long dresses, frizzin my red curly hair into a 'Princess May' fringe, and tyin the rest in rags to make ringluts. I were never a Lily Longtree [*Langtry*] but I've always 'ad rich 'air.

With all these growed-oops I were over-loaded. I longed for my little brothers. I missed their little 'ands in mine and their warm bodies snugglin oop to me at night. I missed bein my Mum's right 'and. I missed goin with my Dad of a n'early morn to fetch our old Ilda, gearin her oop, and leadin her along the towpath.

I can't recall any of us takin over Troy from Mr Statham. *Somebody* must of done from time to time. I can see Old Man Statham now, thin and wiry, ploddin on and on, his winluss humped over his shoulder under his jacket, stickin out like a clockwork key. How he kept goin on and on all day at the same steady pace, I don't know. He must of wound his-self oop! He never cast a clout. Year in year out he seemed to always wear the same barley-boyer [*small brimmed hat*], scarf, jackut, weskut, yorks—not the strings, the proper yorks, thick worsted britches buttoned at the knee—and gaiters. He was the only boatman I ever seed wearin gaiters. He seemed to be a throwback to some landed gent. He were very quiet-spoken. Not that he spake much, Granny done all the talkin. He looked askant from me at first, as if I were Granny's pidgin, women's worry, none of his concern; but he tooked to me at the finish.

I slept in the cabin with Granny and Old Man Statham. I slept on the sidebed and the old 'uns slept on the crossbed in the bedroom. It wasn't really a room but once the crossbed was let down from the bed-'ole cupboard, the flockroll mattress made oop, and the crosher [*crotcheted*] curtains let to fall across that end of the cabin we always called it the bedroom.

I can't ever remember Old Man Statham comin to berth; he slid in and out like a skiff in the night. He can't of had much leeway, the crossbed was only four feet wide, but it's surprisin how many can fit, sardine fashion on a four foot crossbed, and on a sidebed. There was always the cabin floor if you was pushed. I had the sidebed to myself. I was made to lie towards the tumble'ome, the little slantin eave over the sidebed, so I never seed Granny ungirdin her stays. I seed her lacin 'em oop once, criss-cross on hooks acraws her stummick like rinky-boots [*ice skating boots*].

It was a terrible long time before I seed my Mum and Dad and little brothers again, and then only in passin; we was passin out of Hillmorton double locks as they was passin in. Mum fetched my little sister out to show us how she'd got on. 'Managin all right?' she calls to me.

We was brung oop never to kick oop a fuss but I couldn't help cryin.

'Rally at Christmas!' Mum promised. 'H'Oxford! Father Christmas! Remember?'

As if I could forget. Last Christmas we was moored at my Granny's at h'Oxford and it had been the first time ever that Father Christmas had left me and my brothers a n'apple and a n'orange and a bright new penny.

We never rallied at Christmas, we was h'iced oop at Tusses Bridge. I were most oopset that Father Christmas wouldn't know where I was and which boat I was on. I needn't of worried, Granny was strict and gruff but I never went short. On Christmas mornin, soon as the lamp were lit, I spied across the foot of my bed a new pair of h'Oxford blue knitted stockins. In the toe of one were a n'apple and a n'orange and a bright new penny; and in the toe of the other a crosherook [*crotchet hook*]. I were cock-a-noop! It were fashioned out of bone with a little pricked pattern wot said 'ROSE'.

Very old it was. Granny was gived it when she was a little girl. She learned me to crosher no end on that crosherook, all the old patterns, 'the filet', 'the heart', 'the 'orseshoe', 'the rose', 'the lady's loop', and 'the pointed Rover'. Some called it 'the Vandyke' but Granny always called it 'the pointed Rover'. She learned me to make edgins, shelvins, runners, box covers, boatee belts and boatee braces, 'orses' earcaps, the lot.

I picked oop how to knit on four needles just by watchin her steel needles flashin in and out of her golden rings. I was watchin her turnin the n'eel of a sock one day. I'd seed her turn so many n'eels. I plucked oop courage.

'I can turn that n'eel.'

'Goo on!' she never believed me. She handed it over. I done it. Matched every stitch, neat as a fishtail. It's terrible important for a n'eel to mesh smooth. A stitch out of true can soon raise a blister, all boatwomen knowed that, but Granny plyed ern almost invisible. I done mine zackly like ern. I'd picked it oop just by watchin. When you can't read you has to watch. *Watch* as careful as if yer life depended on it; sometimes it *do*! I must of been about nine when I turned that n'eel. Granny were *that* chuffed. Poor Granny! Her own girls could do nothin tiddly [*fancy work*], they was all thumbs, thick thumbs, strong for turnin a winluss, 'opeless for turnin a n'eel.

From then on Granny tooked to me. I becomed less of a skivvy more of a n'andymaid. She parted to me all her boatwoman knowledge. She done all her stockins in boatee-blue with the welts and toes in white. Boatwomen on the h'Oxford done 'em like that for generations. They was special yarns for boot-walkin. You could get it from little 'abberdashers here and there along the Cut. They sold it on the Grand Junction too. We got it from 'top o' Buckby' when we was on the Junction, and from Banbury when we was on the h'Oxford. The 'abberdashers in Banbury was handy to the saddler wot stitched the leather straps and buckles on the spider-work belts and braces she learned me to 'broider. Banbury was famous for 'orse fairs in them days, and the saddlers was famous for webbins and 'orseclawths as well as harness. It was close to the 'erbalist where Granny bought the same potions for Troy as she dished out to the rest of us.

I have a fleetin memory of Granny bendin over me in the middle of the night tendin me for ear-ache, heatin erbaloyal [*herbal oil*] in a spoon with a candle, fillin the cabin with healin fumes; Granny in her nightshift, her head shoved into a 'basket'. The 'basket' was her hair, strings and strings of thin dark plaits, moored and looped about her old scalp. I loved to watch her plaitin her hair, her defty old fingers crossin and criss-crossin, and then usin a single strand of her own hair to neatly splice the end. She done the front plaits independent of the back so she could wash the front at one go and the back at the next. She reckoned it were less of a shock to her system.

She learned me no end how to scrape and do, to make the most of a bit of meat or bones with yer pertaters and potterbs [*root vegetables*], to pluck a partridge and skin a rabbit, to make spotted dick and bacon jack. She done more bakin than my Mum because she had more time and a bigger range. It had space for three pots on the top and a good oven at the side. The inside of her food-cupboard door was covered in nilonum [*linoleum*]. She could sit on the sidebed, let down the cupboard door, roll out her suet-crust on that nilonum—easy to wipe and keep clean—and all her ingrediments was to hand in her food cupboard. She never baked bread, there was no end of good bakers along the Cut and she reckoned to store enough bread in her starn cupboard [*cool cupboard built to store food in the stern of a narrow-boat*] to last the trip; and she never kept a side of bacon hangin oop like some boatwomen did. She kept ern at Mrs Beesley's, Sutton Stop. They killed and cured their own pigs. The Beesleys kept the shop *and* the 'Greyhound' in them days, they was joined by a long stone passage at the back. Each woman saved the money with Mrs Beesley to pay for their own flitch. All these bacon flitches belongin to the boatwomen was kep hangin oop along the passage. Mrs Beesley kep 'em safe and hacked orf a piece as each woman wanted.

Granny was borned Rose Lookit [*Luckett*] in a 'kit [*basket*] on a boat on the canal at h'Oxford. Her old Grandfather Lookit come oop to fame [*was well known*] as a 'kitmaker on the river at h'Oxford. He bought rads [*reeds, osiers*] all along the Thames, and his family-band peeled and plaited, weaved and woved, creels and eel-traps for Thames fishermen. He even sent lobster 'kits down to the coast. Peelin those rads was cruel work on the fingers of the women and children. Granny's fingers still showed the shrivel marks from where she used to pull the rads out of the boilin hot coppers to pull them through the strippin iron when she was a child.

When the railway came, bringin the cheap sea-fish to h'Oxford, Grandfather Lookit changed from makin 'kits for the river fishermen to makin pedders and panyers [*market baskets and panniers*]. Everythin in them days was hawked in 'kits none of yer plarstic containers. He had his yard this side of Hythe Bridge agen Jacob Beesley's. He had boats on the river for tradin the rads and set up his son, Granny's father, with a pair of boats to trade the 'kits along the canal. Granny's Mum and Dad traded 'kits all over the navigation. I don't know zackly which wharf she was borned at along the h'Oxford but she always used to say, 'I was born within the sound of the little bell of St Barnabas'.

Years after Granny was dead-n-gorn, when I was married, we'd moor at them Juxon Street or Walton Street wharfs, in the '20's and '30's, waitin to be unloaded on the morrow. I'd lie in the cabin listenin for the little bell of St Barnabas tellin the hours of the night, and I'd think of Granny Statham and all she learned me.

She never had no schoolin—didn't hold with it—'*All schoolin teaches yer is dis!con!tent!*'—but she had a well-wore game of 'Planks-n-Snubbers', like the Snakes-n-Ladders wot came in later. A snubber was the heavy rope we used for towin. We'd land on all sorts of 'hold-oops', 'wait to load', 'drought', 'h'iced-oop'—and slide down the snubber; or land on a bonus, 'lock ready', 'get ahead', 'road clear'—and shoot along the plank. That's how she learned me to count.

I can *count* just so far but I can't read all them big numbers by sight. I knowed by heart the bridges but I couldn't read their big numbers. I knowed by heart 'Ten Green Bottles' and how many locks or milestumps between places, a n'oondred milestumps from Branston [*Braunston*] to Paddinton, a n'oondred locks from Branston to Brentford. I knowed that from Bulls Bridge there were no locks tween h'Uxbridge to Paddinton, but to Brentford you had yer 'twelve', 'the two', 'the six', 'the h'odds', and 'the Thames-two-together', that makes oop yer oondred locks. But if I was to see all these numbers in a throng I'd be stemmed-oop [*stuck*]. I couldn't read no pattern for knittin or crosher, I learned by heart how many to cast on and orf, and I followed me loops-n-chains, me doubles-ntrebles from the little scrapbag of lacets [*sample patterns*] Granny's mother had made for her when she was a child.

Most of all she learned me how to cope with cabin work. '*Never leave till mornin wot yer can get done tonight.*' Even if we didn't tie-oop till midnight she'd want everythin ready for cast orf, sticks for the fire, kettle topped oop, water can filled. Old Man Statham, soon as Troy was bedded down for the night at the 'public', would have his shave in the lamplight, mix Troy's breakfast in the nostern and polish the hanimal's gear and brightwork. All our lives was geared to gettin the boats forward, gettin 'em ahead. The sooner we loosed away in the mornin, the first we'd be through the lock, the first in the queue to be orf-loaded, the first in the toll h'office to present our tickut or collect another order.

We never stopped for breakfast we had our 'bait' on the go, a chunk of bread and lard, good home-made lard, proper lard, nourishin lard, you can face oop to all weathers with a bit of good lard behind yer. I'd help to steer or get the range goin or the tea brewed or the bait larded, '*corners first, middle after*'.

It was always 'corners first' with Granny's beady eyes on yer, specially when yer cleaned the cabin. A cabin's all corners, cupboards, draws, lockers, bed-'ole, monkey-'ole, soap-'ole. '*With rags in the soap-'ole and water in the Cut cleanliness don't cost yer nothin.*'

While I beavered, cleanin the cabin, she'd sit throned in the starn steerin, so's I didn't have to keep workin round her. Sometimes, if the weather were fine and the pound [*stretch of water between two locks*] were plain sailin, she'd make me mop down the slide and the outside of the cabin so the paintwork was clean and smilin, and she'd have her stoof [*sewing material*] and sewin machine on the roof and do her 'sheenin. She'd have the tiller under one great arm and turn the handle with the other. It was only a chain stitch but the thread were good-n-strong and, providin you finished it orf good-n-proper by hand, it worked woonders. *Woonders!* She made all our frockses, petticuts, drawses, *lovely!* And she made all Old Man Statham's h'Oxford shirtses. There was a ware'us wharf down Manchester way where she'd collar whole bolts of stoof from the mills at fourpence a yard. Good, strong, cotton prints, calico, flannel, flannelette, *fourpence a yard!* Corse, it were *blighted*, but not so's you'd notice. The dooks never noticed!

In them days you weared wot you could lay yer hands on. You couldn't afford to be choosy, just as long as it covered yer back. She never needed no pattern, she knowed the ropes by heart. All she had to do was to cut each shaped piece full enough. Fullness was everythin; fullness in the upper arm for steerin and makin the locks, fullness in the bodice and across the back for castin ropes and bowallin [*bow hauling: towing a boat manually*], fullness in the skirt for stridin the planks and leapin the gates. Most 'dresses' she made for the twins was skirt with separate blouse top, less room needed in the cabin for cuttin out, less depth on the washin line for dryin.

We often had to dry the clothes goin along with a washin line rigged oop along the length of the hold. It was easiest when we was travellin empty, of course. We dropped the post into two special ring-'oles fixed on the forend of the cabin, laid the planks along the beams, and dolly-pegged the washin all along the line to the mast. When me and the twins was all garbed oop in Granny's latest big blowsy print with washin to match you could see us blowin along the Cut a mile orf.

She made all our stays. There was little shops all over the Cut, within walkin distance of the lock, Banbury, Bedderth, Buckby, where she'd send me to sought out a packet of welbons [*whalebones*].

She learned me to splice and knot the ropes and to scrub the plaits [*decorative ropework on the rudder and tiller of a horse-drawn boat*]. She learned me no end but she didn't hold with schoolin. She used to keep me out of sight of Miss Sticks when we was on the Coventry, and the kidcatchers [*school attendance officers*] at h'Oxford, Birnigum, wot-av-yer, hadn't no notion a n'old lady like Granny had a little runnerboat stowed aboard. She let me go once or twice, but the raggin [*persecution*] got worser as I got older. In them days you was 'ranged in Standards. I was way 'low standard. They'd all gang oop in the playground, 'Duncey boatee! Pee in the Cut!' I were terrified. I were brought oop on the quoyet of the Cut, I weren't used to racket, that yard were like a syloom [*lunatic asylum*].

We didn't pee in the Cut, we peed in the po, real chiner an' all. We kept it in the po cupboard with roses painted on the door, and emptied it, modest-like, when nobody was lookin. 'Course, yer dooks gived yer away; eats anythin, does dooks! Our po were cleaner than the stinkin privies shared by oompteen families, wot we used to glimpse sometimes along the backs of them tenements at Bethnal Green and Birnigum. We used the privy at the 'public' when we was moored, the stench was pretty bad at the so-called 'Sanity' Stations the Company provided along the Cut; but I was always more at 'ome on me own pot. We wore divided drawses, easier to squat behind the hedge if you was walkin the towpath. I favoured them calico divided drawses for years, till the celanese came in and I changed to the ready-made deerecters [*directoire, a style of knickers reaching down to the top of the knees; celanese, synthetic silk*]. Years later when I was married and we had a moty-boat we had a dubba in the hinjin-'ole, but on the butty I still clung to me pot [*dubba derived from double-U.C. but actually an Elsan; hinjin-'ole, engine cabin*].

All the time I stroved for Granny we kept in touch with my Mum and Dad by words-a-mouth passed along the Cut by boaters, lock-keepers, lengthsmen, and toll clirks. We rallied as often as we could at h'Oxford where my Mum's family, Granny Fisher and Aunt Polly, had two rooms in a house belongin to Granny Statham's family, the Lookits. We rallied at Stowell too [*Stowe Hill*] on the Grand Junction, where my Dad's mother, Granny Mella, rented a one-oop-one-down, a little thatched roost, where my Stowell Great Aunt Ilda and any of the rest of the family could stop and tie-oop. There was a whole row of these little cots at Stowell, all joined under the one thatch, all rented by boat families, the Mellas, the Ramlins, the Ojits [*Hodgetts*], the Littlemores. All gone now, and a big motor-road whizzin over the top. In the main we carried grain from the docks to the mills and coal from the coaleries to the coal wharfs and factries. All sorts of coal, from the dusty slack and 'sweepins' to the big glossy 'anpix' [*hand-picked*]. We carried tons of stone and timber for buildin fine mansions. Other loads was more unusual, [*see map on p. xix*] madderoots to Manchester for dyin in the mills, oakum to Banbury for pickin in the work'us.

I 'mind' [*remember*] loadin pot-pipes [*glazed pottery drainage pipes*] from way oop the Moira, the Ashby, before it was silted oop, and deliverin them way down the old Stratford Arm before *that* were silted oop. They were shamrock fashioned, three pipes in one, and packed in straw. That straw were buckshee, valuable on our

way back for tradin with the 'public' for stablin Troy. I mind carryin
dusty slack and sweepins to the Cement Works at 'Arefield on the
Grand Junction, Shadbolt's we used to call the Arm, and fetchin a
backload [*return load*] of dabbas, big blue-grey-white cobbles from
the chalk mountains 'gen there, and carryin them oop the Junction,
the h'Oxford, the Coventry, the Trent and Mersey, to the potteries
agen Stoke.

I mind carryin coke, pig iron, and sand from Staffordshire to
Sammerson's [*Samuelson's Foundry*] in Banbury, to make reapers,
mowers, chaff-cutters. I mind helpin out other Number Ones when
there was a throng on [*rush of orders*] carryin beans [*small coal*] to
the paper mills at Croxley where the big tidal barges would come
oop from the London docks with great big bales of foreign pulp and
grasses for makin fine paper. The throng were for the old King's
mournin [*Edward VII*] and the new King's coronation [*George V*].

Beautiful them court papers was! Handmade. Court black with
gold swirls for the old King's mournin, and lovely coloured shiny
papers for the new King's coronation. They allowed us to have
some cutorfs [*off-cuts*] from their royal roobish-'eap. Me and
Granny started the craze in every cabin along the Cut with these
posh papers. She learned me to make fancy paper bows for the top
of each of her ribbin plates, and let me use her stiletto-scissors, tiny
sharp pointed blades, to fret along the folds to make pretty edgins
for shelfs and lacey-daceys [*paper doyleys*] for 'er h'ornamentals
[*cabin ornaments*].

Granny's h'ornamentals was of brass. There wasn't a lot. There
wasn't the space, only a set of shallow corner shelfs between the
range and her food cupboard. I mind polishin a tiny toy-size water
can, a frog box, a horse brass of the old Queen's coronation, and a
tiny pair of Cooke's winlusses, made at Willooks on the Chester
Canal. I coveted them Cooke's winlusses no end. They shined oop
beautiful with 'Bluebell' polish and slid through yer 'ands like silk.
On the top shelf of all were her Measham tea-pot, her 'Live and let
live' she called it. She brought it from Ashby Deller's 'ouse [*Ashby
de la Zouch*]. It were guarded from fallin by a polished brass chain
threaded with a n'eart, a spade, a club, and a dimunt. We saved
the biggest paper bow of all for the gimbal, the fancy brass bracket
wot held yer oil lamp level. It were all lampwicks and candles in
them days.

The 'lectric were flowin in fast to the towns. We was throngin the wharfs with ballast and timber and stone to build 'Lectric Light factries [*power stations*]. Every big town made its own 'lectric, they wasn't all the same strength. The one at Coventry kept growin and growin and powered the trams and the oyists at Robinson Powers. I helped to build that 'Lectric Light and when, later, they got too big and steamy for the town and they had to shift out to Longford, I helped to build *that* one too. I mind rallyin once with my Mum and Dad at Banbury Fair and bein taken to see the new 'Lectric Seminer [*Cinematograph*], flickerin pictures of the old Boer War. I can't tell you which year. It's a job to tally the years when yer can't read-n-rite and yer days is cast without number. The *boats* was all numbered and 'counted for, of course; who they belonged to, where they comed from, where they was registered. I couldn't read the boats. I went by the people. To me the people was always more important. Without the people the boats would go nowheres.

It was easier to note the passin of days once the wireless came in. The man's voice [*BBC News*] gave yer somethin to anker on. Granny had no wireless, that was *ages* to come, but she had a Pandorus [*Pandora's Box*], a lovely polished box with a high curved lid.

'I bought this Pandorus from a soldier wot brought it all the way from the Boer War', she sez. That was acraws the High Seas, the Boer War. 'Moy-hoy!', she sez, givin me a n'old fashion' look with her old beady eyes, 'If only this box could talk!'

And it did. She opened it oop, fixed a little tin 'orn on the side, pushed on one of them roly-poly reckerds, and this little chap's voice wavered out, 'The Wonderful History of Tom Thumb'. I were *captified*! There was me frettin I'd never hear the last of that little chap oop in the 'orse's ear, and *there* was he workin his way along inside this reckerd. She had only the two roly-reckerds, 'Tom Thumb' and 'See me Dance the Poker'.

I don't know wot happened to her Pandorus. I expect her Girls had it when she died. I were very fond of Granny. I worked for her for years. I were most oopset when she fell sick and couldn't take nothin. She had cancer of the stummick. She didn't want nobody to tend her 'cept me. She could of been nursed proper at the Lookits' on the bank at h'Oxford but she wanted to die at 'ome and 'ome were the 'Victoria'.

'I was born on a boat, Rose,' she used to say to me, 'I shall die on a boat.'

She dwindled right away to skin and bone at the finish. She had a lot of bodily sufferin. Mr Statham and the Girls couldn't stand it; they was all at sea. I done everythin for her. She were light as a child. I must of been about fourteen by then, not much more than a child meself. I helped her on the po, kept her fresh and clean, and done her plaits. Sometimes she'd bear the pain, lyin taut, grippin her old wooden-'andled winluss. When it was really bad she'd turn wild, strugglin against me to get out and 'make the lock'.

The day she died we was travellin back empty from h'Oxford, 'Ayfield wharf, 'gen the old Radiators [*near where the Oxford Radiators Factory was later*]. We'd stabled overnight 'gen the 'Strugglers' in Banbury, and were well on our way back oop the 'Claydon Five' for Wyken. I was steerin, keepin my weather eye on Granny in the cabin. We'd locked 'Claydon Bottom', 'Claydon Middle', and the ones between, and were wendin our way round the big bend to 'Claydon Top'. Granny was lyin very small and still, starin oop at the open slide and clutchin her winluss as if strainin to make the summit. They'd got the lock all ready for us. As we quoyetly floated-in her winluss dropped to the floor. She'd made her final lock.

I can't remember the name of the ganger in charge of the yard, it was before Mr Donovan and Mr Bloomfield's time, but he were daycent to us. There was a marster carpenter at the yard, come from a family of coffin makers named Gilkes, and the ganger allowed him to measure Granny and go home and prepare a coffin for her. We had to travel on to Fenny [*Compton*] to wind the boats round. On the way along 'the Tunnel' to Fenny we met the Coleses of Thrupp. They was carryin goods to Youbert 'Awkins [*Hubert Hawkins, Builder, Hayfield Wharf, Oxford*]. Their daughter, Rosie Coles, becomed Rose Beauchamp later, 'Queen of Thrupp'. They promised to spread the news along the 'road' to the Lookits at h'Oxford.

As soon as we moored back at Claydon we stroved to make the 'Victoria' and the 'Princess May' look their very best. I scrubbed the plaits and polished the brasses, and decked the cabin with the old King's mournin papers wot we'd saved in the best box. We done out the hold extra special for the coffin to travel in state, slung from the planks, back o' the mast. Old Man Statham groomed Troy and polished his best brightwork. We was determined to do the old lady proud. We was lucky to be travellin empty else I don't know how we'd of managed. Last of all I tied the big black-n-gold bow from the gimbal on to her old winluss and fixed it on the top of her coffin. *Lovely* it looked!

They loosed us through all the way along the h'Oxford [*gave us precedence through the locks*]. Granny Statham were well-knowed for miles, all over the Navigation, but the h'Oxford were her 'ome-Cut. There was hardly a wharf nor a yard, a lock nor a bridge—even some of they little lift bridges way out in the fields—without somebody, sometimes whole families, on a boat or on a bank, standin in respect to mark the old lady's passin.

On the last stretch into h'Oxford the Lookit menfolk came to meet us and took over in the old boatee way, bowallin the boat to its final moorin. Me and the twins followed in the butty, drawn by Troy. Old Man Statham plodded bravely alongside but Troy needed no leadin, he knowed by heart where he was headin; only his 'clip-clop' and the song of the birds could be heard as we glided past they last few wharfs, thronged with folk, caps orf, silent as statues.

Moored at last where she was borned, Granny's life had come full-ring, and the little bell of St Barnabas welcomed her back.

Number Ones

'AND this is yer h'Oxford Great Aunt Rose, *Kitsy* Rosie, yer Granny Fisher's *sixth* sister, wot lives agen The Row and 'awks the 'kits along the Cut. *Her* Rose, *Greyhound* Rosie, is married to Abel Beesley, brother of Ben, wot keeps the "Greyhound" at Sutton Stop, and carries the coals to the new Foze'll Gasworks . . . This is yer h'Oxford Great Aunt Kilby, yer Granny Fisher's *seventh* sister, wot's married to Great Uncle Kilby and has the coalboats carryin for the bewry. *Their* Rose, yer Auntie "Tarboats" Rosie, married yer Dad's oldest brother, yer Uncle Jack Mella, wot runs the tarboats oop Obry. *Their* Rose—'

At Granny Statham's funeral I gathered the rigmaroles of me relations, Roses, Roses, all the way. I gathered I was borned, like Granny, within sound of the little bell of St Barnabas, and the two big soldiers carryin Granny's coffin were my two older brothers Eloy and Aymus. There was a war started. Been started for weeks. Nobody told *me*.

I'm sure I was about fourteen. I know I'd started me 'anky-panky [*menstruation*]. It came on me sudden-like, on a tram, oop Coventry. I'd never been on wheels in my life, not a bike, not a cart, not a waggon, let alone a n'opentop tram. I were terrified. I were used to bein 'orsedrawed, peaceful, down on Cut level; not perched oop in the air, clangin and bangin along setted streets, swayin and swervin round corners, 'lightnin' flashin all over me. When I got back to the boat I were in a 'eck of a state. I thought the tram had finished orf my insides. Granny put me straight, put me in the picture-like, learned me how to go on, burnin me waddins, boilin me rags, keepin me growed-oop parts to meself.

Now I was really growed oop Mum and Dad needed me back. Old Man Statham was sellin oop, goin to live 'on the bank' at Jericho in h'Oxford. The Girls was goin to tend their Dad and earn a livin takin in washin for the prisoners at h'Oxford Castle. Since our old mule, Ilda, had died, catchin cold from another duckin,

Dad had found life all oop 'ill with a string of 'ap'azard 'orses. Dad decided to take on the Statham's 'Victoria' as butty with Troy into the bargain. This was a big step-oop for my Dad, takin on a butty-boat. By then Alby and Ezme my two younger brothers was away workin on other boats, my little sister Arryut was Mum's right 'and, just like I used to be when I was her age, helpin with the steerin and lookin after my other two little sisters, Lizer and Suey. Without me on the butty they hadn't 'the strength' [*enough crew*].

When I next boarded the 'Victoria' I had a terrible shock. All Granny Statham's lovely cabin 'ome had been stripped to the dusty shelfs, the dead range. All her fine crosher, 'er ribbin plates, 'er shiny h'ornamentals—gorn. The Girls had tooked the lot, even her sewin machine.

'Rose,' Granny used to say to me, 'when I'm dead-n-gorn this sewin-sheen will be yourn.' But, of course, nothin in real writin.

I grant it was all theirn by rights, but I'd *stroved* for her all them years, it was me she sought for comfort at the end. I'd of loved just one little keepsafe. All I had now of Granny was wot she'd learned me.

'*Corners first, middles after.*' I set to and cleaned oop. At least they'd left me 'Bluebell' and polishes in the monkey-box and me brushes and rags in the soap-'ole. '*With rags in the soap-'ole and water in the Cut, cleanliness don't cost yer nothin.*' I was just givin the floorplate behind the range a good wipe—you can only get right into the cranny at the back when yer stove's out—when I hit somethin loose, somethin metal. It was one of her little brass winlusses. I had a good weep over it. True, it should of been a pair, but it *was* Granny's.

'Finders—keepers', I sez to meself. I polished it oop, polished the shelf, fetched one of my lacey-daceys, and set the winluss on it, *just so*. Granny Statham's little Cooke's winluss were my very first h'ornamental.

It was lovely workin with my Mum and Dad again, even though it seemed strange at first with no little brothers only little sisters aboard. Lizer and Suey slept with Mum and Dad on the 'Percy Veruns' and me and Arryut had the butty 'Victoria' all to us-selfs. We always slept with the boats breasted-oop at night so the two cabins lay 'gen-side each other. Me and my sister Arryut got on well. She was half my age but she'd been Mum's little runnerboat

for so long we made a good team together. She wasn't stout enough
to shift paddles but she could pull her weight in the cabin, share
the steerin, moor the ropes, help Mum with the littleones or walk
Troy for Dad.

We was lucky to hang on to Troy, 'They' nearly nabbed him for
the war. The clirk at Long Buckby pleaded for Dad, that 'Troy was
already troopin for the war, carryin coals to fuel the Ordnance
Works and inkits [*metal ingots*] to supply the munitions factries'.
'They' gave Dad a special letter of permission to keep Troy and we
kept it safe in the ticket drawer.

We was lucky to hang on to our Dad too. So many men from the
Cut had been taken away to the wars, boatmen and maintenance
men. Old boats was abandoomed, lockgates was left leakin, paddles
un-oiled, arms and channels siltin-oop. Some women with families
left the boats, just couldn't cope without their chap, others stroved
to be Captain *and* Best-Mate.

Dad would always stop and lend a n'and if a boat were oop the
crick or stemmed-oop, even it it were a dirty stinkin Rodney-boat.
You never knowed when *you* might need a n'extra hand to block-
and-pulley you through or shaft yer orf the mud. You was all in the
same boat,—if yer gets my drift. Some wouldn't lift a shaft nor raise
a paddle to help but most boat families, though we was rooff-n-
ready and unscholared, was brung oop to use yer boatin manners,
leave the lock ready as you would like to find it, nod 'Ah do!' to
passin crew, signal how many locks was set for 'em, or warn 'em of
hidden perils and scour-puds [*heaps of sediment built up by a side
current*].

Us Number Ones flourished in the war. For years the Cut had
been fightin the railways, then comed the motor lorries. Before the
war they was startin to poach our orders, then war broke out and
they was needed for carryin soldiers. Motor lorries needed precious
fuel whereas 'orse-drawed transport needed no fuel, 'cept grub for
the hanimal. We had the orders, as long as we had 'the strength'
and a clear 'road' we could make a good livin. We toiled 'ard,
specially unloadin. Sometimes we'd get to a wharf with two
boatloads of coal to find a queue waitin to be orf-loaded, shortage of
labour and wharfingers [*overseers*]. Delay wasn't so bad for crews
workin for big companies or on Joey-boats [*open day-boats*], they
was on a 'basic' [*regular minimum wage*]. Dad was paid only for

delivery. The sooner we orf-loaded the sooner we could wind [*turn the boats round*] and seek another order. '*You can always lose time but you can't make time*', as Granny used to say.

We'd get stuck-in and orf-load on our own. Even the littlest was made to help, fillin her little tin bookit and tippin it into Mum's barrer. Sometimes if we had to walk the planks from the boat to the wharf it would take us two days or more. A lick-n-a-promise [*quick wash*] before we dropped into bed last thing at night, then oop at first light and into stinkin coaly clothes to start shovellin all over again. It was back-achin work liftin shovels and bookits of coal into them barrers. They was heavy wooden barrers belongin to the wharf, with iron wheels, weighed a ton before yer started. Mum and Dad would push them acraws the planks to the wharf. Dad would never allow Mum to tip a full barrer, he always done it. He weared a strong leather boatee-belt to stanch [*support*] his stummick. As soon as he'd emptied her barrer she'd start back with it. They was a close team, true mates, swearin blue murders at each other sometimes but never knockin each other about like some of the Rodneys and bargees we seed sometimes along the backs in London. She was his Best-Mate for over forty years and in the war they was in their prime, Captain Dick Mella, Number One, and his Best-Mate, Rose, of the 'orseboat 'Percy Veruns' and the butty 'Victoria'.

We'd help out the other Number Ones if there was a throng on. Dad loaned me to Auntie 'Tarboats' Rosie for a while when Uncle Jack, Dad's oldest brother, had his accident. The 'orse's gears snapped when the 'orse was pullin, a strap hit Uncle Jack with such force his stummick was cut, even through his thick cord trousers. When the bruise came out he couldn't straighten his-self, had to lie in the cabin for six weeks. It was just the 'andlin of the 'orse Auntie needed help with, there was no loadin nor unloadin on them tarboats. We was filled and emptied by a big round pipe let into the lid-'ole. The tarboats was all one hold then, but they was dangerous with all that tar sloppin about, specially on rivers. Soon after, a tarboat *did* capsize over a weir from the River Soar into the River Trent. After that the hold was divided into two sep'rate stanks, each with their own lid-'ole, and this was much safer. We carried the tar from the gasworks agen Manchester to the chemical gas tanks at Obry [*Oldbury*]. Obry was all gas tanks in them days, miles of 'em, stinkin summat terrible. We went on the Manchester Ship Canal but we didn't turn into the docks we kept on the canal over a big bridge wot we called 'the tank' [*Barton Aqueduct*], it was a n'ackerdook, and if a big ship wanted to come past under the ackerdook the water was trapped on this bridge, with us and the 'orse still on it and we was swung round with the bridge in the middle of the river and the big ships had right of way to pass on either side. It was a WOONDERFUL thing! You'd 'ave to be very clever to think oop a gadget like that before anybody else thinked of it.

Auntie Rosie and Uncle Jack wanted me to stop with them for always but I wanted to go back to my Dad. I loved my Dad. 'Sides, the tarboat-run was always the same, whereas Dad helped out all over the Cut. I mind us helpin out old Boatee Own [*Alfred Hone, senior*] who later had the 'White City' and the 'Cylgate', Rose Skinner's grandad, not Rose Skinner of the 'Friendship' but Rose Skinner wot later had the 'Rose and Bet' ['*Rose and Betty'*]—carryin coals to Banbury Co-op and Banbury Light.

I mind workin for Captain Coles of Thrupp, Rose 'Coles' Beauchamp's grandad, carryin coals to the h'Oxford Colleges, and for Captain Peter Littlemore of Stowell, Captain Dick Littlemore's dad, carryin coals from Polesworth down the old Stratford Arm on the Grand Junction to Robert's foundry, Dinzinger [*Deanshanger*].

We arrived one day at Dinzinger to find the foundrymen had just finished unloadin the Littlemores' boats and were ranged round the Littlemores' new grammerfone havin their picture tooked. A newspaper man had turned oop to take a fota of them all. Mr Peter Littlemore were a very short-tempered man yet his wife, Minnie, were just the opposite, patient and hard workin. She had to be. She had eight sons and seven daughters. Though they had that little house at Stowell Mrs Littlemore always went on the boats with her Number One husband. Her children were borned all over the Cut. She used to boast to me, 'They was all borned, Rose, and they was all christened'.

Lizzie, her eldest daughter, nearly wasn't borned, She had her opposite the pub at Cosgrove on the Grand Junction. She were that weak after, with her hands still full of little boys, she just couldn't pluck oop the h'extra strength to feed this tiny new baby. The old couple at the pub acraws the way hadn't any children, they tooked to the babe for a while, feedin her on the bottle, fostered her like, until Minnie had gotten more strength. Every time Minnie called back to collect her little Lizzie they used to plead, 'Just a little while longer' 'Just a little while longer' till in the end more babies came along for Minnie and Lizzie never was gived back. She was the only one of Minnie's children to be proper schooled. She came oop to fame later—married the Curate of Cosgrove.

Five of Mrs Littlemore's sons went to the war and five came back yet Mum lost all of ern; Eloy and Aymus in the fightin, Alby and Ezme in the wicker-fire at Birnigum. They was workin on the boats, Fellas Morton, general carryin. Late one winter's afternoon they delivered a cargo of big wicker carbies to a factry ware'us [*glass carboys of acid or other chemicals, packed in wicker containers*]. One of the carbies was leakin but it was too dark to see which one. Somebody struck a—'NO!'

Too late. The match lit the air. 'Flame-able'—see? But nobody couldn't read. The 'ole ware'us went oop. Alby and Ezme were never found.

I'd never knowed my other two brothers wot was killed in the fightin but Alby and Ezme I'd cuddled when young and tooked by the hand when they was learnin to toddle. I would yearn for them always as the little chaps they used to be.

Mrs Littlemore still had her three youngest sons at home, Tom, Dick, and little Charlie. We all loved baby Charlie, he'd sit in yer arms good as gold in his frilly bonnet and little white petticuts. Mrs Littlemore used to let us look after him while she and Mum did their washin. That was one of the best things about deliverin to the foundries, there was always plenty of hot water for the women to do their washin. Out would come the dolly tubs, the dolly sticks, the wash boards. Mrs Littlemore did her washin so regler at Roberts's they rigged oop a permanent washline for her. There was also plenty of foundrymen to do the unloadin so us kiddies could play.

Me and Annie Littlemore was about the same age. We got on well together. Her little sisters, Nell, Sarah, and little Alice fitted in well with our Arryut, Lizer, and Suey. Eight little girls all playin 'Mothers and Babies' and 'Cleanin out the Cabins', the only games we knowed. Me and Annie was the mothers and all the others was our children and Charlie was our baby. We had no books, no pictures, no telly, just the Littlemores' grammerfone. It played the one old plate reckerd over and over, 'Home sweet Home'; with our boats and cabins moored alongside we was as much at 'ome at Dinzinger as anywhere, and the Littlemores had their fota tooked with it.

The Littlemores was lucky to have a regler contract supplyin Roberts's. Dad had no regler contract he was always chasin orders. He never turned his nose oop at anythin. He picked oop every little didgy-dodgy load the big chaps like the 'Joshers' [*Joshua Fellows, Morton and Clayton Carrying Company*] and the 'Limited' [*Samuel Barlow Coal Carrying Company*] wasn't so bothered about; and the ones some family boats wasn't keen on in wartime, like fuellin the Ordnance at Coventry and the Gun Factory in Birnigum. They reckoned them places 'drawed' the Zeppeleens. We seed quite a few Zeppeleens, but not like all them bombers in 'Er 'Itler's War. We seed one Zepp, agen Birnigum, a big silver hull of a 'boat' in the moonlight with a chap under-deck, leanin out over a balcony with his 'shoppin'—a bomb in a net.

'S'orlright,' sez Dad, 'we'm safe, he's aimin at us, so he's bound to miss.'

They told us afterwards the only casualty he caused were somebody's pet monkey, even then he never hit it, it died of shock.

At first the war was 'far away and over the seas'. We couldn't read no papers, we hadn't heard of no wireless. There *was* one bridge on the South h'Oxford near a village where the big 'ouse had been turned into a n'orspital for the wounded where we used to pick oop stray convers [*convalescents*]. We'd give 'em a ride down to the next lock or drawbridge, just for the fun of it, and they'd 'obble back. They learned our Lizer to sing 'Sister Susie's Sewing Shirts for Soldiers' because she hadn't got no front teeth. Suey used to copy her, 'lithp' an' all, she thought that was how it was supposed to went. Larf!

'Put 'em on the Music Hall,' them convers told Dad, 'they'd make you a fortune!'

They used to give us pennies and sweets. They'd offer Dad money for the ride. He'd never take it, even though he needed every penny he could save in his stockin in the best box under the bed. In them days folks like us had never heard of banks. Arryut once heard this chap say to Dad, 'You wants to put yer money in the bank, Dick, it would make more there'. Without tellin nobody Arryut pushed her precious Christmas penny into the muddy bank at the entrance to the tunnel at Noble [*Newbold-on-Avon*]. The next trip it were still there doin nothin, she never trusted no bank after that.

Besides keepin us lot, Dad had to pay orf the Stathams, put some by for dockin [*boat repairs*], and pay his tolls. Every canal charged yer on the tonnage carried. Every time we loaded we had to travel to the next stop-lock, and this measurin chap would have this dipstick marked in feets. He'd stick it in the water agen the sides of the boat and red orf how much depth the boat was drawrin. He knowed how much it drawed empty, that was on yer registration, so he could fathom out how much you was carryin. He'd write it on Dad's ticket, and they'd write it in their big ledger in the h'office, and Dad would have to pay the Canal Company accordin. If he went on to another canal that Company would want their toll too. Only if you paid yer tolls was you allowed to travel. The dreaded day of all for a Number One were to be black-masted. The Company man came and nailed a notice to yer mast tellin the 'ole world you hadn't paid yer way and until you *did* that boat was goin nowheres. Dad couldn't read-n-rite but he could always 'turn 'is stockin out' [*count his money*].

Ilda Gamble were good at figurin out. She were the clever daughter of the 'Barley Mow' pub agen the entrance to the tunnel at Noble. She wasn't much older than me, about sixteen. She always had a word [*spoke to me*]. She went out to work, addin oop all day, in a n'office at Ruckby [*Rugby*]. I used to envy Ilda no end. She always looked smart. I used to lie in bed in the cabin at night dreamin wot it was like to live on the bank and go out to work in a smart costoom. I knew I had it in me like, but I hadn't the figures. Ilda were bound oop in figures. 'Figures fastenate me', she used to say. She done all the business-side of the pub in this big ledger for her Mum and Dad. They kep the 'Barley Mow' at Noble for years. They had just the two children, Ilda and Erbert. They was good to us boat people and gived the poorest families good growed-out clothes. The pub were very 'andy, right alongside the Cut. They had the latest marvel, the new gaslight, and a lovely old stone standpipe with a lion's mouth spout, very easy to fill yer water cans, and good clean stables for yer hanimal. It was one of the few pubs where the boatwomen could enjoy a drink and still keep their eye on their children. A tankard of fore-ale were only a penny a pint, but there weren't a lot of pennies to slosh about. 'Spite of all you hears about 'drunken boatwomen' most of 'em was content of a n'evenin to loose their chaps orf to the pub while they stayed tied to their kiddies and the cabin. It was a chance for Mum to catch oop on her chores ready for mornin and catch oop with news of the Cut with the women moored alongside.

One summer's evenin there was us and the Sherwoods and the Coleses tied oop there. The Coleses was Number Ones too, not the Coles wot carried the cement from 'the Rock of Gibraltar' to the h'Oxford Cement Company's ware'us at the basin in Coventry, but the ones wot carried the coals to the Ruckby Co-op. H'Arthur Coles was about my age, he was always threatnin, 'I'm gonna marry you, Rose'. But 'e never.

Mum and Dad was in the pub with the others while we was playin outside, lookin after the littleones. Mrs Gamble had a great big curly-wurly dog, 'Hairdale' it was called, most unusual. All the boat children loved playin with Hairdale, chuckin sticks into the water for him to fetch. SPLASH! in he went. Even great big stones he'd bring oop from the bottom. SPLASH! in toppled our little Suey. Before we could yell 'Dad!' Hairdale duv in, hauled her out, dumped her at h'Arthur's feet, and were waitin for him to chuck her back in again.

All of us at some time and another have fallen into the Cut, 'tooken a look'. However funny it is lookin back, it were never funny at the time, always a shock. Most of us can't swim, never had the chance nor the time to learn. Though the Cut in most places weren't all that deep, often only a few feets, it were h'icy cold in winter, and too slimey-clayey to scrabble out in summer. Drownins happened all too quick. In them days of big families boat kiddies was drowned two-a-penny. 'They' sometimes didn't even bother to hold a proper h'inquest.

'Was she a boatwoman's child? What can you expect? Case forgot.'

But *you* never forgets that child. *Never.*

Mum gives me a clout for lettin my little sister fall in and sends us all to bed. I have to be oop at crack of dawn for my usual trek, walkin Troy the three miles round the road. Though there were a n'orse path through the Noble Tunnel Troy would *not* go through. Our old mule Ilda would tow yer right through without a n'itch, even though the 'orse path were slippery with drippins from the roof and the echo of boots and hoofs was deafenin, specially if another 'orse was close behind. It's a very short tunnel yet Troy would *not* 'ave it. Troy would not *never* 'ave it.

Though the tunnel wasn't all that long the bank beyond was steep with great oakses and I couldn't get down until I'd walked him round the road and down agen the 'orse bridge over the old Noble Arm. They'd have to keep bowallin along to meet us. Troy could of taken his-self round to the Arm, he knowed the way well enough, but there was a war on, good 'orses was scarce and meat was scarce too, we didn't want nobody nabbin him for 'orseflesh.

'Mr Mella,' h'Arthur sez, presentin his-self polite as yer like to my Dad first thing that mornin, *'might* I walk along of your Rose?'

'No, she's got enough hanimal to look after.'

He were only fifteen but I were chuffed, it was the first time of 'bein asked for' by a chap. If Dad of said yes I *might* of gotten in tow with h'Arthur Coles. I'd of done well for meself. He prospered as a Number One when he growed oop, carried best 'ousecoal from Badgely [*Baddesley*] to Ruckby Co-op for years, bought his-self no end of little properties along the Cut.

'When I'm eighteen my Dad's gonna buy me a pair o' boats, I'll be me own Number One, then I'm gonna *marry* you, Rose.'

But 'e never.

Moy-chap did.

Moy-Chap's War

'CATCH, Rose!'

A moorin rope came sailin out of the dusk. I caught it. Never let
go. And that's how me and Moy-chap came to get in tow.

I was sixteen, standin under the lamplight on the quay at Banbury
Basin that dusky October evenin. I'd no idea wot chap's rope I'd
catched till he leapt from his boat into the lamplight and took the
rope from me.

'Thanks, Rose.'

'Ah do, Syer!'

Me and Syer Ramlin knowed each other, comin and goin, all our
lives. His family had one of the cottages agen my Granny Mella at
Stowell, next but one to the Littlemores'. The Ramlins was all boys,
seven boys, and Moy-chap were the middle'un. They kep a coalyard
agen Weedon Wharf on the Grand Junction and hardly ever worked
the South h'Oxford. We'd seed each other from time to time
through the years, havin a word in passin—

'Ah do, Rose!'

'Ah do, Syer.'

Never much more than that; gettin older, gettin shyer—

'Ah do, Rose!'

'Ah do, Syer.'

We hadn't kept close comp'ny since I was eight and he was ten
and he was blowed-oop by my Granny Mella for cuttin my 'air into
a cock'rel [*cockscomb*]. It had growed a lot since then. He'd growed
a lot an' all, I had to look oop to him in the lamplight and his voice
in the dusk were manly. "Ow yer blowin, Rose?"

"Ow did yer know I were me?"

'Know that 'air anywheres', he sez; 'I've come to take yer to
Banbury Fair.'

He were eighteen, about to be called oop. His brother had
already gone, leavin Syer to work their boats on his own. It's hard

work on yer own, steerin, strappin, paddles, locks. Syer was a strong chap.

'Comin to the Fair with me, Rose?'

'You'll 'ave to ask me Dad.'

'We'll all go together', Dad sez.

Banbury Fair were a 'must' with the boat people, even in wartime. Every year we'd aim to rally for all the big fairs, Coventry, Branston, h'Oxford, but Coventry and Banbury were the best. At Coventry we'd all moor alongside the timber yards, Trenery's or Cartwright's or Smith's, and walk along to the Fair on Paul Meadow—all bus station now. The Coventry were held at Whitsun but the Banbury was held in October. It were held in the Market Square and all oop the main street, and it were the boat people's final fling before winter set in.

It was quite a sight that October night to see the dark shapes of all the workin boats moored along the quay as far as the eye could see and packed into the basin—where the bus station is now—their chimneys lit, the lamplight glowin in their cabins, their tillers curvin high into the smokey dusk 'at rest' for the night. Number Ones took a pride in their boats, boats and boat families would be all dressed oop, spit-n-polished, lookin their best; the Coleses, the Skinners, the Granthams, the Fishers, the 'Ambridges, the Beauchamps, the Brummidges, the Beecheys, the Littlemores, the Humphries, the Wilsons—they had relations among the fairground folk—and the Ownses [*Hones*]. The Ownses was well-orf, they had boats *and* a house down Factry Street—all 'sinked' now [*shopping precinct*]. We all troops to the fair. Though it was war there was hardly any black-out; not like 'Er 'Itler's War, one little insey-winsey chink of candlelight in the cabin and 'they'd' bawl at yer—'PUT THAT LIGHT OUT!'

We had a few go's on the whirlygigs and the sideshows but the biggest side-show of all were the crowd. All them PEOPLES! we never seed many crowds on the Cut. We all clinged together threadin our way through the fair, Syer, me, Mum and Dad and my three sisters, samplin the crowds all round the Town 'All, oop the Street and packed in the Market Square.

At last Mum and Dad vowed they'd had enough, all that racket from the barrel-organs and smoke from the flares, and were all for goin 'ome to the boats. Mum wanted to get the little'uns to bed and Dad wanted to go for his usual pint at the 'Strugglers', the boatmen's pub. He sometimes honnered the 'Leather-nd-Bottle' [*Leathern Bottle*] but the 'Strugglers' was his favourite. It was very 'andy to the Cut, on the corner of Mill Lane with two front entrances, one in each street. It had a big sign outside of a man strugglin through the globe o' the world with his head stuck out one side and his legs stuck out the other, just like our old Dad, leggin it through life, strugglin to get orders and keep his head above waters.

Syer asked Dad if I could stop out with him for a bit longer. Dad threatened him with blue murders if I wasn't back in the cabin by the strike of ten by the Town 'All clock.

Syer didn't even put his arm round me at first—you *didn't* in them days—but in the end, as the crowds got more packed, we was throwed together and got carried away till we ended oop 'and-in-'and in front of these oops [*hoop ear-rings*], rows and rows of golden oops glintin in the lamplight, every size and style you could dream of, on this velvit, *real* velvit. *Lovely!* I'd ankered after a pair of them oops for years. Mum said I wasn't old enough and Dad said he hadn't the money.

'You'd look 'ansome in a pair o' them oops, Rose.'

'You has to 'ave yer ears bored.'

'Do yer do the ear-borin?' he sez, straight out, to this old woman sittin beside the stall on her caravan steps.

'One ear thrippence. Two ears sixpence.'

'Would yer like a pair o' them oops, Rose?'

Them oops was winkin, temptin me like mad.

'I'll pay for yer, Rose.'

'My Mum'll *kill* me.'

'Which ones do yer fancy?'

'Them little pretty-patterned ones.'

She done me quick. She pricked a bit but it was worth it.

'Sixpence for the borin. One-n-ninepence for the oops.'

It was the first present I ever was gived by a chap.

'Let me look at yer, Rose,' Moy-chap sez, drawrin me into his arms under the street lamp. I let him 'ave a good look. 'When I'm away in the war, Rose, I shall always picture yer loike this, in the lamplight at Banbury Fair, with yer pretty 'air and yer golden oops.'

[37]

He was strong and warm, his eyes was yearnin, and his curls was jet-black.

'I shall picture yer loike this, Syer, with yer arms tight round me.'

Nothin was promised but we both knowed we was bound by them oops. From then on I were to be 'is Rose, he were to be Moy-chap.

Very early next mornin I felt our boat rock gently and knew he was orf to his war. I lay on my bed in the cabin turnin them oops in my ears like mad, wishin him luck. All through Moy-chap's war I 'kep-in-touch' with him like that. 'Goin to marry 'im then, ay?' Our Dad would tease every time he caught me at it. '*Wait till we gets there*, Dad', I used to flash, shakin them oops real ladyfied. I knowed in my heart if we *did* tie the knot, Dad would be pleased. He'd knowed Syer since a baby; we was both from long-lasted boatin stock; and we wasn't close-blooded.

I started the craze for small oops on the Cut. They was all the rage after mine. They wasn't just sleeper-rings, they was real gold, patterned oops. They cost Moy-chap all of two-n-thrippence at Banbury Fair and I had 'em in night and day for nineteen years.

He was sent for h'army trainin out h'Oxford way. Several weeks later I was standin with Troy waitin to cross the road at Nell Bridge, where the towpath changes over on the South h'Oxford. Dad had shafted the boats through the bridge-'ole and was waitin, wonderin where the 'eck me and Troy was but we was held oop, waitin for all these Tommies marchin past in bunches.

'HALT!' This Captain-chap bawls out.

All these soldiers holds back.

'Advance, Miss Mella', he bows at me, nice and gentleman-like. *Advance*, Miss Mella! In front of all these soldiers! I could of died! I tossed me golden oops and led the hanimal across, right under their noses! I stole a glance—*Syer*! He never batted a n'eyelid, not a flicker, eyes front, straight as a boat-shaft.

'*Why* didn't he look at me, Dad?'

'He's keepin comp'ny with the *army* now, gal.'

'*How* did that Captain-chap know my *name*?'

'—Seed it on the 'orseclawth', Dad pointed to the letters on the corner of Troy's canvers [*waterproof canvas*], 'RICHARD MELLOR—that's me; and you're me daughter—I 'opes!'

It was the first time I learned that our Dad were writ Richard.
He were always called Dick. That's the trouble with words, you sez
one thing they writs another. It's no wonder I gets mismuddled!

All through Moy-chap's war I kep 'in touch', turnin them oops
and hopin for the best. He couldn't write and neither could I. He
were so good all round in the army they kep wantin to promote
him, but he hadn't a word o' schoolin. It was a proper let-down for
him. Some boatmen in the army brought themselves to ask another
soldier to write for them and sent their letters to a toll-office or
lock-keeper's cottage or favourite pub where they knew a trusted
clirk or lock-keeper's wife or publican's wife would read it to their
family when they next called.

I remember one of the Oofs [*Hough family*] sendin a letter to
'Granny' Keys who kep the 'Three Pigeons' by the lock-side at
Kirtlington 'gen h'Oxford. Mrs Oof kindly let Granny Keys read it
to the rest of us wot hadn't got no letter.

The 'Pigeons' was really a n'ale-us [*ale-house*]. It wasn't dressed
as a pub. To us it was Granny Key's Front Room and you felt you
was welcome and could turn to her. Our Lizer turned to her once,
full pelt, and buried her head in her apron. She'd seed a ghost-lady
trailin along in the gloamin, ghastly grey from bonnet to boot. It
was only a woman from the cement works comin along the lane in
the dusk, covered all over in cement dust. All through the war
them women did the men's work, quarryin the clay, baggin the
cement, they was just as thirsty as men after a long day's work. But
not many of the village people came along to the 'Pigeons', mostly

us-selfs, boat people. It was set back a little way from the Lock with a little green in front where we children could play, and a lovely tree with a seat all round it where the men could sit and smoke and quaff their ale of a summer's evenin while the womenfolk chatted with Granny Keys and her growed-oop daughters.

Some people was racketeerin in the war but Granny got eggs and bread and stores at fair prices for us. You could order it on yer way past, and she'd have it ready for yer to collect on yer way back from h'Oxford. Sometimes she'd buy fresh greenstuff for us from the allotments. You do miss a bit of fresh greenstuff on a boat, lettuce and wot-av-yer. I *love* lettuce, but it makes yer sleepy, all that laud'num in it. If you was 'short', hadn't been paid for yer trip, she'd let yer tide the bill over till you was next passin. You couldn't always tie-oop there, yer 'orse could do only so much in a day, but we'd try to make it because Mrs Keys were 'Granny' to all of us and her stables was only thrippence a night, penny cheaper than most people's.

When we was loaded Troy managed about thirty miles a day at the most. When you was empty a good 'orse could manage fifty miles in a day. A n'empty boat rides high in the water, almost skims the surface, a loaded boat were often travellin so deep it were almost awash. We used to say 'the sparrers be drinkin from the gunnles' [*gunwales*]. We stroved to deliver before the wharfinger were gone home and the wharf were locked oop for the night. Us Number Ones was always *strovin* to get loaded or orf-loaded, to get 'em ahead down to h'Oxford back to Branston, down to London back to Coventry, down to London back to Birnigum, or Northampton, or Leicester. In them days us Number Ones traded all over the different Cuts. Much later as trade dwindled we dwindled more and more to workin the Grand Union and, last of all, the h'Oxford.

Most wharfs were locked orf at night. Some couldn't be locked and were out in the open. Dad didn't like orf-loadin at them out of workin hours. There was one at Wilstone on the Wendover Arm where he had a contract for a while to deliver coal but he never renewed it. Folk kep pilferin that coal at night when the wharf was unguarded and we was blamed for short delivery. Number Ones don't want no iggle like that [*higgling or haggling, dispute*], they has to *strove* to get a contract, they has to make sure all their dealins is kep straight forard and above-board else they don't get no more orders from that party. Dad got another contract instead, deliverin to the Condensed Milk factry along the Aylesbury Arm, but it was bad-goin along there. The mud-'oppers [*dredger-men*] had gone to the war, the bank was siltin oop, and you couldn't draw the loaded boats in close enough. You had to lay out several lengths of planks from boat to shore and wheel it along in them heavy iron-wheeled barrers.

We was workin all the daylight God sent for the war, coal, inkits, stone, sand, timber, grain. Then they brings in 'the clocks' [*British Summer Time*], 'daylight savin' they called it, daylight *slavin* more like! another hour of strovin on the boatworkers' day. I hadn't much spare time to dwell on Moy-chap, I just 'kep-in-touch' whenever I could.

''Undreds of thousands killed on the Somme! Read all about it!' this newspaper boy was shoutin one Sunday mornin outside Berkers Station [*Berkhamstead*]. The station isn't far from the moorins and Dad had gived me some pennies to fetch the *News of the World* for Mrs Ojits [*Hodgett*] who was moored along of us. Mrs Ojits could 'pick out words'. We all gathered round to hear the news of the war as managed by Mrs Ojits. No matter how much she skipped she brought it home to us. The war was goin in a bad way, whole armies gone, 'Kitchendor' gone, battleships gone. I covered my oops with my 'ands and prayed and prayed for Moy-chap.

Soon after, my Uncle Frank, Dad's younger brother, was called oop. It didn't count no more that he was already doin valuble warwork, they was gettin desp'rat for fightin men. His Best-Mate, Aunt Rose, were big and raw-boned with a deep voice. I spose 'They' thought she were man enough to manage on her own, she still had four children at home; but Gladys, the eldest at thirteen, was as'matic, Kenny was ten, and the twin girls was five. They worked a pair of boats for John Griffiths on the North Coventry. Their 'orseboat was the 'Severn' but I've forgot wot their butty was. My Granny Mella had worked for Old Man Griffiths, carryin best buildin stone from Runcorn to build fine mansions and churches. Uncle Frank had carried on with Gran's boats. He'd worked for that same firm all his life, he were born and bred under Griffiths of Bedderth. Aunt Rose were determined to keep the boats goin for when he comed back. Dad loaned me to Aunt Rose to help her get on her feet. I walked *miles* for Aunt Rose. Griffiths was very perticler with their 'orses. If we was moored within walkin distance of Bedderth the 'orse was never allowed to stay more than one night in the public stable, they wanted it back in their own medders at Bedderth.

Coal down to London and grain oop to Coventry was our main 'road'. Coventry Basin was like today's car parkin, you was only allowed to moor in the Basin while you was bein orf-loaded at one of the ware'ouses, you'd be fined if you moored beyond yer time. All them wharfs was that busy they didn't want idle boats clutterin oop the Basin, and at night *no* boats was allowed in there, they dropped a big beam of wood into the grooves of the bridge-'ole and we all had to moor outside. Robinson Powers' cornmills could only deal with so much cargo at a time at their ware'us in the Basin. In Moy-chap's war we was often laid oop outside the Basin for several days, sometimes a whole week, waitin for our turn to be orf-loaded. As soon as we reached Coventry I'd help Aunt Rose to moor the boats then I'd set orf for Bedderth, walkin the 'orse along the road, window-shoppin all along them little Coventry shops wot was bombed in 'Er 'Itler's war and never comed back. We walked craws-country through all them little 'amlets wot's part of the city today. Granny Mella used to tell me that before the trams came along the only way them 'amlets' people could get to Coventry was to walk acraws the medders or ride a n'orse. I never rode a n'orse, we was never encouraged 'cept when we was little. The hanimal had enough, drawrin the load, without you a-top. It was six miles to Bedderth. I'd hand over the 'orse to Griffiths' h'ostler, and walk the six miles back. I could of went back by tram then, but I 'adn't a n'igh h'opinion of trams.

When our turn came to be orf-loaded, I'd help Aunt Rose to shaft the two boats through the bridge-'ole into the basin to Robinson Powers' wharf. At Robinson's their men unloaded the full sacks to the top of the oyist. The sack was untied and the wheat fell loose, helta-skelta, down the chute into the yooge big waggon underneath, where two big dray-'orses with a poleshaft between 'em was waitin patient to thunder out with the loaded waggon into the narrow Leicester Row drawrin the grain to the mills. And if the water-cart 'orses was comin the h'opposite way a-sprayin the dusty Row, moy-hoy! didn't the language fly!

I'd walk again to fetch the 'orse back from Bedderth—this time it may not be the same hanimal, it depended on which one the h'ostler wanted worked. The 'orse would draw the empty boats back to Bedderth to be loaded with coal and several sacks of provender, mixed by Griffiths' own forager to suit that perticler 'orse and last him the fortnight down to the docks in the East End and back with another load of grain.

We was at the 'Front' carryin the grain yet we was at the back when it came to gettin a loaf. Bread were the shaft-o'-life on the boats. In peacetime we prided ourselves on stockin the starn with bread to last the trip. The kind of flour, the way it was milled and baked, kept bread 'fresh' for far longer in them days than it does today. In Moy-chap's war we had a constant battle gettin a loaf. I walked miles for bread. When they brought in the rationin 'for regler customers only' we was all over the shops. If it wasn't for our old friends the lock-keepers' wives and the publicans' wives gar-nerin vittles for us we could of starved for all 'They' cared. It was fairer in 'Er 'Itler's war, we was alleycated [*rations were allocated to boat people*]. In Moy-chap's war I once queued for a loaf all mornin in the East End until I just fainted away. When I came to, all I got was 'That's it for today. Come again tomorrow'. Just as well we moved on, the next day the first bombs ever dropped from aeroplanes on ordinary people landed there, flattened the bakery, killed and injured no end of kiddies in the school acraws the street and people in the station nearby.

I walked miles to find food, and miles to get round troubles, fallen trees, caved-in banks, and sinkin bridges. So many lengths-men and maintenance men was away at the war, some parts was gettin impassable, some Arms got growed in and was never used again. The Northamton Arm were in a terrible state. Griffiths tried to get a contract with Whitworths at Wellinbrer [*Wellingborough*]. We got as far as we could but the Cut beyond the Devil's Elbow was all silted oop and they had to send their 'orse-n-carts to unload us. The Elbow itself were a nightmare, a *terrible* tight fit to turn a pair of loaded narrow-boats. You ent got no 'hinges' on a boat, you can't fold it in half, you has to wind all 70 feets of it round the bend at once, or nothin.

As for the sinkin bridges, if it was a case of 'goin over the top' Kenny could manage to take the 'orse while me and Aunt Rose shafted the boats through the bridge-'ole to meet him. The water takes the main weight of the boat, of course, but it's still a killin strain on yer shoulders and back shaftin two loaded 70 ft boats. Yer shaft's long and heavy. You has to plunge it into the Cut, push on the bottom with all yer might to send the boat along, then pull it out hand over hand and plunge it in again. Sometimes the mineworkins had made the bridges sink so low we couldn't shaft, nor stand oop. We'd have to wind the ropes round us and bowall the boats through. It's cruel 'ard on yer breasts, bowallin a loaded boat.

The bridge-'ole at Longford on the Coventry was one of the worst. We always had to unhitch the 'orse and walk him over the top, dodgin the trams all the way down the road to New Inn bridge. All the boat people was gettin fed oop with the hold-oop. The Longford were a very important bridge-'ole leadin to the Gasworks, the Ordnance, the Lectric Light, the Co-op, and all the other famous mills, timber wharfs, and factries into the heart of the city. They *had* to raise it at the finish.

Other bridges on other Cuts like the end of the Moira was let to sink till none of us could even crawl through and the Cut beyond were gradually abandoomed. That Cut belonged to the railway so it paid 'em to let it silt to ruin so goods would be transferred to rail. This was a shame, Dad always got a drawback [*toll rebate*] for carryin Moira coals all the way to the h'Oxford colleges.

Aunt Rose never paid no tolls, Griffiths done all that, but wherever we roved we had to get the boat tickets signed at the toll h'office. Just inside yer cabin door, nice-n-andy, high oop, between the wall and yer cabin top, was yer ticket draw. Under that were yer soap-'ole for yer cleanin clobber, and under that yer monkey-'ole for yer winlusses. Aunt Rose had a n'ansome brass drop-'andle on her ticket draw. The backplate were a battered old h'Oxford Canal Company badge, Britannia showin a leg in front of h'Oxford city with her shield, boat shaft, and navvy shovel. Uncle Frank fashioned that 'andle for her. She thought the world of it and kep it polished 'for when he come back'.

Though Griffiths owned the boats all they was compelled to supply was a water can and a warmin stove, not even a *cookin* range. They let yer make yer own cabin-'ome, do-it-yerself like. Uncle Frank could turn his hand to anythin, and he always prided his-self on his 'finish'. He done all his own tiddly-work [*decorative*

ropework], the fenders, the Swan's neck, the Turk's head, and the plaits around the tingles. They plaits *flowed*. They wasn't just for decoration, the plaits on yer tingles protected yer woodwork, and the ones on yer tiller not only protected the paintwork on yer cabin top when you laid the tiller on the roof in the locks but also stopped the water from drippin down yer tiller into yer tiller socket and rottin yer elum. Uncle Frank's plaits was gettin worn and wiskery now but it's bad luck to renew them without the Captain's say-so. Aunt Rose wouldn't dream of it, she sez we must go on scrubbin the old ones, keep 'em white and smilin 'for when he come back'. She *strove* and *strove* to keep everythin smilin 'for when he come back'.

He never come back. Dad and Mum were waitin with the 'Percy Veruns' and the 'Victoria' at top o' Buckby locks to break the news to Aunt Rose, 'Missin, believed killed'. All Uncle Frank's lot had been wiped out. Many had no known grave. I was feared about poor Syer, prayin he was still alive. So many men had been lost they was threatenin to call oop the 50s. We was dreadin it would be Dad's turn in the end.

Aunt Rose, always so buxom and bustlin, just croompled-oop. Tears and tears, tumblin like a weir. Dad said it wasn't only because of losin Uncle Frank it were the strain of keepin on strovin and strovin 'for when he come back'. Her deepest grief were that he'd had no proper burial. 'No proper finish,' she kep on, 'Frank would be oopset about that.'

Me and Aunt Rose was loaded with coal for the Maypole Dock, the big factry they'd built for the Dairy Margarine just before the war, just orf the Grand Junction before you gets to Norwood Lock.

Dad and Mum were loaded for Fountain's Mill, h'Uxbridge. Dad decided we'd work the four boats down together between us, the kiddies could play together, me and Kenny and Arryut could help work the boats and we'd all be company-like for Aunt Rose.

News travels fast on the Cut. They had a bounty [*collection*] for her at the Fountain's; and they gived her a whole pound of margarine at the Maypole. In Moy-chap's war margarine were like gold dust. She were still grievin 'no proper finish' when we tied-oop at Brentford for a backload of timber. There was a collection tin for her already in the h'office at Brentford and all the boatmen were puttin in their few precious pennies for her. The Mission-man came acraws from the 'Boatman's Mission'. He'd heard about Uncle Frank and knew him well. He asked Aunt Rose if she'd like a special service for him in the Chapel.

That chapel were choc-a-bloc and overflowin; boat people, chaps from the docks, and even some wounded soldiers home on leave from France. They gived the boat kiddies a bunfight [*tea-party*] afterwards in the h'Institute. Kenny broke his leg playin 'Boofs' [*Blindman's Buff*], and had to be carted orf to 'orspital. Poor Aunt Rose! As if she hadn't enough to worry about, and her all loombered oop with timber for Coventry. She were tore both ways, whether to get the boats ahead or stay with her only son. She needed her wages from Griffiths more than ever but she didn't like leavin Kenny behind all by his-self in 'orspital.

'You go ahead, Mrs Mellor', the Mission Man said, 'Kenny will be well looked after in that hospital. *I'll* keep an eye on him every day until you get back.'

Aunt Rose trusted him. He kep his special eye on Kenny, visited him every day in that 'orspital, and Kenny looked upon him as a spare h'Uncle for the rest of his born days.

Soon after, Aunt Rose packed oop workin for Griffiths and teamed oop with her widowed sister, Bertha Stoutback, workin on the tarboats for Thomas Clayton of Obry. They collected the raw tar from Birnigum Gasworks and took it to Obry to be 'worked' [*distilled*]. They tarboats was a lot easier in many ways for women. There was no hand-loadin, the tar was pumped in and out. There was no sheetin-oop, the decks was sealed and flat; and the men at the Works done all the cleanin out in special clothes and gas masks. But it were hard on yer cabins and paintwork because it were a dirty old 'road' to travel, stinkin chimneys and 'poison' works, we used to call it 'the Chemical'. Aunt Bertha once told me that her late husband used to keep his shiny silver pocket-watch tucked away in his innermost pocket, yet he'd only to walk the towpath at Obry for that watch to turn black with 'chemical'.

'If that chemical does that to moy watch,' he used to wheeze, 'wot must it do to *moy* works?'

He were always very chesty, couldn't draw full-breath. He died of the new monia, the bronical. Yet my cousin Gladys and her asthma ran on that 'Chemical' for years.

They gived Aunt Rose a medal for Uncle Frank, a big heavy copper thing, all the chaps wot died in the war had it. They called it 'the Deadman's Penny'. Aunt Rose gived me her Britannia 'andle orf her ticket draw as a special keepsafe for helpin her in the war, and I went back to workin the 'Victoria' with Arryut for my Mum and Dad.

That last winter of the war was bad [*Jan. 1918*]. People had got right down low for lack of food. To cap it all the Cut h'iced oop. We was tied oop at Sutton Stop loaded with coal for London. They had a job to sought out enough 'orses to draw the h'ice boat. It took anythin from twelve to twenty 'orses to drag the heavy iron-hulled boat through the h'ice, crackin open a passage for the rest of us. It was a job to sought out enough men to 'andle the 'orses and man the boat, the young was all away at the war, and the old was all down with the 'flu. They had to call out the h'army, the raw recruits, to 'andle the 'orses and rock the big iron handrail that ran shoulder high, from stem to starn along the boat, rockin the boat from gunnle to gunnle, breakin the h'ice right out to the banks. On the still frosty air you could hear that h'ice boat comin from a mile orf; whips, boots, hoofs, shouts, h'ice crackin in all directions like sharp pistol shots and above it all the bawl of the sergeant-major. Best drill they recruits could ever have, rollickin that heavy boat— put no end of muscle into their 'mooskits'!

By the time we was on the move again I was struck with the 'flu. Then all my sisters had it. When we got to the Blizzerth [*Blisworth*] Tunnel none of us was strong enough to walk the 'orse over the top. Mum had to walk it by herself through the snow. To cap it all the tug wasn't workin, the snow was blockin the air-'oles in the tunnel and they daren't risk suffocatin us in smoke. The tunnel-chaps had to get out their old wings [*legging boards*] and leg us through. Poor Mum were frozen, waitin for us in the lobby at the other end.

I'd just about got oop on my feet again by the time we tied-oop at last on the Paddinton Arm, between the Mitre and the Ladbroke, waitin to unload. That night Mum and Dad went down with it. It was said to be borne over on the stench of the battlefields in Flanders. Judgin by the stench on the Paddinton Arm I could believe it. We was used to smells—everybody was in them days— none of yer 'dodorans' [*deodorants*]—but on that built-oop slum of the Cut the pong was shockin. People worked where they lived, squeezed in between gasworks, sugarworks, paintworks, glueworks, oondreds of chimneys, factries and houses, belchin smoke and flumes, and the everlastin stench of the boats clip-cloppin past carryin in their open holds the rottin roobish of London.

Mum and Dad had the 'flu real bad. No end of people was dyin of it. I went trekkin round all they little back streets in the cold queuein for bread, pertaters, tripe, oonyuns. I got back to the boat to find Arryut was all alone cryin her eyes out. The 'Croolty Man' [*NSPCC Inspector*] had been and carted Mum and Dad orf to 'orspital. Lizer and Suey had scarpered because he was comin back to take them into care if nobody was lookin after 'em. She flung her arms round me, 'O, Rose! I'm so glad we've got you. I told 'im you was out buyin food for us and you was over twenty-one.'

I was eighteen. I felt oondred. I were worried about Lizer and Suey. They hadn't long got oop from 'flu, 'Where could they be?'

'Don't know. I've looked all along the wharfs. They've been gone ages.'

Lizer must of been about nine and Suey were seven. We lived very close on the boats, boat children hardly ever strayed from the Cut on their own, specially in London. I suddenly had a good idea.

'*Oonyuns!* Get the pan on, Arryut. They'll be back when they whiff fried oonyuns.'

I made oop the range—at least we had coal, sixty ton of it—left Arryut mindin the pan and set out to find them. 'They can't of gone far.'

They'd trailed the red-crossers [*ambulances*] all the way to that 'orspital. I met a bobby bringin 'em back. He'd found 'em on the 'orspital steps askin everybody, 'Please can we 'ave our Mum and Dad back?'

Day after day that were *my* prayer too as I watched the never-endin 'ersts' [*hearses*], black draped motors, black plumed 'orses, on the opposite bank waitin to go into Kensal Green Cemetery. In them days 'ow many plumes showed how important the dead was. I couldn't think wot I'd do if Mum and Dad died. My Granny Mella hadn't long died at Stowell. She lay there in her coffin with us in the little downstairs room at Stowell. She looked lovely. We had our dinner and done everythin round her on the first day, Granny were 'closed' on the second day, and buried on the third. Wot would happen to us if Mum and Dad died? My Granny Fisher on the bank at h'Oxford were poorly. We couldn't go and live with her. The boats was our only 'ome. We'd have to hang on to the boats between us *somehow*. One thing was sure.

'Yer not goin in no work'us', I promised my three sisters; 'they'll have to drag yer out of this cabin over my dead body!'

And still the ersts lined oop. And still the stinkin roobish boats went past. Some of 'em was wide boats but most of 'em was narrow-boats like ourn, 'Monkey boats' them Londoners called us. I've learned since that a chap oop North called Monk built the first ever narrow-boat, but in them days I'd no idea why they called us monkeys. We never had no monkey. We had a thrush.

'Thrushy' were our Mum's pride and joy. She'd brung him oop from a weaklin on the towpath last summer on the South h'Oxford, the dillun [*weakling*] of a late brood. We had to crush 'empseed with a bottle till it was fine as dust, and she'd mix it with crushed croombs and a little milk. She fashioned a thin hollow twig into a tiny scoop and fed him like that. 'Ah-ah-ah!' his little beak went, 'ah-ah-ah!', everlastin. It were a job to keep oop with him. Dad made him a woven wicker cage, *lovely!* And Mum made him a crosher cover to shade him from the sun and to 'tuck him oop' at night. Every time we went past the Sand-'ole at Garsides or Arnold's sandworks at Leighton Buzzid Mum used to say, 'Take a bookit and fetch Thrushy some of that sand'. Lovely sand they had at the Sand-'ole, all silvery. She'd bake it in a tin in the oven and then spread it on newspaper in the bottom of his cage—didn't have no ready-made sandsheets like you buys nowadays. He'd sing on the cabin top all day and sleep in the cabin at night. We used to search the grassy verges along the towpath for snails for him. He'd get *that* h'excited. 'Thwack! Thwack!' you'd hear him breakin his snail on the bottom of his cage.

Poor Thrushy were pinin. There was no grassy verges where we was moored, no snails, no Mum to feed him the way he liked, no Mum to say 'Night-night, Thrushy', and cover him oop. On the way down to London she'd been offered a fortune for him by a big-business-bloke wot kep 'The Packet Boat', the big inn just before you gets to the Slough Arm but she wouldn't part with him. Thrushy died the day Mum and Dad came back from 'orspital. We owed no end for Troy's stablin.

'There!' Mum sez, 'we ought to of tooked that fortune that big-business-bloke offered us.'

'Don't worry', sez Dad, 'he's offered us another—*cartin roobish!*'

It wasn't yer common roobish, it was the posh h'offal from the kitchens of the big London 'otels, and all the left-overs the fine-mouthed left on their plates. We collected it from the 'orse-n-carts at the dock wot's called Porta Bella and took it down to Squires', 'the Trout' we used to call it, on the Slough Arm. They boiled it into pigs' swill, dogs' dinners, and h'artificial manure. Moy-hoy! Didn't it stink! We dumped it out at the factry in fish-barrels, sluiced out the empty holds, and took the clean scalded barrels back. Took us ages to sluice out. We'd tie the bookits on ropes, sling 'em over the side to fill in the Cut, tip 'em in the hold, mop down and pump out. While we were at it we washed down the cabin top, the paintwork, the ropework an all. We may be oop to the gunnles in roobish travellin along to the Trout but we was the cleanest pair o' monkeys on the Arm travellin back.

That run lasted us to the end of the war when the roobish—like millions of tons of other cargo—was switched to surplus army lorries. Lots of didgy-dodgy loads us boaters had sneaked durin the war to out-of-the-way wharfs and factries went over to the lorry-chaps. Lots of the boatmen wot came back from the war never went back to the Cut, they joined the lorry-chaps. We didn't know it at the time but Moy-chap's war and the comin of the owner-lorries was the beginnin of the end for us Number Ones.

I can't remember zackly where we was moored for the h'Armis-tist. It was somewhere on the Grand Junction. I can only remember we was tied oop along of the Smiths' dirty old boat with their beautiful tame blackbird in a cage on their cabin top, whistlin for all he was worth, 'Inky, pinky, par-ly-voo!'

It belonged to George Smith, father of the George Smith who later married Sonia, who later married Mr Rolt. George senior, like our Mum, had brung this tame bird oop from a weaklin and taught him to whistle. All the chaps whistled in them days but George senior had the clearest whistle of all. No matter which wharf you was loadin at you'd hear his whistle above all the din, and his bird echoin him, 'Inky, pinky, par-ly-voo!'

George Smith senior married Anna Statham, and his brother Solomon married her sister. Anna's mother, Mrs Statham, used to despair of her daughter keepin such a slap-dash boat. 'I can't understand our Anna, she wasn't brung-oop "Rodney" like that!'

Yet Anna and George produced seven or eight *beautiful* children, real nice kiddies, deep red 'air, *lovely*! They all went on to do well. While George junior was married to Sonia he had the spickest pair o' boats on the Cut. When he lost Sonia he sank right back into his mother's old ways. Such is life.

Moy-chap came home at last but he would never tell me nothin about his war. He said it was somethin so terrible that women should not never know about it. '*Never!*' But sometimes I'd catch him, on the quoyet, tears runnin down his cheeks, whistlin soft to his-self, '*Inky, pinky, par-ly-voo!*'

Gettin in Tow

I WERE married in blue with button-strap shoes and a closh-'at.

We was married at Banbury Registry h'Office. I were nineteen and Syer were twenty-one. I were too worked-oop to take-in the goins-on; that Registry chap talked 'with a ploom in 'is mouth' and Syer had a new pair of boots from the 'Workers' Boon', a shop in Banbury, and they creaked chronic. They boots put me orf proper. All I remember is Moy-chap promised 'I do' and I promised 'I do' back.

We had a job to rally two witnesses. None of our families was come. My Mum and Dad was 'oop the crick' with a stoppage at Branston Tunnel, his Mum and Dad had 'gone' in the 'flu at the end of the war, his two older brothers was killed in the war and the others was strugglin to earn a livin all over the Cut. In the end Mr and Mrs Ambridge, the landlord and his Missis from the 'Strugglers', h'obliged. They was Uncle and Aunt to Rosie Coles of Thrupp. They was scholared, they could read and sign for us. They wanted to take us back to the pub for a quick drink but we was wantin to get started on our first trip. Our honeymoon were a load of coal to deliver to Dolly's 'Ut [*a wharf near Hayfield Wharf, Oxford*]. Work was very short, we was lucky to get a load. It was all boarded and waitin for us agen Banbury lock.

Our marriage-'ome were the 'Britannia', a 72 ft, wooden-hulled narrow-boat, a dumb boat [*without an engine*], drawed by a n'orse. It were to be our 'ome for the next thirty-five years. It had taken Syer two years of hard work to get enough money to put a deposit on her. She'd had another life in tow with the 'Providence', worked regler by Emmanuel Tooley and his younger son 'Mr George', carryin moldin sand and steel bars twixt Birnigum and Sammerson's, the big foundry on the side of the Cut on the outskirts of Banbury. You always seed important machines, reapers, binders, chaff-cutters, wot-av-yer, ranked in rows along there. When 'Mr George' took on the Banbury boatyard in 1900 from the Comp'ny

[*Oxford Canal Company*] he kep on the 'Sammerson run' but he had change-boats as well, for hirin when yourn was in his dock. 'Mr George' offered Syer the 'Britannia' for one oondred pounds, to do oop at his yard, providin he helped out with the Sammerson run whenever there was a throng on.

Syer had worked on 'Britannia's' timbers, corkin [*caulking*] and tarrin. He'd even done some of the scumblin [*thin overlayers of colour*] for some of 'Mr George's' fancy paintwork. Last of all he'd fixed Uncle Frank's 'Britannia' drop-'andle, wot Aunt Rose gived me, on our ticket draw. Now she were ourn, all decked-out and waterproof, fifty pounds paid and fifty to go. Syer Ramlin were her Captain and, for better for worser, for richer for poorer, I were his Best-Mate, Rose.

Mrs Syer Ramlin! I stowed our precious weddin soostificut safely away at the back of the ticket draw. Some said boat couples never bothered to wed. I were now wed and, though I'd no idea wot it said, I were now Mrs Syer Ramlin and I were going to cherish that soostificut to prove it. I were vowed to be a good wife, to stick by Moy-chap through all weathers, keepin the boats always ahead, always on the go. As Granny would say, '*An idle boat puts no bread on the loaf*'.

While the Captain went to fetch the 'orse from Tooley's stables I stowed my weddin-gear away in the best-box under the crossbed. My blue costoom, my closh-'at and strap shoes had cost me all of 'ten-n-eleven' and they lasted me for best, lettin out the seams, for years. I donned my workin-wife gear, long black skirt, long-sleeved blouse, long white apron, workin boots and workin 'at. In them days no daycent boatwoman ever went about outside her cabin without a n'at. Some still weared the sunbonnet, but I never, sunbonnets was beginnin to be old fashion' amongst us young boatwomen after Moy-chap's war.

I knowed everythin about runnin a boat. The only thing I knowed nothin about were 'IT' [*sexual intercourse*]. Neither of us had had much chance to get to know each other, let alone at close quarters. Neither of us had knowed nobody without our clothes on. Ye'd think we'd learn as children from close-livin in our cabins but I never seed my Mum and Dad at 'IT'. They must of done it when I was asleep. If yer can sleep through a swan takin orf, whack-whackin its great wings all along the water beside yer, yer can sleep through anythin. Nobody learned yer nothin in them days but I'd gleaned at a very early age that 'IT' were sweet and 'IT' were dangerous.

I must of been about four at the time. We was tied-oop way-out in the country at one of they little drawbridges on the South h'Oxford. Very early in the mornin a woman came runnin down the dewy grass in the risin sun. I don't think they was related yet she and my Mum seemed to run into each other's arms. The woman was crying. Somebody oop in the lone farm'ouse was havin twins *'and it's all gone wrong!'*

Mum hurried away with her oop the fields. 'He ought not to have done it to her,' the woman kep on, 'He was told when they married she mustn't have children. He *knew* she was too delicate.'

All day long me and my Dad was left tied-oop at this bridge waitin for Mum. In the evening we wandered oop to the farm. It was a big ramlin place. All we could hear was women wailin oopstairs. Dad told me to stop downstairs. Downstairs was very quoyet 'cept for a yooge tickin clock. A door was ajar. I peeked in. Two little waxy babes, wispy red 'air, was swaddled, stiff as candles in their little home-made coffins of sweet new wood. I wandered out into the courtyard. I could hear somebody planin wood in one of the 'ovels. A man was in there, red curly 'air, fashionin a bigger coffin and cryin over it. The settin sun was glancin through the dust in the doorway, fallin on the 'rings' of sweet smellin wood driftin from his bench on to the cobbles. I mind playin with them, child-like, curlin 'em in and out of my fingers and tossin 'em to float down red in the settin sun. And all the while he were planin and sobbin over this coffin, 'It wasn't my fault. I loved her. She wanted it. She begged for it.'

We nearly didn't get round to 'IT' that night. We was wore-out with the hanimal. It were a 'thirty shillin 'orse' [*no good for the job*], called Ambo [*Ambrose*], bought as a bargain orf a milkman in Banbury. We found out too late that he wouldn't keep goin, kep stoppin for us to 'ladle out the milk'. There's a spate of them wooden drawbridges all along that part of the South h'Oxford. Nowadays they'm often left oop because people no longer use them as regler footpaths and bridleways, but in them days they was in almost constant use and left down. Every time you raised the bridge you had to watch out for a load of cow muck or 'orse muck fallin on yer. Every time Moy-chap loosed the bridle to go and raise the next bridge, expectin Ambo to carry on, the soppy hanimal came to a n'alt, the boat would glide on and the line would come orf the looby [*spring-hook on top of the mast*]. In the end we had to use the short shaft as a 'Banbury stick' to prop-oop the bridge and shift the 'orse.

We was glad to tie-oop late that night 'gen Somerton. While Moy-chap walked Ambo along the path and oop over the bridge to Charley Eagle's stables 'gen the paper mill—Charley owned the 'public' and the coalyard—I had a good wash and made our marriage bed with the lovely bedcover my blind Aunt Polly had croshered for us. She were my Granny Fisher's only unmarried daughter, and she kep on the little 'ome at h'Oxford for us all after Granny died. She'd lived there all her life. She was blinded by quicklime when she was a child. A workman h'accidently dropped it on her not knowing she were down below lookin oop at him daubin the underside of a roof. A lady at one of them big 'ouses in Walton Street learned her to read brailes. Aunt Polly worked for her all her life, bathin her children an' all. They all thought the world of her. Even though the children was now growed-oop and gone away she still went along there every day to do the h'oddjobs. She knowed every inch of the way along Robinson's wharf and all them little jitty-ways around St Barnabas. Everybody knowed her by sight and she knowed everybody by voice.

"Mornin, Polly!'

"Mornin, Mr Aymus!'

"Mornin, Polly!'

"Mornin, Mrs Beesley! Lovely weather for the time of year.'

She could knit and crosher *lovely*! I smoothed our bedcover, 'Peace at Home' it said, in brailes, and we spent half the night 'avin a row 'cos he wanted to sleep in his workshirt. It was all he'd got. *He'd never had a nightshirt*! I asked him wot he weared in the h'army. He said he'd never slept proper in the h'army.

'We was forever on the go.'

I could believe it. Never had I seed such *gallded* feets, *never*! 'Wherever did yer catch them feets?'

'In the trenches.'

'We'll have to *strove* with *them*!'

[55]

He wanted to keep them boots, them awful stinkin creaky boots, beside him all night.

'I en't 'avin them boots in my cabin. They can go outside in the 'atches.'

'Wot if it rains?'

'Nonsense! T'ent gonna rain. I can see the moon through the crack in the slide.'

'*I'm* Captain of this 'ere boat.'

'*I'm* First-Mate in the cabin. That's 'ow *my* Mum and Dad always works it and that's 'ow I means to go on.'

He wouldn't give in, tried to come over all lovey-dovey.

'No lovey-dovey along of them boots!'

He give in, put 'em outside in the moonlight. I came over all sorry then, watchin him tyin them boots to the step so's nobody could creep 'em away in the night. They was all he'd got. He'd put his all into makin the boat into a n'ome for us, he'd nothin to spend on his-self. Them poor feets! No chap should have to suffer feets like that. No chap should have to suffer such terrible things in the trenches that he could never bear to tell his Best-Mate. I drawed him into my arms, he deserved all the lovey-dovey I could give. Neither of us knowed how you was sposed to set about 'IT'. Us managed.

Them boots was puddled with rain in the mornin. I felt awful mean. I let him keep 'em in the coalbox after that. It were a posh coalbox, pretty-painted, like a deep wooden cradle. The low bit held yer coals and pushed under the step, the hood become another useful bottom step. The wet cured the creak out of them boots and we worked on 'em with 'orsegrease to make 'em supple. I stroved 'ard with his feets, permangeenate and Fuller's Earth, the sippy-tated [*precipitated*]. We cured 'em. I knitted him the special h'Oxford socks, turnin the n'eel smooth as silk as Granny learned me, and I always made sure he had good soles to his boots. He flit about the locks like a gnat-fly from then on, boundin down on to the cabin top, jumpin the gates, stridin the planks. Never seed nobody like Moy-chap in his younger days for steppin out along the top planks—'cept young h'Arthur Bray. In his young days h'Arthur were that wiry and spring-footed, he bounded rather than walked. Even in his seventies, to see h'Arthur stridin out along the top planks ye'd think he were orf to the end of the Cut.

We had a nice surprise when we opened the side locker. 'Mr George' had made a n'andmade stool for us. The boatbuilder always used to give yer a stool as a good-luck souvenir when he built yer a new boat, but we never expected one for doin the old boat over. He'd painted it with roses on the sides and the head of a span'll dog on top, big brown eyes gazin oop at yer, *lovely*! I have that stool yet. His nose is wore, one eye's a gonner, but the stool's as steady as ever. Over the years it's been stool, step, dolly's cradle, ride-a-cock 'orse, wot-av-yer. It's seed us through the good times and the bad.

Times was very 'ard when we was first in tow. In them run-down days after the war it was frightenin how many Number Ones and little Carryin Comp'nies was goin under. We got back to Sutton Stop one day to find Mr Veaters [*Veater*], the young traffic manager from the toll h'office, most oopset. Cox's hadn't paid their tolls. They was bankrupt, and Mr Veaters had the sad task of nailin a writ to the masts of Cox's boats. All my life I'd seed Cox's boats plyin the Coventry Cut. They was day-boats, without families livin on 'em, 'double-ended' with a rudder and a mast you could fix to either end to save windin [*turning the boat round*]. Tons and tons of coal and stone Cox's had carried over the years to Cash's, the Coventry Light and the Tramways. Now Cash's was goin over to rail, motor buses was challengin the trams, and the Coventry Lectric Light were shiftin out of the town centre to bigger premises. Cox's was finished, black-masted.

We stroved all the hours we could, me and Moy-chap, to keep *our* mast clear; and Mr Veaters was a good friend to us over the years. No matter wot little you earned you always stroved to put a bit aside for dockin, and for yer lines [*ropes*]. A 94 ft towline for the 'orse set yer back about twelve-n-sixpence. Lines was made of hemp or cotton. Hemp was all right for moorin or a checkin-strap, to hold the boat in the lock, but it was terrible splintery to yer 'ands, heavy when wet, yet limp as a reed, wouldn't 'whip' to zackly where you wanted. Cotton's nice and smooth, scrubs oop white, and whips to zackly where yer wants it. I always remembers how awful I felt when I made-do with the wrong tow-rope for the 'orse and watched 'elpless as it swept everythin orf the top of Suey Beechey's cabin as I went past. Suey were on the Clayton tarboats, carryin between Leaminton Gasworks and the Banbury Tar Distil-lery, just by the drawbridge; and from h'Oxford Gasworks, back o' Christchurch, to the Banbury Distillery. Her boat was the 'Leam' after the river at Leaminton. She were moored at Itchindon that day [*Long Itchington*] and had just finished spring-cleanin her cabin-top, polishin the brasses on her chimney, settin oop her fresh flowers and her clean water can. I walked past with the 'orse on the wrong line, wouldn't 'whip' clear, and swept orf the lot into the 'atches. I went back as soon as I could to make amends. She were seein the funny side of it, she were very good like that.

Mind you, she could be very outspoke'. The Boat h'Inspector came along the towpath. 'I've come to inspect your boats, Mrs Beechey.'

'That you won't, h'Inspector', she sez. 'I know my rights. It's Sunday. No boat h'inspections on a Sunday.'

She was right, they wasn't allowed by lor to poke their noses in on a Sunday.

'You can come tomorrer', she says, 'I'll be gorn by then!'

She was big, with a tremenjous voice. You could hear her callin her husband a mile orf. 'AL-BERT!'—and this tiny little chap would pop his head out of the cabin in front of her and pipe-oop, 'Yes, dear?'

No wonder most of us boatwomen ends-oop gruff. Most of yer life was spent strovin out of doors tryin to make yerself heard over the wind and the rain. It isn't easy, even in the best of weathers, to talk ladyfied to your belovid when there's seventy feets of boat and

almost ninety feets of towstring between you on the steerin and
him ploddin along on the towpath. If you wants a word you has to
bellow. I were often lonely when we was first married, with him
'miles ahead' on the towpath or away chasin orders. I missed
chatterin with my Mum and my sisters. You was used to close-
comp'ny all day with a family on board.

We was both so happy when we knew we was havin a baby. My
Mum were *that* h'excited over havin her first grandchild. I longed
for a little boy but Syer wanted a girl, he'd seed enough of boy-
babies with all his brothers. I was relieved that Mum was goin to
be with me for the birth. She knowed well how to manage, she'd
had eight of us, all borned on the Cut. I were plannin to have the
baby in me own cabin, moored at Aunt Polly's. There was a little
kitsy-cradle all ready and waitin for us at Aunt Polly's. In the best-
box under the bed I'd got everythin made wot Mum learned me,
binders, bonnets, vests, pilchers, back-flannels, the nightgowns
with the strings, and the daygowns with 'the posh'—tiny tucks and
lace—along the little yoke and all round the bottom. All new, made
'em meself, never been wore. Mum was makin me a shawl.
Everybody wot seed it told me how fine it was. Mum wouldn't let
me see it. 'It's bad luck to see the shawl before you has the baby',
Mum sez.

A few days before I were due to 'come to town', Mum and Dad
and the girls were ahead of us with the 'Percy Veruns' and the
'Victoria' loaded with sacks of wheat for Banbury Co-op. We was
followin with a load of coal for a private wharf near Little Bourton,
just before you gets to Banbury. We had Charley by then. We'd
sold Ambo after he bolted near Ruckby. We was goin under the
Grand Central railway bridge when a train suddenly shrieked over.
Orf he bolted. The towstring snapped, whippin round Syer's ankle
and bowlin him along like a ninepin into the Cut. I were nearly
widowed the year I were wed. We bought Charley cheap from a
farmer ruined by 'foot-n-mouth'. There was terrible plagues of foot-
n-mouth breakin out over and over again all over the country after
the war. *That* was sposed to of been brought over on the stench
from Flanders too. We used to deliver steamcoal to several farms
along the Cut for ploughin with traction hinjins, then we had to
change to coal for burnin the foot-n-mouth carcases. They used to
dig out a long hollow, line it with coals and burn the stock. Only

the cloven-'oofed stock were affected. The burnin stink of 'oof-n-'orn clung for miles along the Cut.

Charley were fourteen, on the small side, ideal for fittin under the bridges. He never forgot his old farm, he'd always perk-oop along there. Once he'd trod a 'road' he knowed it for always. He were just like old Troy used to be, take his-self oop over the 'orsebridges and 'bacca' for miles [*tow by himself while his master had a rest and a smoke on board*]. Troy had long since dead-departed. Only his long black tail still braved the Cut, flowin down the back of the elum of the 'Percy Veruns'. When you lost a good 'orse wot had served yer faithful for years you asked the knacker to keep and cure the tail with a patch of hide in-tact. You tact that patch of leather to yer rams'ead, the top of yer big rudder post, and the tail would flow down, and the spirit of that 'orse would stay with yer and bring yer luck.

Cobber the mule followed Troy. I can see Dad now, leadin Cobber ahead of us that day with a jaunty gait, boastin proud as proud to the chaps he knowed along the Cut, 'Our Rose is comin to town! We'm a-goin to 'ave us a gran'child!' Dad were goin to warn Mr Plester, the Banbury blacksmith, to get Charley's shoes ready. Mr Plester had his smithy 'gen Tooley's yard. There'd been a smith there since the Cut were first cut, and many of 'em was Plesters. Folk had only to say, 'Boatee Ramlin's Charley needs shoddin' and Mr Plester would know zackly how much iron was needed. 'Once shod, never forgot', yet he shod oondreds of 'orses, bewry 'orses, coal 'orses, boat 'orses in them days.

We had only the one boat to unload whereas Dad and Mum had the two. We was hopin to unload, get to Banbury, get Charley shod, catch them oop and work the three boats through together to h'Oxford. We was held oop waitin for somebody to help Syer unload. He was shovellin all by his-self. I couldn't help, I were spare h'admiral, all blowed-oop and useless. At this rate, I thinks to meself, by the time we gets to Banbury Mum and Dad will be halfway to h'Oxford! 'Don't you dare 'ave that babby before we gets to h'Oxford!' Mum had shouted as they left us and I laughed.

When I seed their boats still at the Co-op wharf and a crowd gathered underneath the ware'us gantry I knowed somethin terrible had happened. We tied oop quickly opposite Edmunds and Kench's Mill. Syer ran along to look. I were pluckin oop courage to clomber out and foller when he came runnin back. I were not to look. He made me go back down into the cabin and sit on the bench. He put his arms right round me and held me close.

'I loves yer, Rose', he sez. He were tremblin all over. 'It's yer Mum. She've broke 'er neck.'

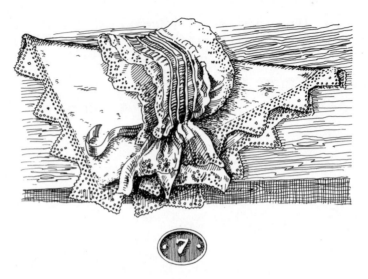

7

'Comin to Town'

THE Co-op ware'us had a n'overhead gantry with the chains comin down through the high platform for unloadin. On the end of yer chains comed yer 'dogs', strong nipper-'ooks like the one on the end of a dog's lead, for clippin on to yer sack. Each one of them sacks of wheat weighed two and a quarter oondred weight and took some handlin. While yer chap was sweatin, shiftin each sack acraws to the side of the boat, it were woman's work to clamp the dogs on to the sacks, lift a hand to the chap on the gantry above to 'haul away'—and busy yerself with the next sack. Either Mum didn't clamp enough sack or the gantry chap hauled too soon—we never knowed—but the heavy sack swung ockerd [*awkwardly*], hit the gantry platform at the top, slipped the dogs and fell, killin Mum outright.

I fought to go to her but they wouldn't let me. I fought to go to her funeral at h'Oxford, but I were stuck behind in Banbury Basin tryin to born the baby. Mrs Minnie Littlemore stopped with me. I was lucky she happened to be tied-oop in Banbury. The old Stratford Arm where they used to ply regler to the foundry at Dinzinger was all silted oop, the foundry abandoomed; the Littlemores, like many another old boatin family, was havin to seek work further and further afield.

I was two days walkin fore and aft the cabin, tryin to born the baby. My veins stood out on my body like 'awsers. Mrs Tooley kep lookin in and so did Mrs Plester. They kep tellin me I must 'let go', cry for my Mum, then the baby would come. I couldn't cry and I couldn't born the baby.

Mum had a nurse all lined oop for me to 'come to town' at h'Oxford, a good nurse, used to deliverin boat babies. I never knowed no nurse at Banbury. One nurse came. I shouldn't think she'd ever set foot on a boat, let alone tended a boatwoman. She didn't even ask my name. It were 'my good woman' this, and 'my good woman' that. She brought all this pannerfernalia, a load of old clothes in a draw.

'Wot's *them* for?'

'My good woman, you'll need *something* to clothe the baby.'

'You can take them back, I've got me own.'

She'd brought this *draw* for a cradle.

'You can take *that* back an all. I've got a brand new kitsy-cradle at my Aunt Polly's at h'Oxford.'

She refused to deliver me in the cabin—said I'd got to go to the h'Infirmary. 'You don't want your baby born on a *boat!*'

She spake as if it were the lowest of the low. I let loose at her.

'*I* were born on a boat! My *Mother* were born on a boat! My *grand*mother were born on a boat! My *great*—' by then she were fled oop the steps, out the 'atches. If Mrs Littlemore hadn't stayed my 'and I'd of chooked the flat-iron after her.

I were amazed to see it were night outside. I'd lost all sense of time. After that I lay on my bed numbed. The baby took me over. Mrs Littlemore peeped between my legs.

'I can see the top of its head, Rose! It's got lovely black 'air!'

It could of been sky-blue-pink for all I cared. At last old Mrs Boatee Own [*Hone*], from along Factry Street, mother of Alf who had the 'Cylgate', found a good nurse and brought her along in the middle of the night.

'My! You *have* got it clean and cosy in here, Mrs Ramlin', was the first thing Nurse said. Her name was Cope. And she did. At last our Rose was borned. Nurse drawed back the slide so I could hear the bells of Banbury town. It was Sunday morn.

[63]

Moy-chap were over the moon. Nurse wrapped her in the beautiful sawft shawl my Mum had made with such care for her first grandchild. I thought of Mum's 'ard 'ands managin such fine yarn in the lamplight when she were wore out with work at the end of the day. Big broad 'ands from all those years of workin the tiller, the locks, the ropes, wringin the washin, and tendin us kiddies. I thought of the tons of coal and stone them 'ands had shovelled, the oondreds of sacks she had clamped with the dogs. The tears came then.

We called her Rose Matilder after my Mum. I were hopin for a boy but I wouldn't of swopped our Rose for all the tea in chiner. It were a beautiful mornin. Suddenly in the blue sky beyond the slide were a sight I've never forgot, a yooge silver sky-ship with people, *real* people, havin their breakfast in the winders. We was already worried about the lorries takin away our trade, if you was to of told me then that 'oop there' were the carryin of the future, I'd of told yer to 'go and joomp in the Cut!'

'She's gotta be christened', I sez to Moy-chap. '*I* was christened, my Mum was christened, and my Gran. It's summat wot oughter be done, oughter come in somewheres. You never knows how long a baby's goin to live.'

Moy-chap was anxious to get the boat ahead, get on the move again. We'd already lost a whole ten days at Banbury, tied-oop havin the baby. The Littlemores with Dick and his sisters had already moved on. Dick was about sixteen then. He and Syer had been earnin a bob or two while I was laid oop, shovellin spent hops at the bewry, Oont Edmunts [*Hunt Edmunds*]. Spent hops was used a lot on the farms and the farmers would line oop with their 'orses-n-carts to be loaded.

In them days you was sposed to stop three weeks where you was havin the baby so they could keep their eyes on yer and take yer stitches out, but I wasn't registered to come to town at Banbury, and my Dad and my sisters wanted sortin out at h'Oxford. Dad had had a stroke and was in a bad way. I was twenty-one. I'd have to be Mum to 'em all now. I still felt weak and wantly after losin Mum and havin the baby but I was young, I gotter buck-oop. In them days if yer gived in yer went under.

'And I'd better be churched', I sez to Moy-chap. 'Aunt Polly won't 'ave me in the 'ouse until I've been churched.'

'Roight!' Moy-chap sez. 'Let's get it all sorted out now, whiles we be still tied-oop, then there's no more 'angin about!'

That's how our Rose come to be christened Rose Matilder at Banbury Big Church instead of St Barnabas.

Dad was lyin in the cabin of the 'Percy Veruns' at h'Oxford. I couldn't believe it were Dad. My poor father were struck down, couldn't move, couldn't speak, seemed to be seein nothin. They said it were delayed shock. Without Mum he were barely alive. He and Mum had been in tow for over forty-three years. Every day of those forty-three years they'd stroved together as one, best-mates in every way, sometimes yellin, sometimes laughin, workin the boats, raisin us children, raggin themselves out fetchin and carryin for other people all their lives.

It was less than two weeks since we'd all been jokin, lookin forward to the baby.

Mum laughin, 'Don't you dare 'ave that babby before we gets to h'Oxford!'

Dad steppin out so jaunty, 'We'm goin to 'ave us a gran'child!'

Now Mum was oop the Cemetery, and Dad were a pralasee [*paralysed person*].

Nowadays there'd be all the rigmaroles of 'sueing' and 'compensation'. In them days you tooked wot life chooked at yer and came back fightin. Some of the big firms like 'Fellas Morton' sometimes gived h'accident or sick pay to their boatmen but not to their womenfolk. There was one firm wot gived 'stamps' to their boatwomen for a while. I can just remember Ada Monk as was, showin me ern, stamps on a card, then comed the boatmen's strike and they took 'em all back. Ada was now happily married to Number One, Jack Skinner, brother to Joe who later had the 'Friendship', and had to manage like the rest of us. Us Number Ones just *had* to manage, put a bit by for when yer boat was laid-oop, and pray to God that *you* was never laid-oop. Every doctor cost a crown, every stitch a guinea. You spent more on yer hanimal than you spent on yerselfs. By the time you'd put aside money for fodderin, shoddin, and stablin there was nothin left for insurans. We just did our best in bad times to comfort each other and help each other to bear it.

Dad didn't seem to take anythin in, yet I'm sure he knew that the little warm bundle I lay close to his cheek was his first longed-

for grandchild. One tear gathered at the outer corner of his eye and
trickled down over the bare patch behind his ear. Over the years
my strong Dad had carried oondreds of sacks of corn, sand, cement,
on his shoulder, restin against that side of his head. He were
completely bald behind that ear. You never noticed when he
weared his old boatman's cap, but as he lay there in the dim cabin
of the 'Percy Veruns' it showed oop so weak and white I've never
forgot. I were tore wot to do with him. I knew it would be hard
copin with a pralasee and a new-borned babe on the boat. Dad
would hate to finish his days stuck inside, whether it be in a cabin
or in rooms on the built-in wharf at h'Oxford or Stowell. He loved
the open countryside. He were marster of all he viewed from the
towpath. Then I thought of Aunt Tovey.

Aunt Tovey, Dad's sister Thirza, were the dillun of my Granny
Mella's family. She wasn't a dwarf but she was under-sized and
bow-legged. She'd been terrible ricketsy as a child because my
Granny Mella had lacked nourishment when she was carryin her.
She done all the 'rough' in the house and the coalyard at Stowell
when she was young yet she were knowed for her healin hands
with people and hanimals. All her life she'd longed to be a nurse
but the look of them legs let her down and she hadn't the schoolin.
When the 'Fourteen War broke out a posh mansion agen Stowell
was turned into a n'orspital for h'officers. The nurses there was all
anpix [hand-picked], they wasn't only h'eddicated but 'igh-borned.
She just turns oop one day on her little bow-legs with her willin
hands, and begs to be allowed to nurse. They takes her on as
'General', skivvyin and wot-av-yer, and with her skilful 'ands she
works herself right oop from General to hawkzillery [auxiliary
nurse]. She hadn't the 'letters' she hadn't the legs but she lapped-
oop the lore, the practical.

A n'ordinary Tommy, h'officer's batman, fell in love with her.
They never married, she were old enough to be his grandmother,
but he thought the world of her. He was gived only two months to
live, he'd lost most of his stummick in the war and his lungs was
badly gassed. She coddled him along for another year in his little
cottage on the bank of the River Tove just above the wharf at
Yerdley on the Grand Junction. When he died he left her the
cottage and a nice little nest-egg to last to the end of her days as
long as she were fewgal [frugal]. She was now 'the woman wot

does' in them parts, deliverin babies, layin out the dead, wot-av-yer. If only we could get Dad to Aunt Tovey's before it were too late, *she*'d bring him back to the land of the livin if anybody could. At Aunt Tovey's he'd be in good hands, out in the country, within sight of all the boats comin and goin along the Cut.

Aunt Polly's lady-she-worked-for at h'Oxford telegraphed the wharfinger at Yerdley to ask Aunt Tovey. Aunt Tovey were only too willin to try her skills, she were very fond of our Dad. Now it were oop to us to keep him hangin on to life until we got there.

Of the three boats the 'Victoria', Granny Statham's old boat, needed most docktorin. Moy-chap decided it would be best to sell 'Victoria' to Mr Tooley to pay orf the last of wot we still owed him for the 'Britannia'. We'd carry on workin the 'Britannia' as 'orseboat and the girls could carry on workin the 'Percy Veruns' as butty. Arryut was about fourteen by then, Lizer twelve and Suey ten. We was all brung oop to work; come rain or come shine we'd strove to get a livin for all of us.

Moy-chap were all for sellin Cobber but Arryut were most oopset, she'd always helped Dad with him, she couldn't bear to part with him. 'We'll keep him for just a bit longer', Moy-chap gives in, just to comfort her. Lucky we did, comin through Wolvercote with the three empty boats at the start of that trip Moy-chap managed to pick oop a n'order for coals for the new road-bridges they was buildin at Duke's Cut to carry more and more motor-traffic to and fro into h'Oxford. The road-makin machinery in them days, lorries, rollers, wot-av-yer was still mostly coal-driven. Piles of coals had to be dumped on the sides of roads and wharfs for refuelin. My heart sinked, it would mean partin comp'ny at Branston while he went oop the North h'Oxford to Coventry leavin me single-handed to cope with Dad along the Grand Junction to Aunt Tovey's.

'I'll manage', I sez.

We couldn't afford to turn nothin down. You never knowed when you'd earn another chance. The work at Duke's Cut was just startin, with luck there'd be more orders to follow. In them days if yer didn't work yer didn't eat and there was the baby and the girls to keep now. I was lookin forward to reachin Banbury; it would be a big relief to pay orf Mr Tooley with the 'Victoria'.

We never got nothin for the 'Victoria'. Mr Tooley was cluttered-oop with hulks nobody wanted. Too many boats was chasin fewer and fewer orders. All he wanted was her stove, he could get a quid or two for that. He had quite a choice of old boat stoves standin round his yard. This was a 'Larbut', Granny Statham's old range, one of the best, wider than most, with a good oven, brass fittins galore, drawed well, heated even, and polished oop beautiful. If times had been more favourable I'd of had the one taken out of the 'Britannia' and kep Granny's for myself.

We stripped the rest of 'Victoria's' h'ornamentals, brasswork, ropework, wot-av-yer, and left her to rot in Banbury Basin. Providin they're not holed, it's amazin how long they old elm bottoms last in water. Yet if you was to beach her oop on the bank, dry her out in the sun, she'd crumble to dust. The 'Victoria' lay there for years. A bomb nearly scuttled her in 'Er 'Itler's War but she wouldn't 'ave it. She was still there when they filled in the basin after the war. She's probably *still* there under the bus station.

We was both oopset at splittin-oop at Branston. It was the first time we'd been single-parted. He didn't want to leave me, and he didn't want to leave the baby. He were *that* soft over the baby. He went orf to Coventry with Charley towin the 'Britannia' and young Suey as crew. She was only ten, a bit of a chatterchops but a good little runnerboat. Mum had brung her oop like the rest of us, she could steer, help with the locks, keep the cabin ship-shape, and manage a range. There was hardly any locks to be worked oop that 'road', and no shovellin. The bogey-waggons loaded the coal at the coalery—Syer had only to trim the boat, make sure the load were safe and level on the water—and the meechanical 'grabs' unloaded the coals straight from the hold oop on to the road at Duke's Cut.

Me and Arryut and Lizer worked the 'Percy Veruns' towed by Dad's mule, Cobber. Arryut was good at handlin Cobber. Me and her had went with Dad to buy him just after the war. There was a glut of hanimals come back from the war. Some of 'em was pitiful to be'old, branded with arrers all over 'em like convicks, and lousy. I reckon most of 'em was lousy because their tails was docked, 'buck-tailed' we called 'em, and they couldn't flick the lice orf. You'd see them driven wild, scratchin themselves raw against the arches of the bridges. I think it's terrible crool to dock a n'orse. We believed the strength of the 'orse lies in its tail. Cobber had been in the war in Turkey and was blinded in one eye. He didn't like yer comin at him from that side, specially in the stable. He'd 'tickle' yer [*pin you to the side of the stall*]. When we first had him he kicked. Moy-hoy! Cobber could kick! Backwards, sidewards, forwards, and his forwards—pardon me!—were the booger of 'em all.

Only once he had me in the Cut. It was just before I left home to get married. Oop the North h'Oxford it was, Coventry side of Noble, where the towpath's very narrow and the great oakses crowd oop the steep banks and roof over to meet each other like in church. It was a lovely bakin hot afternoon, flies buzzin, dooks snoozin, all was peace and ripple as me and Cobber plodded along. I were leadin him from his good side, next the Cut. Suddenly he jibbed. In I went. Lucky I was clad only in a cotton dress, and the tussocky bank was close to hand. He'd shied at a chap comin along the towpath. He was wearin one of them big Aussie-brimmed soldier hats some of our chaps brought home as souvenirs from the Turkey war. That hat were like a red rag to a bull to our Cobber. He were all for chargin at this h'innercent chap. He wasn't a proper chap he were a h'artist. He were no mountaineer, that's a fack!—took him no end of a struggle to scramble oop into one of these oakses while Dad coaxed Cobber past.

We was to keep him to the end of his days. Him and Charley worked well together. Handled right, Cobber were meek and mild. He was cheap to keep; mules have very hard 'oofs and need little shoddin, and he was never so greedy for fodder and water as Charley was. Charley was always nudgin the water panner on top of the cabin to tell me he wanted a drink. I'd offer one to Cobber while we was at it but he often wasn't bothered. He was every mite as strong as Charley and very sure-footed.

When we'd parted at Branston me and Syer had split our money, three quid and a few pennies, between us. He had tolls to pay, I had tugs to pay through the tunnels, we both had the hanimal to stable and feed ourselves. Every penny counted in them days. You could get a meal, a good chunk of fillin bread-puddin, for a penny.

I were anxious to get Dad to Aunt Tovey's as soon as possible but it was a job to get away from Branston. News travels fast on the Cut. Everybody knew about Mum, and Dad, and the baby. They cheered at the line of nappies blowin on the line along the hold. The Mellas and the Ramlins was well-respected along the Cut. The women on the banks and on the boats, the men from the pubs and along the wharfs wanted to say how sorry they were about Mum, and where was we takin Dad? 'Where's the "Victoria"?' 'Let's see the new little Rose.'

There hadn't been a Ramlin Rose for ages. Moy-chap was one of seven boys and both his married brothers had boys. I kep fetchin her out of the cabin and tuckin her back. People kep givin me things for her. Nobody had a lot to spare in them days, the Fellas Morton boats was even on strike, fightin their own firm's lorries, wantin paid 'olidays and daft things like that, yet our Rose was 'showered' with pennies, thrippny-joeys [*silver threepenny bits*], tins of Nestles milk and wot-av-yer. By the time we at last got away and worked oop the Branston flight to the summit, we was only just in time to catch the last tug of the day through the Branston tunnel.

It was our Rose's first tunnel and she cried all the way through. I was on the steerin and I didn't want to fetch her out of the cabin to cuddle her in the stink and the smuts and the smoke of the tug. The tunnel's not all that long but it's not straight like the Blizzerth, it wendy-bows in the middle and you can find yerself bumpin from side to side if you don't watch out, specially if yer the last in the tow as we was. It's best to take yer water cans and wot-av-yer orf the roof for safe keepin, so they don't bump orf, but it's not worth takin down all yer cabin h'ornamentals. It got on my raw nerves with the baby cryin and our Dad lyin there 'elpless but I were single-'anded. I'd sent our Lizer with Arryut to walk Cobber over the top. By the time we'd joined on the tug at the tunnel all the other women and children had already set orf with their hanimals. It wasn't all that far but it was only a farm track between fields, away from everywheres, very pleasant when you was all in a throng walkin together in broad daylight but a bit scary on yer own in the gatherin dusk.

I'd walked it all on my own in thick fog once when I was Lizer's age. I just clung to Troy and he led by h'instink. I heard this slow clankin comin nearer and nearer. I was terrified.—Sounded just like a convick draggin a ball and chain. It was a bull, a big beefy fella, with a tin 'blindfold' over his eyes, draggin this chain with a stake at the end. He must of slipped his moorins. He couldn't see nothin from under his tin lid but he could smell us. He stopped stock-still snortin the air. I wondered wot old Troy would do, he was nearest. Troy never give a toss, just tugged me past. He'd of kep goin however many old bulls was a-snortin after him.

We tied oop that night agen Welton and stabled Cobber at the wharf. There was no end of stablin about in them days, wharfs, ware'ouses, public 'ouses, builders' yards. None of 'em more than sixpence a night. Some farmers let you stable yer hanimal for nothin. You got to know the good stables. At the 'public' you supplied yer own feed and hung oop yer own haynet. You was payin for a nice clean stable and some straw. You was nearly always away early the next mornin so the publican had plenty of time to get the stables cleaned out, free manure for his garden, and ready for the next hanimal. We always stabled ourn, no matter how mild the night; hanimals, like 'yumans', need to know when their labour's done and they can be at rest.

I sent Lizer with Arryut to the stable that night. Stablin was man's work really, the rubbin down, the 'orseclawth, the feedin, wot-av-yer. Stables wasn't the place for young girls, all them h'ostlers and rooff chaps, but we had no chap of our own to do it. Cobber could be ockerd to stable if yer didn't know him. Dad once delivered a load of wheat oop the Warwick to Emscott Mills for a Major Gibbs—big chap he was, 'h'Empire Made', given to orderin about.

'Put him in my stable for the night, boatman!'

'If yer don't mind, Sir,' Dad sez, 'I'd rather stable him at the "public". He knows the "public", he'll settle there.'

'Nonsense! He'll settle here. No mule ever bested *me*!' I'm a *cavalry* man!'

Dad had hardly started back down the field to the Cut when he heard the Major 'ollerin—and it weren't the King's h'Inglish. He'd gone to feed him on his blind side and Cobber had pinned him 'right where his medals shouldn't be'.

We never got much rest that night, all in the one cabin. The girls had to make do on the narrow sidebed after bein used to the wide crossbed on the 'Victoria'. Dad were on the crossbed. I had to lie alongside him and get wot rest I could with baby Rose in her little kitsy-cradle on the floor beside me. I'd got a n'old pozzit [*invalid cup with a spout*] and managed to get some nourishment into Dad durin the day but it was a slow job. I was so lucky to have my sisters to cope with the boat while I had my hands free to feed Dad and the baby and keep oop with all the washin and hangin-out.

We was glad to call in at Stowell, Dad's old home, the next day, even though it weren't the same with Granny Mella gone. The Cut could be pretty lonely at times when you was on the go, specially when you was forced to tie-oop miles from nowheres at night. To tie oop at yer own folks on the bank was a rare treat. We couldn't read, we hadn't got no wireless, no telly, all we'd got was talk. We was often tongue-tied with 'furriners' on the bank, but with our 'own' we was chatterchops, chatterchops, shovel-n-tongs. I'd of given anythin to have back my Gran, chatterin away to my Mum and Dad, dandlin their new little grandchild. Mr and Mrs Ramlin were gone from their cottage too, died in the 'flu at the end of the war. They would never know now that they had a little grand-Rose come into the world. You *do* miss the old 'uns to talk with when a new baby comes along. Great Aunt Ilda was still there, flappin about in her long black skirts and black sunbonnet. No end of old people round there still remember her, in her eighties, humpin coals to the 'ouses out Weedon way and round Stowell.

The rest of the Ramlins and Ojits was pleased to see the baby, and shocked to see Dad. None of the Littlemores was at home, they was all workin their way oop to Tring and down to h'Uxbridge for Peter's weddin that weekend. Peter was marryin the lovely Alice Mees, and the young couple was workin their own boat to the weddin.

We was castin orf very early the next morning—I was vowed to get Dad to Aunt Tovey's that night—when the lengthsman wot looked after that stretch of the Cut came along with the sad news. The lovely Alice Mees had drowned the day before just beyond Lady Capewell's Lock, goin into Watford. There's a great big bend round there, the 'orse has to go oop over the 'orsebridge and you have to work the tiller hard round, but you mustn't shove it right over. The trainee boatwomen in 'Er 'Itler's War often made that mistake. It's no use shovin yer elum flat against the starn, you lose the steer of yer boat, you can't make the weight of the water work for you. You and yer elum work best when you keeps the tiller within bounds, usin the full power of the water. Alice was a borned boatwoman, she must of knowed this, but the big wooden tiller must of dried out in the long spell of dry weather and worked loose.

It went further than she meant and it jumped right out of the rams'ead and pitched her into the water. In dry weather we always soaked that end of the tiller in the water last thing at night and again first thing in the mornin, then banged it home into its socket. Alice couldn't swim, couldn't fetch herself along. Peter saw the tragedy happen, he was with the 'orse on the towpath, but there's a big broad sweep of water between the bank and the boat just there, Peter couldn't get to her. He never got over losin her, mourned her for years. He did marry in the end, but not for years after.

It seemed as if the whole of the Cut were in mournin that day, Stowe, Heyford, all the way to Bugbrook we hardly seed a soul. There's not even lock-keepers to pass the time o' day along there. Arryut plodded along with Cobber while Lizer done the steerin, and I looked after Dad and the baby and got a bite for us to eat. Dad were fast losin h'interest; we *had* to get to Aunt Tovey's that night.

We got to the Blizzerth Tunnel to find the tug had broken down. They was tyin it oop agen the windy-'ole [*turning place*]. They didn't hold out no 'ope of a replacement that day. There was four of us waitin to be towed, the two Wilson boats, the Bodley's one, and ourn, all of us anxious to get through without delay. The four Wilson chaps was loaded with anpix coals for some important customer, Mrs Bodley had just given birth to a baby, her twenty-secund, so she knowed how to go on. He were so tiny and blue, no bigger than a pound bag o' sugar—didn't look as if he'd last the tunnel, let alone 'life'. She were callin him Alf. Nar a one of his sisters lived beyond the age of seven yet little Alf Bodley growed oop to be champion pile-driver-ganger on the Grand Union.

Lizer had gone over the top with Cobber along with the other boat'orses. It were a two-mile trek all along the Stoke Road until you beared orf along the bridleway and down to the brick lobby just beyond the openin of the tunnel at Stoke Bruin. There was no 'orsepath through the tunnel at Blizzerth, and very few moty-boats to hitch yer a tow in them days. It were no use shaftin through neither, even though the roof is high enough; the tunnel is clever-built, round as the inside of a barrel, and yer shaft keeps slippin into yer hull. There were nothin for it, the Wilson chaps decided, but to leg through.

Though leggin had gone out of practice with the comin of the tugs, we still kep our 'wings', our leggin boards, in the loomber-'ole in case we was ever caught out without a tow. You wasn't allowed to leg durin tug-hours, leggin took over two hours and the tug was comin through one way or the other bout every hour. 'Sides, they wasn't goin to be done out of their three bob tow money. They tug chaps mostly lived at Stoke. Their last tug to Stoke was usually about half past six, whereas the boatman's day still had hours to go.

The brave Wilson chaps was willin to leg us all through together, lockin their boards on to their boats first, towin the Bodleys', then the 'Percy Veruns' on the tail. They wasn't wore in to that sort o' caper, clingin flat on their backs to their boards stuck out over the water, with their legs and heavy boots in the air 'walkin' the weight of those boats, boot over boot along the slimy wall, prayin no rare moty-boat would come the other way. Arryut was on the steerin. She knowed how to help by keepin in the 'flow' without 'drag', but it takes some doin, steerin in the dark with very little light. You can't use yer parafeen headlamp because it makes black'oles ahead for the steerer in front. I gived Arryut the candle lantern to give a n'extra bit of light on the cabin top, and the trap-brolly, a yooge affair, for when she went under the air-'oles.

Those air-'oles vented into the roof of the tunnel not only let out the smoke and steam of the tugs but let in the air and water from above as well. No matter how dry the weather was oop a-top there was always no end of hidden runnles of water that found their way down into them air-'oles. In times of heavy storm it could almost flood yer orf the tiller, you'd hear 'em torrentin down in the darkness ahead. They poor chaps leggin-it just had to put oop with it, but you was all right on the steerin as long as you put yer brolly oop.

I lit Mum's little lamp in the cabin and stayed down with Dad and the little 'un. I kep bathin Dad's eyes, they kep runnin and makin his face sore. I had a job to shave him. I kep talkin to him, tryin to explain where he was, and how we were takin him to Aunt Tovey to be made better, but all the time his eyes were unseein and I were beginnin to feel at the end of my tether. The slow 'Clap! Clap!' of the leggers' boots built oop louder and louder in the brick-built tunnel. Suddenly I noticed that Dad's eyes were 'listenin' tryin to make out that din he had known so well in his younger days. He still didn't move his head, but his eyes looked at me, strainin like.

'*Blizzerth*, Dad. The Wilsons are leggin us through.'

The din filled the cabin. Suddenly his eyes were 'follerin' it.

'You've got it, Dad! *Leggin*!'

I honestly believe it was them Wilsons' boots wot hommered through to Dad's senses, and brung him 'back' to us. They wouldn't take a penny for leggin us through, and they worked the locks for us, loosin us through to the bottom of Stoke. We stopped at the little cottage at the bottom of Stoke, wot we called 'the Navigation', and bought them a full jug of foamin ale. It was fourpence for a full jug. I think it was brewed on the premises. It wasn't a proper pub, it were a n'outside pub [*off-licence*] and a little shop. It was almost hidden behind a high hedge but us boat people knowed it were there and the lady was very good to us. There was a big farm'ouse standin just behind it. She got fresh milk for us from there and she made big rice puddins. She baked it stiff in a tin like cake and sold it to us, penny a choonk, *lovely*!

Very late that night we got Dad into Aunt Tovey's. His eyes told us he was more than content to trust his-self into his sister's sure keepin. Within a month Aunt Tovey had got him shufflin with two sticks to his chair by the window, where he could see all the comin and goin along the Cut. He shuffled like that with two sticks to the end of his life. His talkin never came back, but he could foller yer drift and take an interest, and he always done his slow best to be a help to Aunt Tovey.

Never have I been so relieved as when I handed Dad over to Aunt Tovey. I was *that* tired. I were frayed out with worryin, whether we'd ever get him there, whether I was makin enough milk for the baby, whether I could be a good 'Mum' to my sisters, whether I'd ever see Moy-chap again. I burst into tears when I seed him at last with our Suey safe and sound, with the 'Britannia' tied-oop agen the bottom lock at Branston. It was lovely bein 'in tow' together again. Syer couldn't believe how baby Rose had 'come on' in the long days and nights he'd been away from her. He felt cheated some'ow that she'd managed to keep goin without her Dad bein around.

The Dad was always around on the boats. On the bank most

Dads don't see their spouses and kiddies in daylight in the winter from one weekend to the next. They leave for work before they're oop and don't get home till they've gone to bed. On the boats the Dad is there from morn till night. Some was bloody miseries, always knockin their Missis and kiddies about; but Moy-chap were a good Dad as far as Dads went in them days. Havin been brung oop with no sisters to help out he'd had to help his Mum more than most lads. As a husband he were more considerate than most.

I'd never expect him to lift a hand in the cabin, look after the baby on his own, or do the shoppin. *That* were woman's work. Woman's work must be done on the go, or when tied oop at night, and meant plannin ahead. There must be no stoppin the boat. With Syer, as was only right and proper, the boat comed *first*. 'The boat, the hanimal, and my Best-Mate', in that order. That's how it were with all the best Captains. He had to keep the boat and the hanimal in good order and in work to provide a n'ome for us all. It was the only 'ome we'd got. There can be only one Captain on a boat—but *I* were First Mate in the cabin. Never shall I forget comin to town with our Rose. After that one trip with my Dad we vowed never again to be single-parted.

Suey were full of her latest jink, she'd 'lifted' a bike.

'Where d'yer lift that, ay?' I sez.

'Out the Cut.'

In them days it was still possible on certain stretches of the Cut to see clear to the bottom, the roach, the gudgin, the 'bandoomed bikes. This one Suey had collared were a rusty 'igh-'andled affair with a low-slung seat. 'The Rover' they called it. Both wheels was still on it.

''Ow yer gonna ride a bike on a boat?'

'Along the towpath, Rose. It's all the rage; ride ahead, get the locks ready.'

'Oo, I don't know, our Suey . . .' I were worried stiff, 'Wot'll the *'thorities* say?'

We never reckoned to draw the 'tention of the 'thorities, the Comp'ny [*Canal Company*], the Sanity [*Sanitary Inspector*], the Lor. In them days you wasn't sposed to ride even a n'orse along the towpath. Only the Comp'ny men, lengthsmen, lock-keepers, wot-av-yer, wot looked after the banks and sluices was allowed a pushbike.

'All the boats is takin to it, Rose,' Moy-chap sez, 'they calls it lock-wheelin.'

'*Whatever next?*' I remember thinkin to meself. '*Two legs was enough in my day, now the youngsters want two wheels!*'

Every generation wot's borned to life wants to live it faster. I expect if we was back workin the boats today they'd be lock-wheelin with *wings*!

No end of folk roved into the Cut learnin to master that old bike. It speeded oop proceedins no end. You could ride ahead, get the lock ready, dash to the nearest lockside butcher or shop, hand the shoppin back to whoever was in the cabin, finish the lock, and push on to the next. You had to watch for them 'igh 'andles under the bridges. When it wasn't in use we just propped it aboard anywhere we could. It was no use tryin to fit it into the laid-'ole. Our'un was already choc-a-bloc with dolly-tub, tin bath, tarpourlins, wot-av-yer. The laid-'ole was a cubby-'ole, back o' the mast, with boards laid loose so you could get through to the bottom of the boat. If you had trouble down below and needed to get to it quick you just had to turf everythin out. If we was moored at night in a real rooff place we'd tether the bike safe on board and hide it under the old 'orseblanket so's no other light-fingered so-n-so could lift it. 'The Rover' lasted us for years. I even took meself to Coventry 'orspital on it some years later. That was when I were pretty stout. I'd come to have me 'pendix drawed out.

Doctor nearly had a fit, 'You've come on *that*, Mrs Ramlin?'

'Let's get on with it, Doctor,' I sez. 'We'm only tied-oop for three days, then we wants to get the boats ahead.'

We was all for 'gettin 'em ahead'.

'Gettin 'em Ahead'

THEY called it the 'Depression', to us it was 'The Strikes'.

It was a job to keep our heads above water durin those bad years between the wars. Even the big chaps, those wot worked for 'Fellas Morton', was cut to fifteen bob a week and fourpence a ton. They was lucky to be tided over [*given an allowance*]. We had no big 'Fellas' to tide us over, just Moy-chap. He were a marster-daddy at ferretin out orders. The first whiff of a rumour that a bridge were to be widened to take more traffic, a new factry was sproutin oop along the Cut, a Lectric Light was shiftin to larger premises, he'd be there, scramblin oop the bank on to the site. He'd look for the 'arditter' [*hard hitter—bowler hat*], the chap in the bowlerat, 'ave a bit of a banter, put him in a good mood like, and wangle a n'order for sand or stone or ballast or steamcoal. He kep his ear to the talk at the locks, along the wharfs, at the pub. Moy-chap never went overboard for drink. He once got fisticoof-drunk on porter. After that *I* kept the purse strings.

The trouble was, you'd get a good order for stone or coals, then find the quarry or the mine was on strike. You'd get to the docks for grain to find—dockers 'out'; to the factry for goods—factry closed, no coal to drive their boilers. You'd hear the dockers was back, you'd go to the docks, still no load—seamen on strike, or tugmen on strike, or barges on strike. And all the time there was the boats to keep goin, Charley and Cobber to feed and stable, and us and the kiddies and my sisters to feed. True, stablin were hardly ever more than fourpence a night, and small herrin were 3-a-penny, but out of yer average two quid per boat per trip it was a job to put a bit by for bein laid-oop at Lime'us or Brentford doin nothin.

Us boats had to wait our turn at Brentford to get the import-coals from the barges. They couldn't load us when the tide was out, we had to wait for 'em to come oop river on the tide to the Cut. We was dependent on them barges. We wasn't built to go on tidal waters. The big ships from the 'igh seas would come oop river to London and be orf-loaded on to the barges. The barges would be tugged oop to the Canal basin and be orf-loaded on to us. Some h'ignor'uns calls us 'barges', we'm *narrow*-boats and proud of it! We'm built only 7 feets wide to fit the tunnels, locks, bridges, and waterways deep into the heart of the country and the cities. They barges was more than twice as wide as us, they was too wide to squeeze oop the Cut much further than h'Uxbridge. Durin the Strikes some barges 'done the dirty' on us, poached our usual trip, went right oop to h'Uxbridge with h'import coals for the gasworks. Them gasworks never again went back to havin their coals from the Midlands out of us narrow-boats.

In them topsy-turvy times between the wars we'd often find ourselves 'gettin ahead' wrong-way-rounded. Instead of carryin grain from the docks of London to the mills of the Midlands we'd be pickin oop odd loads from the farms along the h'Oxford and carryin 'em to the mills agen London. Instead of coals from the mines in the Midlands to the factries agen London, we'd be carryin h'import coals from London to the factries agen Birnigum. You knowed times was bad when men came limpin miles out from the towns to meet yer, if yer had a load on, beggin to help you unload or work the locks for very little money. 'Obblers' we used to call them. I mind once when we was tied oop in Birnigum, I think it must of been Sandy Lane or Campill—one of them dark places under the city with the streetlamps on all day long. We'd had to tie-oop because the lock was locked oop on the Sunday. It was a filthy dirty 'road', I was still weak after losin my second baby, and we hated doin the dirty old locks along there. A n'old out-of-work obbler came to the boat.

'Wot time you orf in the mornin, Captain? Just give me the lip if yer wantin my help with the locks.'

'Five o'clock the lock's unlocked', Moy-chap tells him.

'I'll be here, Captain', the obbler sez.

'I can't afford to pay yer much; we ent so floosh ourselfs.'

The poor old obbler was glad of *anythin*. There's always some-body worser orf than yerself.

We knowed we wasn't the only poor. There was poor a-plenty on the bank. We heard of the men with no work walkin to London but we never seed them. You can't see many main roads from the Cut,

[79]

we're tucked away out in the wilds, or behind tall ware'ouses or under the city. Half the folk on the bank don't even know the Cut exists, to them we'm non-exist'uns. To us *they* was non-exist'uns. In them days with no wireless, no telly, no newspapers, we was cut orf from most folks beyond the towpath—'cept when they drownded theyselfs in the Cut. The harder the times the more there was drownded. We never made no fuss when a bloated body came bobbin oop to the boat. They was past bein done good to. We just dropped a quiet word to the keeper at the next lock, *'There's a gone'un a while back.'*

We never reckoned to draw the 'tention of the 'thorities. 'They' could hinder yer trip, make yer give h'evidence, tie yer oop in knots, h'interfere with yer way o' life. They could put yer in the work'us, part yer from yer mate and children. We didn't want no 'bein done good to', not even when we was at rock bottom, though I wished afterwards that we had got help sooner for our Suey's TB. They said it wouldn't of made no difference.

I reckon it started with that bee-bite. We was sheetin-oop some special coals from Badgeley for this private coal-chap oop the Slough Arm. We didn't usually sheet-oop coal, but in the Strikes there was a lot of pilferin of coal from boats, and this chap—'Mazlin' I think his name was, his wharf was right oop a private arm at the end—always made sure he wasn't one knob short. He was worth the 'assle of sheetin-oop because he always paid yer on the dot.

A sheeted-oop boat were a marsterpiece when it were done proper. Boat people always prided 'emselves on their sheetin-oop. The heavy sheets are waterproof canvers [*canvas*] poured all over with st'collum tar [*Stockholm tar*], that's why they're called 'tar-pourlins'; and when you unrolls 'em they lets out a stream of filthy brown water wot we calls 'gravy'. You always donned a n'erden or hessun [*hessian*] apron to do the sheetin-oop. First yer beams, chains, stands, top-planks, have to be fixed—that's yer scaffold-like. Then comes yer side-clawths, yer top-clawths, yer five flats— some boats has only four flat sheets but we always had five—and that's yer tort [*taut cover over all the cargo*]. With every string lashed and coiled, tiddly-fashion, all along yer boat, you could be proud of yer sheetin-oop.

Suey was untyin one of the kneestrings wot held the side-clawth when a bee flew out and bit her on the neck. She seemed all right

at the time, livin in the open she was used to bites, we all was. For
the next few trips she kep goin, but gradually she chattered less
and 'er 'ealth began to 'fall away'. She was twelve. I thought it was
the start of her 'anky-panky. Some girls are like that, all wan and
listless, before they starts. That winter I took her to the doctor agen
Paradise in Birnigum [*Paradise Row*], the canal wharf was still
runnin right oop to Paradise in them days. He could find nothin
wrong. He were more concerned about me. He was the same
doctor wot had tooked me into the Birnigum 'Orspital when I lost
my second baby. I were standin on that wharf when the tow-rope
snapped from a passin pair o' boats, hit me in the stummick like a
sledge-'ommock [*sledge-hammer*], tossed me in the Cut. I were in
that Birnigum 'Orspital for six weeks. The doctor wot stitched me
oop said I were lucky not to lose me life. I took Suey to another
doctor in the spring.

'A day at the *Seaside*, that's wot she needs.—Put some roses in
her cheeks.'

In them bad times it was all we could do to live a day on the Cut
let alone a day at 'the Seaside'. None of us had ever been to the
Seaside, didn't even know which Cut it were on.

That August Bank 'Oliday we was all tied-oop along of the other
boats at Banbury Basin. We was strung out, two abreast, stem to
starn, all along the quay as well. There was no end of workin boats
still strovin to make a livin along the h'Oxford in them days. No
pleasure craft. The first pleasure craft I ever remember on the Cut,
years later, was young Mr Rolt's 'Cressy' bein converted at Tooley's
dock. We always tried to rally somewhere like Banbury for the
Bank 'Oliday. There was plenty of space along the quay to do our
washin. Us women enjoyed chattin and workin, sprucin oop our
cabins for the Sunday and Monday, moppin down the outside
paintwork, polishin the brasses, and scrubbin the plaits. The men
would catch oop on the rope splicin, the harness, the shoddin,
havin a shave, and goin for a pint. The kiddies could play with each
other as long as they didn't went down 'the Marshes', the derelick
wilds on the far side of the Cut away from the town.

'Granny Gore'll get yer if yer goes down them marshes', we used
to threaten.

Granny Gore was a widder-woman, some called her a witch. She
lived in a big tumbledown farmhouse with a small holdin down there.

When we was workin and tyin-oop for only the one night at
Banbury, the men would go to the nearest pubs, the 'Strugglers' or
the 'Leather-n-Bottle', but on a Bank 'Oliday weekend they had the
time to have a shave, don polished boots, and clatter further afield,
along 'The Paves' [*pavemented area along the front of the shops in
Bridge Street*], and over the railway bridge to the 'Albion' further
along the Cut. The entrance was just over the bridge but it backed
on to the Cut. Everso pretty the back of the 'Albion' was from the
Cut in them days, little balconies and hangin flowers, *lovely*! The
'Albion' was really the railmen's pub, but the boatmen and the
railmen was much alike in their ways, always 'on the move', takin a
pride, and often workin lonely hours. There was many a gap along
the Cut where we'd look out for the big engines steamin along the
bank or high over the bridges. We'd wave to the driver and firemen
and they'd wave back, and the guard at the end would be lookin
out to wave to us too. There was special gaps where we'd always
look out for the lone lampman ploddin along the track takin his
signal lamps out at dusk and fetchin them back at daylight.

'Wave to the lampman, Rose!' I'd say to our little Rose, harnessed
close to me on the cabin top, and we'd wave, just as me and *my*
Mum used to wave when I was a kiddy, just as *she* and Gran used
to wave. Small pleasure, wavin to the lampman, but it never cost
yer nothin and it gived yer a warm glow, comp'ny like. It wasn't
always the same lampman, of course, over the years over the miles,
but they was all 'our lampman'.

Mr Wyatt was our lampman agen Banbury. He told Moy-chap in
the 'Albion' about this special 'scursion [*excursion train*] wot was
goin on the Monday from Banbury.

Moy-chap came back full of it, 'Takes yer straight to the Seaside'.

The *Seaside*!—Should of seed Suey's face light oop. We *had* to
afford it.

It was the Sunday night. We all sits round the table-flap in
'Britannia's' cabin. There was six of us, me and Moy-chap, Suey,
Lizer, Arryut, and our little Rose squashed oop fast asleep on the
sidebed behind us. There was no question of some goin and some
not, we always shared everythin we got. Moy-chap turns out his
stockin and counts the pennies. If we all went to the Seaside we'd
have zackly five-n-sixpence to feed the lot of us. As luck would 'ave
it, I'd made a set of souse [*a brawn of pig's head, ears, and trotters*]

as a special Bank 'Oliday treat. I packed sandwiches of that and mixed oop a big bottle of lemonade crystals for our Seaside dinner. The five-n-sixpence would cover a good feast of fish-n-chips before we came home.

We was oop at dawn to catch the train. I felt 'any'ow', I'd been oop with our Rose in the night. It was the first time we'd been on a train. When it stopped we thought we was there, but they was only hinjin-swoppin, halfway. By the time we *did* get there we'd already scoffed our Seaside dinner, we was that hungry. We still had our fortune of five-n-six to blow on fish-n-chips.

We had no idea where we was sposed to be walkin we just followed the crowds. It was quite a walk and our Suey had a job to keep goin, her legs was givin out. Me and Arryut made a 'chair' and carried her on our hands between us. She was light as a bubble, buoyed oop to see the Seaside. Moy-chap carried Rose, she were only three and very fretful, not at all her usual sunny self. We was walkin along this big wide 'pave' when this chap came oop to us with a live parrot on his shoulder. He put it on Suey's head. I were worried, she weren't oop to havin high jinks played on her.

'Smile!' he sez.

She were brave, and she did.

'That'll be five shillings', he sez.

He'd tooked our fota! Five shillins! We had to pay for it 'by *lor*' he sez.

'What's your address?' he sez.

'Aunt Polly's, St Barnabas, h'Oxford.'

'I'll send it to you.'

I didn't believe a word of 'im.

We had only the sixpence left. You can't 'ave much of a n'igh old time on a sixpence. Syer took Arryut and Lizer orf to see the sights. I sat on this seat, with Suey restin against me on one side and our Rose fast asleep on the other. I reckoned she were sickenin for somethin. The Seaside was a big grey field of water beyond a bank of dabbas [*large cobbles*]. I didn't think a lot to it. Neither did our Suey. We seed far prettier sights on the Cut. By dinnertime it had started to rain. Our Suey wanted to go back 'ome. Our Rose wanted to go 'ome. We all wanted to go 'ome. We blowed the sixpence on six pennorth o' chips—you could get a lot for a penny in them days—and struggled back through the rain to the trains. We thought we could just get on a train and go 'ome. We had to sit in the cold on that station till all the people came back at seven o'clock. Our two kiddies looked like death by then. That train was packed but people could see our kiddies was in a poor way and gave us a wide berth. We laid Suey on one side of the 'cabin' and Rose on the other and drawed our coats over 'em.

'So much for a day at the Seaside!' I sez to meself. And I've never been back.

The next mornin, 'Come and take a look at our Rose', I sez to Moy-chap. She were *covered*! Chicken-spots.

Our Suey had a lump come oop on her neck, big as a h'egg, where that bee had bit her the summer before. I took her oop to the 'Orton h'Infirmary. They kept her. Wouldn't let me have her back. Only her boots and clothes. My sisters was terrible oopset when I brung back just her empty clothes.

She'd been in there over a year now, gettin more and more poorly. Arryut and Lizer wasn't allowed in. I'd promised Suey the last time I went that I'd visit her again before Christmas but we'd been held oop by the Strikes and I were about to come to town with my next child. I'd got a good nurse all lined-oop at Sutton Stop. I was hopin to get to Sutton Stop, have the baby, pick oop a load—anythin we could get—for Banbury or h'Oxford, visit Suey at Banbury and then go on to 'winter-quarter' at Aunt Polly's where Moy-chap would have a good chance of pickin oop winter work in h'Oxford.

We was tied-oop on the Ashby. The miners was on strike again, we'd no work, no coal for the range, and the Cut were threatenin to h'ice oop. It was a bitter raw day, freezin fog. Moy-chap was out ferretin for work, he were never a one for sittin waitin for it to turn oop. Me and little Rose and my two sisters was siftin coal by hand, salvagin it orf one of these yooge spoil 'eaps agen Measham. I spose we was stealin but we was workin hard for it, it were no easy pickins. From time to time the fog would shift and they chaps in their minewatchers' 'ut would see us and come out yellin at us to 'Clear orf!' But they never kep it oop because it was too bitter raw for them to keep pokin their noses out of their warm 'ut, so we kep creepin back.

By late afternoon my sisters was out of sight, coal pickin in the fog round the other side of the tip. Only Rose was with me, black as a sweep and wantin to go 'ome. I were strovin to lift the bookit to go back to the boat when I cried out. The baby was startin. When I lost my other baby with the towrope in Birnigum the doctor wot done 'me repairs' made me promise never to born another without a doctor bein there. It was all very well for him, he didn't have to pay for it! Another pain. Rose was only four but she were very brave and sensible for her age. I bundled her towards the little dimlit window of the miner's 'ut: 'Tell "They", "*Mammy sick".'

I didn't want to 'bandoom my precious bookit of coal, and I didn't want the baby borned on the tip. I stroved back down to the boat with first the bookit then the baby tryin to best me. It was dark in the cabin. I sank on the floor, it was cleaner than I was. Only that morn I'd scrubbed the floor and lain a fresh mat, one of the 'Starkey-roons' [*a close-woven sack, stamped STARKEY in red*]. That's the best sort of sack to make a mat. Open it out, scrub it oop white, last for months, *lovely*! A knock on the side of the cabin. A man's voice, kind. It was a Mr Gibbs from that 'ut comed back with our Rose. I told him wot's oop. Our Rose began to cry wantin to come in and stop with me. I didn't want her stoppin with me in my state of 'ealth, I'd enough load on, but I didn't want her left outside 'case she felled in the Cut. Mr Gibbs were goin for the doctor. I could sense he were daycent-like.

'You go along o' the gen'leman, Rose, till yer Auntie Arryut turns oop.'

Arryut was just comin along the towpath with her coals.—Sees strange chap in the gloamin hurryin away with our Rose—no idea of suscumstances—nearly biffs him in the Cut.

Lizer takes our Rose into the butty breasted-oop alongside of 'Britannia'. Arryut lights our lamp, sets the water can on the hob to melt the h'ice, draws oop the range with the big copper drawplate, hangs the little garments, binder, petticuts, back flannel, wot-av-yer over the big brass rail to warm. Back-n-forth her boots reached over me, preparin the sidebed. There's precious little floorspace in the cabin at the best of times. If somebody's lyin there half-havin a baby—*that's* yer floor took oop. She helped me oop on to the sidebed.

'*Mustn't 'ave it till the doctor comes*', I grunts to meself.

She'd hardly got the crossbed down and made it fresh and ready

[85]

when our Syer borns his-self with enough cord to stretch to
'Awkesbury Junction and back. He were still tethered when the
doctor comed. I were shamed for the doctor to tend me that rooff,
straight orf the tip.

'I ent always this rooff, Doctor', I sez. 'I 'as me pride.'

'I can see you have, Mrs Ramlin', he sez, noddin at the baby
garments all along the rail. They was the same ones I'd made for
our Rose. I always washed them by hand, and—though I sez it as
shouldn't—they looked never-been-wore.

He were a young doctor, comed all along the towpath on his
motorbike and sidecar. I don't know how he managed it without
tippin in the Cut. It was everso oopsy-downsy along that part of the
Ashby, all them played-out mines, all them lopsided bridges sinkin
at the sides, sub-side-'uns they calls 'em. I made him laugh, told
him he ought to be a rider at the circus. He had a job to stitch me
oop. He said I had the sort of skin wot tears easy. I've had so many
repairs over the years, I'm everso ruckledy over my stummick. I
can't remember how many repairs he done that time, I know I
could only afford to pay for the one.

'I'm sorry, doctor,' I sez, 'I can't pay for all me stitches at once,
but I'll sees you 'ave it when trade picks oop.'

And I did. I paid it orf, bit by bit. I left it with Mr Gibbs every
time we passed that 'ut.

Moy-chap were *that* chuffed to find he had a son. It's funny how
a chap can be so strong yet right weak and soppy over his first son.
The little chap had the most hair I'd ever seed on a babe, lots of
little wet red-gold curls all over the top of his head and round the
back of his neck. He was the best-lookin of all my babes. 'Syer
Ramlin' he had to be, after his Dad. We always done it that way on
the boats, called the first son after his father.—Took some sortin
out sometimes when three generations, grandad, son, grandson, all
with the same names worked the one firm of boats. At one time I
knowed three sets of h'Arthur Coles, the Coventry, the Banbury,
the Kidlinton, *nine* h'Arthur Coles workin the same Cut, not to
mention their h'Arthur Coles cousin down h'Oxford.

Mr Gibbs got Moy-chap a job shovellin snow. He let us stay agen
the tip and turned a blind eye to coal pickin. Mrs Gibbs sent
helpmeats, rice puddin, home-made lard, wot-av-yer, yet the
Gibbses wasn't much better orf in the Strikes than we was. Even

after all these years I still remember the shame I felt at sendin Mrs Gibbs' basket back empty. I'd nuthin to spare in return. Nuthin.

We didn't want to went from there so soon but Moy-chap were anxious not to get h'iced-oop out there in the wilds. He wanted us to get back to the junction at Sutton Stop where, once the miners went back, and if the Cut stayed open, we'd more chance of pickin oop a n'order from Mr Veaters for Banbury or h'Oxford. I *must* get to see our Suey for Christmas. She was only thirteen. With Mum gone I was the only 'Mum' she'd got. In them days we knowed no other way to get to see her than ploddin with Charley and Cobber for several days along the wanderin Cut. It was years before I found out that Banbury lay less than a n'hour from Coventry by motor. It's no use showin me a map. I wouldn't know head from tail, I hasn't the schoolin. All I knows is the view from the Cut. Show me a fota of a lock, a bridge, a church, a tree, as viewed from the boat, and I'll tell yer zackly which stretch, which Cut.

We was h'iced-oop for nearly a week at Sutton Stop. Moy-chap got a job on the h'ice boat. The miners was back, and a clear road had to be kept open from the h'Ex'all and the 'Awkesbury [*coal mines*] along to the old Lectric Light and the big h'injineerin Works along to Coventry. The h'ice was never so thick along there because of the steam and warm water churnin out from the Lectric Light. In summer it was *that* warm along there the 'oolig'uns would swim in it. They wasn't allowed. Cheeky devils! Rockin the boats, terrifyin the kiddies, h'oopsettin the hanimals. Proper 'eadache they was! They knows you can't run after 'em with a boat. Syer used to scare 'em with his big long smackin-whip. It had a special flat thrum on the end to signal to other boats in fog or round blind bends, and he'd crack it like a shot goin orf, makin them 'oolig'uns nearly jump out of their skinny birthday-suits.

No end of other boat families was h'iced oop with us at Sutton Stop that year; the Littlemores, the Powells, the Atkins, the Brummidges, the Ramlins, the Wilsons, the Humphries, the Granthams, the Beecheys, the Coleses. We was able to catch oop on the news of the world, *our* world, the world of the Cut. We caught oop on the latest news of Dad and Aunt Tovey, the other Mellas, Fishers, Ramlins, *and* our Suey. Rose Brummidge had been to see her.

Rose was a good soul. She was then pledged to wed Joe Skinner.

They was havin the two boats, the 'Elizabeth' and the 'Friendship' built at Sephton's yard, acraws the way at Sutton Stop.—Took some courage, settin on new boats to be built in the Strikes, but Sephtons, keen to stay in business, kep the price down, and the young couple was going to pay-orf accordin to suscumstances. Rose and Joe were goin to work the 'Friendship', with Rose's brother, George Brummidge, on the 'Elizabeth'. They had two hanimals salvaged from the war, Dick and Dolly. Dick was a mule. Some called Dolly a mule. We never. Dolly were sired by a n'ass. Dolly were rightly a fummel. She were slightly smaller than Dick. She were a game little worker. She and Joe kep each other trottin along the towpath to the end of their workin days, drawin timber from London to Coventry and coal from the mines to Banbury and h'Oxford. At the finish she fell in the Cut agen Farmer's Hut, Wormyleighton, and catched the new monia.

Rose was the eldest of a big family. Her mother came from Coventry but she wasn't a boatwoman. They used to work for Cox's dayboats, haulin a lot to Coventry Co-op. All Rose's uncles used to work from Badgeley down to Atherstone. Many a time when I was a little girl and our Dad was waitin for our boat to be loaded at Badgeley I used to like workin the locks for her Uncle Tom and Uncle George. They was very easy locks along there. They'd give me coppers and sweets. Rose was just as kind in her way. The last time her family had tied-oop in Banbury she'd trudged all the way oop that steep Banbury hill to the h'Infirmary specially to see our Suey. She told me Mrs Boatee Own had been too, and Mrs Plester the blacksmith's wife, and Mr Stanley, the young lock-keeper from Claydon. People were very kind if they knowed somebody orf the boats was left behind in 'orspital—specially a child—they'd do their best to visit. It wasn't easy, visitin times was rare and strict, workin folk had a job to fit in a visit.

Rose was only allowed to talk to Suey through a glass wall. In them days the TB was terrible rife. Lots of people, rich and poor, children and growed-oops, was a-dyin of it. They was tryin no end of cures. Rose reckoned Suey was wastin away from loneliness as much as from disease. All her life she'd been used to close comp'ny on the boats, workin in a team. I thought of her as she always used to be, laughin and chatterchops, rattlin along the towpath on that old Rover bike, gettin the locks ready. She were always a one for collectin things, flowers, blackberries, mushrooms, duckdown, feathers. The Cut were her whole world. I couldn't bear to think of her, prisoned all on her lone.

As soon as the Cut were clear to Banbury and the orders came floodin in, the other families knowin how we was fixed about Suey, let us go first. We'd a n'urgent load of coal from the Griff for Juxon Street, h'Oxford. As we neared Banbury I was steerin, sucklin little Syer so I could leave him with our Arryut while I went to see Suey. Moy-chap could only allow me so long. As we come oop agen the last bridge before tyin-oop I seed a n'orse and cart goin over the bridge followed by a small red-crosser bus. A girl's face was peakin out of the window. She waved and waved and were gone. I was sure it was Suey. I knew it couldn't be, I'd been strainin so long to see her I was 'seein' her everywhere.

I trailed oop to that h'Infirmary with her Christmas 'stockin', a big brown paper carrier-bag stuffed with presents people had gived me for her. Pretty picture-cards of birds and flowers, Suey loved birds and flowers. Colourin pencils and a drawrin book. She was good at drawrin, she could draw real dooks and boats. Mr Veaters gived her the drawrin book, *and* he'd crawsed baby Syer's palm with silver, even though I'd borned him on the Ashby and not at Sutton Stop. Mr Veaters reckoned to craws the palm of every boat-baby borned at Sutton Stop. Rose Brummidge had gived me oranges, and Mrs Gamble at the Barley Mow at Noble had gived me a picture-scope [*kaleidoscope*] and a long piece of left-over ribbin from her daughter's weddin frock. Her Ilda were about to wed Lang Clarke. Real satin weddin ribbin for Suey's hair, *lovely*!

I were played out by the time I got oop to that h'Infirmary and the string 'andles of the carrier was cuttin into my fingers. It was only a month since I'd had the baby. I were right glad I were got to Suey at last.

'You've just missed her', they sez. 'She's been sent away to breathe the pines.'

So it *was* our Suey I'd seed wavin on the bridge.

They gives me this ticket. 'Here's her address. It's Farnborough.'

I *think* they sez *Farnbrer*. They could of said Timbuctoo for all I knowed. Even if some kind scholard read the ticket for me I'd no chance of goin there.

'It's lovely there', one of the nurses told me. 'They'll take special care of her at the Pines. They won't let her suffer. She'll look out on to a beautiful garden.'

I told her we was 'orf the boats'. I gave her Suey's Christmas 'stockin' and she pledged to get it to her.

We never seed Suey again. Never got the chance. I kep her Pines address in the ticket draw. Years later 'the Schoolmaster' [*Herbert Dunkley of Coventry*] read it for me and took me there in his motor to where he reckoned Suey were buried by a Charity, and I laid some flowers there.

That Seaside fota *did* land oop at Aunt Polly's. I kep that fota for years at the back of the ticket draw, along of her Pines address and our marriage soostificut. I've still got her, faded but smilin, with her parrot.

Moycle

WHENEVER we was tied-oop at Banbury we never reckoned to go down on the Marshes after dark. Tribes of gypsies was always camped down there and there was tales of terrible fights and goins-on.

Some h'ignor'uns calls us gypsies, water-gypsies. We 'ates that. We'm workin people with a purpose, and proud of it. We'm all for gettin 'em ahead to earn our livin, not cuttin adrift to cadge for it. We has to strove as a team to get the best out of our craft. A boat handles different' in different sets of suscumstances, cargo, weather, the state of the Cut. You gotta be skilled, you gotta be handy, you gotta be limber [*nimble with your limbs*]. There's nothin skilled to bein a wanderin gypsy, tethered on the Marshes.

Granny Gore lived on the Marshes in the scullery of her big tumbledown farm'ouse. She wasn't a gypsy but she traded with 'em. She were dirty, fat, and shapeless, clad always in old sacks and shawls. She could of been fifty, she could of been 'oondred, widders aged before their years in them days. She lived alone and farmed pigs, poultry, and vegetables. Her name was Waddle [*Woodall*] but she was knowed to all as Gore because she were nearly always oop

[91]

to her elbows in it, guttin fowl and rabbits, 'ready-dressed' she used
to sell them. I never bought 'ready-dressed' from her, didn't fancy
it from that dirty old scullery, but I liked her vegetables, straight
from the garden. Wotever time you tied-oop late at night or had to
cast-orf early in the mornin you could always stock oop from down
there. She never went to bed, just dossed down on the broken
down sofa in her dark scullery. People said she'd seed posher days
and had a lot of money stowed away. She'd been attacked once and
been wary ever since. From then on you always had to show yer
face at the winder, else she wouldn't come out to yer. How she
seed through the cobwebs, I don't know. She'd come waddlin out
in all her shawls with a great carvin knife, ready to carve yer oop or
cut yer a cabbage.

When our Suey was alive and well she and Lizer used to walk
down and get the vegetables. I didn't like them goin down after
dark, not only because of the gypsies but because Granny Gore
sometimes had men-callers. Some said they was payin her the
rents—she owned all sorts of didgy-dodgy properties—but other
men used to come scuttlin out of her scullery, buttonin oop their
trouser-falls, as if they couldn't get out fast enough. We tied-oop
late one night, Syer had to tend the hanimals, me and Arryut had
to tend to all sorts of jobs ready for another early start in the
mornin, so Lizer and Suey *had* to go. I gave them each a candle in
a jamjar and told them to keep together, go straight down and
hurry back. They was back in a mickey [*moment*].

'Granny Gore's been done in, she's lyin in a puddle on her
scullery floor. I think it's *blood!*'

I hurried down. She wasn't done-in. She was havin a baby. She
was just grabbin her carvin knife. I reckon if the girls hadn't turned
oop when they did she'd of had that baby, done away with it, and
nobody would of been none the wiser.

How that baby survived into a toddler, I don't know. She had no
feelins for it, called him 'little booger', and penned him out of her
way in a n'open top tea chest most of the time. Poor Little Booger
could hardly see out.

About a year after our Suey had gone me and our Rose went
down one day and found him danglin from her great rusty-iron
mangle by his dirty petticuts. He must of been about three by then
but he still hadn't been britched [*put into trousers*]. She'd wound

him oop a-purpose to keep him out of her way. Our Rose was only five but she were most oopset.

'Can *we* 'ave Little Booger, Mum, ay? Take Little Booger 'ome to play with me and Syer, ay?'

'No, Rose, I got enough.' Our Syer was toddlin by then, he must of been about eighteen months. He were a proper handful, tryin to clamber about after our Rose all over the place.

We lost our little Syer the next winter when he was two. He died of the new monia, the bronical. We was snowed-oop at Claydon Top Lock and nobody could get through to the doctor at Fenny [*Fenny Compton*]. Not even Mr Bloomfield could get through. He was ganger [*maintenance foreman*] for the Cut from Banbury to Napton and knowed every inch of the lengths. That Top Lock used to be a busy world of its own in them days. The Bloomfields lived in the two top cottages with a big walled gardin. Mr Stanley was the lock-keeper for the Claydon Five but he lived in the village and had his lock-keeper's hut at Top Lock agen the maintenance yard, the blacksmith's shop, and stablin for ten hanimals. All gone now.

Mrs Bloomfield had four boys of her own and had nursed them through the new monia when they was babies. She were a great support to me with our little Syer, showed me how to go on with the mustard poultices on his little chest and the constant steamin kettle on the hob to ease his tight breathin. She had a proper laundry place in the second cottage and allowed us to use her copper and mangle to do the washin. It was a risky job gettin the water at Claydon. The pump was opposite the cottages and you had to flit along the h'icy top of the frozen-oop lock gate to fetch it. Mr Bloomfield or his lads would fetch it for us when they was about but most of the time they was diggin out the drifts.

We had coal that time, thank the Lord! We was able to trade the h'odd bookit with Mrs Bloomfield and she traded potterbs and cabbages. Mr Bloomfield stocked his large gardin full-to-bustin in the summer and knowed well how to garner and store for the winter. In winter they was often cut-orf from the village acraws the fields and was used to bein self-rely'uns. Moy-chap were a marster-daddy with a catty [*catapult*], dooks, pigeons, rabbits dropped to his stone. The only thing we lacked was milk. We was desprat for milk for little Syer. Moy-chap stroved to get to the farm acraws the fields but had to give oop when he were lost in the drifts and nearly done-for. He'd of crawled to the end of the Cut to save his little son but it were of no avail.

I couldn't believe my little boy was dead. I *wouldn't* believe it. They had to prise him out of my arms at the finish. Mr Bloomfield cleaned out a toolchest from the yard and we laid him in that on a little wadded pillow. Mrs Bloomfield offered to have him in her front room but me and Moy-chap couldn't bear for him to be taken from us just yet. He lay in that chest three days and three nights, red-gold curls, so still, so peaceful, like he was havin a little smile to his-self. I kep lookin, longin for a little tell-tale breath, a little tremor of life to come back.

As soon as the thaw set in the maintenance men turned oop at the yard. The marster-carpenter made a proper little coffin. He were another Mr Gilkes, relationed to the old one wot made Granny Statham's coffin all those years before. Moy-chap borned it on his shoulder all acraws the snowy fields to the church and we followed. I never shed a tear. I couldn't. Not until weeks after. We was travellin back from puttin flowers on Mother's grave at h'Oxford when I seed a new-born baby drownded, cord floatin, in the Cut. There was little wet gold curls at the back of his neck. The tears came floodin then, great big black waves, over and over.

Our Arryut had bundled Rose into the cabin of the 'Percy Veruns' so she never seed the drownded baby. When we was sittin oop night after night in 'Britannia's' cabin nursin Syer I'd moved Rose in with her Aunty Arryut and Aunty Lizer into the cabin of the 'Percy Veruns', and she never moved back. They'd made her a Suzy-doll out of a pair of Mrs Bloomfield's old black stockins. She carried that Suzy-doll with her everywhere, specially after Syer died, couldn't bear to be parted from it. Mrs Bloomfield tooked to our Rose. Rose loved to help her with the hens, 'Roland Reds' they was [*Rhode Island Reds*]. Mrs Bloomfield was sad to see us go when the h'ice was cleared and we was on our way again. Some winters if they was snowed-oop and no boats came through she never seed another woman for weeks. Though she loved her husband and four sons very dearly she longed for a little daughter like our Rose to share her skills and keep her comp'ny.

Though she were only six Rose becomed even more growed-oop for her years after she lost her little brother. She were a real mother to the other boat-children. As soon as we tied-oop along of other boat families, sure enough, one of the mothers would come paddlin along the path and knock on one of our cabins.

'Is your Rose comin out to play?'

Out would poke our Rose and all the mothers would heave a sigh of relief knowin she was often more of a mother to their little'uns than wot their own big sisters was. She was always baby-mindin. She was baby mad. We tied-oop at Banbury once just as Boatee Own's daughter's weddin group was bein fota'd 'gen the stablin at Tooley's boatyard. Old Boatee Own's daughter, Bet, was marryin Frank, Lijer Dookit's brother [*Elijah Duckett*]. Alf Own's grand-daughter, Rose, was the littlest bridesmaid. Rose Own and our Rose was about the same size and age. Our Rose were *that* envious of her.

'Will Rosie Own 'ave a baby now she's a bridesmaid, Mum, ay?'

'No. You 'as to be the *bride* to 'ave a baby.'

From then on she were always pesterin me to let her be a bride and have a baby. She were very lost with only us growed-oops and her Suzy-doll to play with.

The next back-end [*latter part of the year*] we was tied-oop again in Banbury on our way to the h'Oxford wharfs. It was one of them dark foggy days, more night than day. *Terrible* dirty fogs we used to have in them days, specially through the towns. Most towns we entered from the Cut was nothin but stinkin gasworks and smokin chimneys, and Banbury was no different. Not only mills, foundries, factries, was belchin smoke, but all those houses along Mill Street and Factry Street wot backed on to the Cut had chimneys and coal-grates galore, fed by all them coal wharfs and coal merchants, 'Adkins', 'Whites', 'Highams', 'Co-op', 'Palmos' [*Palmer's*]. As yer plodded towards the town smuts would settle all over yer paint-work, all over yer hanimals, and sift into the cabin makin all yer crosher and h'ornamentals smeared and greasy. The air would get that dark with soot you couldn't see the forend of yer boat, you'd have to steer 'feelin' yer way with yer senses, smack-smackin the whip on the cabin top, and listenin for the answerin 'smack-smack' from any other boat loomin towards yer. The whip had this silk thrum on the end with three knots. When it was wore down to yer last knot yer needed another thrum.

It was to be only a brief tie-oop at Banbury Lock while Moy-chap got a new packet of thrums. He wanted to keep goin before the fog thickened into night. While he nipped orf to Markby Ploom's [*Mark B. Plumb*] the rope chandlers in the Market Place I sent Lizer and Rose down to Granny Gore's to get some vegetables. Rose came scramblin back breathless into the cabin.

'Mum! Poor Little Booger's goin into a n'Ome. Don't let her put poor Little Booger into a n'Ome, Mum. *I* want 'im.'

It was a terrible bleak day. I didn't like to think of the poor little chap being put into a n'Ome, but I hadn't got over little Syer. I didn't want another to look after. Our Arryut was about nineteen by then. She was bein courted serious by Appy Youet [*'Happy' Hewitt*] orf the boats at Coventry. They was goin to wed as soon as he could afford it, then our Lizer would have her hands full workin the 'Percy Veruns' on her own.

'Oo's gonna look after 'im, Rose, ay?'

'I'll look after 'im, Mum.' She was only six.

'Wot about yer *schoolin*?'

I were fightin a losin battle over our Rose's schoolin. She hated goin to school. It was hard enough in the Strikes to spare the time to tie-oop and give her the chance to 'tend, but when she went orf cryin and came home cryin I had a job to keep forcin her. Moy-chap never backed me oop. He backed me oop on most things but he thought this was crool. Rose were a born boat-child. Next to bein a bride she were going to be a Number One. He loved learnin her everythin to do with boatin. She were fast enough on the ooptake for *that*!

'You'd better ask yer Dad.'

She could twist him round her little finger. She wheedled him into saying 'No' to the schoolin and 'Yes' to Little Booger.

We just fetched him away, dirt an' all, and that was that. No fishal-papers, no nothin [*official adoption papers*]. She said she didn't want no fishal-papers, didn't want to draw the 'tention of the 'thorities. She didn't even say goodbye to the little chap, she were no more bothered than if she were cuttin orf a cabbage. He were very oopset.

'Never mind, son,' Moy-chap sez, pickin him oop in his arms and carryin him. 'We'll stand by yer. From now on yer a *Ramlin*.'

We called him Moycle. Me and Moy-chap had to lay the lor down to him at first, he were that wild. He were almost four but I had to harness him close to me like a baby on the cabin top or tether him like a toddler in the 'atches. On the 'orseboats the 'atches had a high starn like a wall all round and were a safe haven for a toddler. When our Rose was little I got young 'Erbert, one of Mr Tooley's sons, to fit a brass rail acraws with two strong brass curtain rings and I tethered her little harness to that. She had the run of the rail but she was safe. It could be unscrewed and put away when not needed. I'd been glad of it again for little Syer and now it came in handy for our Moycle. He kep 'takin a look' and I hauled him back. He kep chuckin things overboard. I had to put a stop to *that*.

'If you chooks things over them 'atches they goes down a BIG BLACK 'OLE and yer never gets 'em back. If *you* goes over them 'atches *you'll* go down a BIG BLACK 'OLE and never come back.'

I had to learn him. He wasn't brung-oop to it like we was. I couldn't keep him harnessed for ever, and he were too big to dunk in the Cut. I once seed a boatwoman down Manchester way dunkin her two-year-old head-first in the Cut. He were screamin blue murders. Her husband wasn't takin a bit of notice, he were on the hinjin [*steam-boat*] oop front, and she were behind on a long tow on the butty. I thought she were bein crool but Aunt Rose knowed the woman and she told me they'd already lost one child overboard, she couldn't make her husband hear above the wind and he'd just gone on and on. She was determined to teach this one a lesson before she lost him too.

You haven't got no brakes on a boat. You can't stop, turn round, go back and pick things oop. You can't turn a narrow-boat just when you feels like it, the boat's too long for the width of the Cut, you have to wait until you gets to a windy-'ole, a wide place made specially for turnin or 'windin' as we calls it. Sometimes there's not a windy-'ole for miles. If it's a child that's gone over you've 'lost' the spot, it's too late. In our day there were no such things as life-jackuts. We had to learn Moycle to stay 'put', specially when the boat was loaded to the gunnles or ropes was bein cast or paid out. A rope can catch oop a child's foot in a trice and the child be dashed about on the end like a limp rag. A woman's skirts could be caught oop too, specially when you was payin out a long tow from the hatches; you had to watch that when you was long-linin. A taut rope has a n'edge like a knife. It can cut orf a chap's head. I've even seen it sever the roof clean orf a cabin. There was so much danger to guard against on a boat, and on a busy wharf. Most town wharfingers didn't allow kiddies orf the boats. Rose was very good at lookin after Moycle. She soon learned him to do as they was told and stay in the cabin when we was loadin or orf-loadin. They could only 'help' to unload when we was out at a little country wharf doin our own shovellin.

Within a year of Moycle comin to us I had our Alby. Poor Moycle thought we was goin to trade him back. I had to learn him that we would *never* trade him, he was our little boy and so was Alby. I had to learn him to be big brother to Alby. Our Alby comin did Moycle a power of good. They becomed very close. When we had our Alby christened 'gen Coventry we had our Moycle done too. They was a handful at times as they growed oop but our Rose was a good help. We was 'Mum' and 'Dad' to 'em all, and they had their Aunties too. The boys slept on the sidebed in the 'Britannia', and Rose slept with her Auntie Arryut and Auntie Lizer on the 'Percy Veruns'.

Lookin back, those years the children shared were some of the happiest of my life. I can see Rose and Moycle, with young Alby held between 'em, all three grubby and grinnin with delight on the plank-swing Moy-chap used to rig oop for them from the beams in the hold. When the hold was empty they could be let to play in there as we was travellin along. The boys could run about and let orf steam, chasin fore and aft. Alby *loved* bein chased. He'd *chuckle*. They'd help me to clean the hold, their small hands was most useful pickin oop the stray wheat between the cracks-n-crannies. Wheat stinks terrible if it's left to sprout or ferment. I'd lift oop each bit of freeboard in turn and they'd do the pickin-oop from underneath.

They was glad to help with anythin. They had so few toys to play with in them lean times. Rose still had her Suzy-doll with its long black-stockined legs wot her Aunties made her, but there was no money for bought toys nor no room to store 'em. When you have nothin, any mite's a treat; a pile of pea-pods to play patterns, a new cigarette card, a stub of pencil and a piece of paper to drawr on. There wasn't so much waste paper in them days, you saved every bit you could get. Nothin was ever wasted, sacks, paper, rags. A good rag, fished out of the Cut and strong enough to make a rag mop made yer day. I'd save every little bit of rag I could fish oop for Moy-chap to make a rag-mop. He made the children their own little rag-mops so they could help swab down the planks and paintwork. He cut the rags into strips, laid 'em criss-craws-criss acraws the end of the wooden handle, drove the nail through the lot into the handle, bound and spliced 'em with string so that the 'thick' hung down like a big fat tassel.—Last for ages, Moy-chap's mops.

He'd whittle a whip-n-top for the kiddies as he was walkin along the towpath. They could whip-n-top along the false floor of the empty hold. He made 'em a skippin rope, and fashioned 'em no end of make-shift fishin rods. My two little boys would 'fish' for hours danglin a bent nail on a string over the hatches. Never caught nothin, mind—'cept more rags for mops—but it stayed 'em 'put'.

They never played much make-believe. They could make-believe the stool was a n'orse, or a cradle for Suzy-doll, but they hadn't all the make-believes wot children had later from story-books, the wireless, the telly, the pictures. Most picture palaces was away from the Cut in the grander parts of towns and cities, 'cept at Measham. At Measham there was a funny little picture-place so close to the Cut you could almost tie yer starn string to the front door. We never went much oop that Cut when the children were small.

I mind goin to Measham once with my Mum and Dad but we couldn't read the silent pictures. I went later to a talkie with Mary Humphries [later Hartree]. We seed 'Tom Mix'. He called everybody 'Kid' and 'Sport'. For years after, Mary called everybody 'Kid' and 'Sport' and played at bein 'Tom Mix'. It was the only game she knowed. I tried to recall 'Tom Mix' to tell to my kiddies when they was little but it's a job to think oop the words when you've only once and long ago seed the pictures. I tried to think oop the 'Woonderful 'Istry of Tom Thumb' but it was years since I'd last heard it on Granny's Pandorus. Nobody never told us no stories. We was always workin, always on the go, parted early from our Mothers and Grannies. We soon learned not to press questions when nobody knowed the answers.

Moycle was always pressin questions. 'Wot's that bird?' 'Wot's this flower?' He loved flowers. So did Moy-chap. He was always pickin me a bunch of summat from the towpath for my cabin top. I had a real nice stone jamjar from the Jam-'Ole [*Kearley and Tonge's factory at Southall*]. You went right in and under the bridge to deliver coals at the Jam-'Ole. It had its own big basin, tooked two pairs of boats and two big barges. All gone now, just cars where the water used to be. They used to be everso perticler at that jam factry; one little chip in a jar, out it were throwed on their roobish 'eap. We used to ask if we could have it, specially if it were one of them big deep-blue 'andsome stone ones. Crammed with flowers on yer cabin top you never noticed no chips. *Lovely*!

We seed no end of flowers and wildlife from the boat, far more than they ever seed from the bank. 'Wot's this?' 'Wot's that?' Moycle would ask, over and over. I was sorry that I couldn't feed him all the proper answers. Nobody never learned *us* proper. I knowed a mollern [*heron*] from a pigeon-felt [*fieldfare*]; a forget-me-not from a water-blob [*marsh marigold*]. I knowed magpies, stormcocks, dooks, swifts, swans, stoats, snakes. I seed a wonder once, a snake curled-oop sunnin itself afloat in a n'empty moorhen's nest, but there were 'oondreds more wonders baskin, buildin, livin, growin, bornin, dyin all round us.

'All I knows, Moycle, they all draws life from the Cut, same as we. It's *nature*.'

'Wot's nature, ay?'

'We'm nature. You and Alby, me and Dad, Rose and yer Auntie Lizer, Charley and Cobber, the swifts whizzin oop there, the dooks swimmin all round us.'

'Why do dooks swim?'

'Cos they got spread-feet.'

'Why 'aven't we got spread-feet, ay?'

'I dunno.'

'I reckon we all oughter 'ave spread-feet, Mum,' he once said to me, 'then we wouldn't go down the BIG BLACK 'OLE when we takes a look.'

It made sense. He were about seven then. He were a lovely lookin little lad. No matter how grubby Moycle was you could tell there was 'breedin' there. I tried to make him go to school. He liked it when he was there but he was always afraid we would go on without him. Time and again I had to tell him. 'You'm *our* Moycle. We shall *never* go without yer. We shall *never* give yer away.'

He loved goin to the Mission, or the Wyken, or Longford because Rose would go with him. She didn't mind goin to them schools because there was mostly boat children there and the other kids didn't gang-oop on yer. But we was never tied-oop long enough for them to benefit proper, two or three days at the most while we was waitin to be loaded or unloaded, and Rose were always ankerin to get back to help her Auntie Lizer work the boat.

By then Arryut had married Appy Youet and was gone to live with him on the bank in Coventry. Appy had left the boats and got a regler job at the new Lectric Light. Our Lizer missed Arryut no end when they was first parted. My two sisters had shared a cabin all their lives, never been parted before, never sent away when young as I was. From then on our Rose, child though she were, had to be her Auntie Lizer's little runnerboat, sharin the work of the 'Percy Veruns'.

Our Rose were a rare'un. From early years she were completely at one with a boat, it just comed nat'ral. When she was quite small Moy-chap added a n'extrer bit of 'andle so she could fit her little hands on to the winluss to 'help' him with the paddles. For some jobs, heavin coal, shiftin heavy paddles on her own, she just weren't man enough but by the time she were nine she made oop for lack of strength by bein nippy and limber along the planks, oop the lock ladders, steppin on and steppin orf in easy time with the flow of the boat. She lapped-oop all her Dad's lore on splicin and ropework. She took pride in handlin the ropes and loved learnin Moycle to coil the strings and steer the boat to within a n'inch of the gunnle. She were completely fearless at droppin down from the sheer lock side on to the cabin top and would jump the lock-gates—though I'd forbidded her—if I didn't keep my North eye on her.

We was workin flat out when our three kiddies was young, runnin from the coaleries to London, back-loadin with wheat from London oop the Northamton Arm to Wellinbrer, back to Cosgrove to load with ballast for the buildin of the wireless masts at Hillmorton, then on to the Coventry coaleries again to load oop. We seed quite a bit of our old Dad as we to-n-fro'd past Aunt Tovey's. He loved to see the children and though he couldn't speak he were well content to listen to their chatter. He were very happy with Aunt Tovey, his pension, his baccy, and his view of the Cut.

They had proper bogey-trucks on rails to load us with the ballast at Cosgrove but it all had to be shovelled out by hand into the steam lorries at Hillmorton. I felt any'ow when we was shiftin that ballast. I were expectin my next baby and I kep havin these pains. They used to fetch me down summat terrible, these pains, but I kep goin, didn't want to let down Moy-chap, knowin how lucky we was in them bad times to be in work, how hard he'd stroved to wangle the orders.

As luck would 'ave it we was the only pair of boats tied-oop at Sutton Stop the night I were rushed orf to 'orspital. Not even the 'Friendship' and the 'Elizabeth' was tied-oop outside Number 18. We was ready-loaded yet again with coal for London. Our Lizer had gone to stop the night with our Arryut on the bank in Coventry. Whenever we was tied-oop near enough to Coventry our Lizer would squeeze in a quick visit. It was the only way my two sisters could get to see each other. Arryut's chap, Appy Youet, would fetch Lizer in his motorbike and sidecar on his way home from work at the Lectric Light and bring her back when he came to work early in the mornin. Moycle and Alby was asleep on the sidebed in 'Britannia', the 'Percy Veruns' was breasted-oop alongside. Our Rose were about to get ready for bed when these pains fetched me right down. I were only seven months gone yet I feeled I was goin to burst. Moy-chap were in the 'Greyhound'. I remember sayin, 'Rose, fetch yer dad.'

I knowed no more after that.

Fish-outer-Water

'THEY tooked yer away from us in the red-crosser', Moy-chap told me afterwards. 'Our Rose were that oopset, I let her sleep in our bed with the others on the "Britannia". I never went to bed. Never undressed. Couldn't sleep. In the middle of the night the Bobby came for me.'

'It's your wife. You've got to come. It's life or death.'

Poor Syer! He were all shook-oop, tore wot to do about leavin the kiddies. They was all asleep, our Rose were only nine, wot if she waked to no Mum and no Dad? There was no other boats tied-oop, no other boatwoman he could turn to. All the Cut were in darkness save for one little lamp still burnin in the cottages on 'the Waste', the bit of land between the towpath of the h'Oxford and the towpath of the North Coventry. In them days there was quite a smatterin of cottages on there. All gone now. It was the deaf-n-dumb chap's cottage. He worked on the mud-'opper and the kiddies knowed him. He twigged the suscumstances. He settled his-self on guard in the 'atches, case the kiddies waked oop.

'Which do you want saved,' the 'Orspital sez to Moy-chap, 'your baby or your wife?'

[103]

'A babby ent much good without its mother. I ent no good without my Best-Mate. Save moy missis, *please God*, save moy Rose.'

Ever after, whenever we had a tift [*tiff*] he'd boast, 'I *saved* yer, remember!'

It were touch-n-go-go, a *very* near do. I 'ad Hanoverian Sis [*an ovarian cyst*]. *Four pounds* that sis weighed when they cut it out. The baby hadn't a chance. It was a little girl. Even when you lose 'em like that you still pines for 'em, you never forgets she were your little girl. I were in that Coventry 'Orspital six weeks. I were proper fish-outer-water. I used to lie there pinin for my kiddies and my own little cabin 'ome. I'd lie at night picturin my little kerry-lamp with the pretty 'Little Princess' pink glass shade lightin-oop my starched crosher, my polished range with its cinder-guard of plaited brass, my pretty 'swan' ribbin-plate, my 'roses' ribbin-plate wot Aunt Rose gived me when Uncle Frank never come back, and all my h'ornamentals. I had all my Mum's h'ornamentals. Good as gold her brass knobs was, no cheap-jack tin-thins, the best on the Cut. She had 'em from the Bedstid-'Ole 'gen Fazeley Street, Birnigum, in the days when British brass bedstids was sent all over the 'igh seas. Most boatwomen just hung their bedstid knobs on hooks, I got young 'Erbert Tooley, 'Mr George's' younger son, to fix mine proper, on a posh mee'ogany board, just inside the 'atches to catch the lamplight. Night after night in that great ware'us of a ward, I'd strove to picture them shinin knobs with my cabin winkin rosy-gold in each one of 'em. Night after night I'd strain to hear the water lappin the boat, or tricklin in the lock, or tumblin over a weir, or slap-slappin in and out the coolvit [*culvert*]. In the ward night were shut away black outside like a n'emeny [*enemy*], on the Cut night's a close friend, never really dark. The stars above and the rustlins around are all part of yer sleep, the dews-n-damps part of yer breath. I were stuffycated at night in that ward.

Days was no better. I couldn't bear bein shut in. I longed for the open air, the sun, the wind on my face and arms.

'My!' they sez. '*You're* brown! You been on holiday?'

Some 'oliday! I thinks to meself. I kep mum, never let on I was orf the boats. Some folks looks down on yer. There was one nurse, real sneery. One day I heard her sneerin about a 'bunch of urchins' she'd turned away from outside the 'orspital wantin to be let in. I suddenly twigged it were *my* kiddies she'd turned away, *my* kiddies she was goin on about. '*Vagabombs!*' she calls 'em.

'Them's *my* vagabombs!' I claims, proud as proud, and bursts into tears. *My* Rose, *my* Moycle, and my little Alby, *that* near and yet *so far!*

Kiddies wasn't allowed to come and see yer in them days. It wasn't often they was tied-oop that near. Moy-chap couldn't afford to keep two boats tied-oop idle all that time. He and Lizer and the kiddies worked 'em between 'em. Our Rose were worth her skinny weight in gold. Our Moycle took to the steerin. He was only seven but he was gettin a big boy for his age. Our Alby had to stay put, harnessed to the chimney on the cabin top, no more chasin in the hold. Moy-chap came to see me once or twice but he were more fish-outer-water than I were. It worked best for him to stay and mind the kiddies while Lizer came. On the Bank 'Oliday they gave him the slip and turned oop at the 'orspital and that nurse turned 'em away. After that our Lizer always used to leave them with another boatwoman's children, but we was always on edge wonderin wot they was chasin about at. Boat-children love to chase, it's the only way they can work orf miles of stayin 'put'.

Our Arryut was very good to me in that 'orspital, came every chance she got. Visitin times was strict. She had a job to fit in. She toiled at corset-makin for a posh shop in the city. She become very townified, livin on the bank, hair bobbed short and a ducky little hat dippin over one eye; but she were still the same old Arryut underneath. She were always the best lookin of us sisters. She always cut a bit of a dash even when she was on the boats, always dippin her comb in the Cut and settin her quiff into a kiss-curl, specially if there was a chance of seein Appy. Lizer used to tease, 'Where d'yer get that Marshal-wave?'

'Out the Cut.'

'All that fuss for a *chap!*' Lizer never went overboard in them days for chaps. She were always the same even-keel Lizer. At one time I hoped she and Dick Littlemore would of gotten in tow, they knowed each other all their lives, but Dick went overboard for one of our distant relations, Ada Mella. For years our Lizer never wed. I thought she never would, but she did in the end.

Arryut had me home to her place while I was pickin oop me strength to get back on the boats. She and Appy had a nice little 'two-oop two-down' terrist 'ouse [*terrace*] with a proper cellar and their own back yard. That's where Appy moored his motorbike and sidecar. They was joined to the row but they was right at the end with their own back way and washus [*wash-house*]. 'Er and Appy was all the world to each other, yet no babies came along, only 'lectrics'. Appy was well oop in the lectrics, he gave her the lectric light, the lectric door-bell, the h'Empire h'Exhibition washer, and the yoover [*vacuum cleaner*].

When I got back on the boat our Moycle used to pester me no end to talk about 'Aunt Arryut's lectrics'. He'd growed oop a lot while I'd been away. He were very 'mother-dook' to Alby, helpin him to tie his boots and doin oop his braces. He'd still act daft sometimes, chasin Alby to make him chuckle till they drove me mad, but he always put Alby first if they shared anythin and he hardly ever let him out of his sight. That was a glorious summer and he liked me to sit with Alby in the sun on the cabin top doin my crosher while he done the steerin, standin on the stool in the 'atches just like I used to do when I were his age.

'You 'ave a rest, Mum', he'd say. It was as if he couldn't do enough for me after I comed back from that 'orspital. He were a very lovin little lad. I done a lot of crosher for Arryut after I got back, runners for her mantleshelfs, and lacey-daceys for her dressin table.

'Tell us all about her lectrics, Mum.'

'She's got a h'Empire h'Exhibition wash tub wot does its own washin. You just turns a knob and it swishes the washin about just like the dolly does, but you has to do yer own wringin. She's got this ducky little rubber-roller-mangle wot clips on the side. *Lovely!* I don't envy her live dolly-tub but I envies her no end that little rubber-roller.'

Moycle used to promise me, everso manly, standin steerin on that stool with his little brown arm outstretched on the great tiller, 'When I'm a Number One, Mum, with me own put-put, *I'm gonna treat yer to one of them rollers.*'

He kep his promise, but he were never a Number One with his own put-put.

Moycle and Alby was crazy about a put-put [*narrow-boat with a motor engine*].

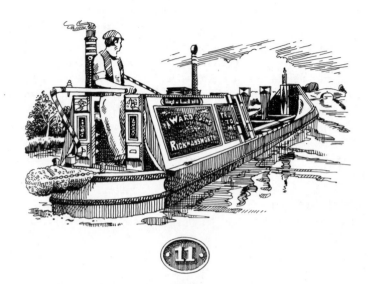

'Put-Put!'

I T was Alby when he was first learnin to talk who dubbed it a 'put-put'.

Whenever he heard a moty-boat hinjin chuggin round the bend to meet us his little cheeky face would light oop. 'Put-put! Put-put!' he'd point, *that* h'excited, jiggin in his harness on the cabin top.

All our lives we'd been used to seein the *steam*-boats, tuggin us through the tunnels or workin 'fly' [*express*] for the big chaps like Fellas Morton. Fellas' steam-boats worked non-stop towin their loaded butties from London droppin 'em orf at the main junctions leadin orf to 'Northamton', or Leicester, or Birnigum. From there on the loaded butties was worked by family crews with 'orses, and the fly boats steamed orf again towin the empties back to London.

The steam-boats made no noise from their 'zaust, just a gurgle of water now and then from the pellers [*propeller blades*]. Syer's Grandfather Ramlin had had his own steam-boat. Syer used to tell the children about the tall brass funnel and the brass steam whistle he loved to help to polish when he were a little lad, and how they had to let the chimney down when they went empty through the low bridge-'oles. It was heavy work. Took oop a lot of cargo space,

yer steam hinjin, yer boiler, yer coke-'ole. We called steam-boats
hinjin boats until the moty-boat came along. They steamers wasn't
for the likes of us Number Ones with families, but the new moty-
boats, the diesels had families aboard. We never dreamed they
moty-boats was come to stay. We laughed at 'em comin round the
bend with their missin-'orse and funny 'phut-phut-phut!'

The big carryin companies had been convertin their 'orseboats
and steam-boats into moty-boats when I was a little girl. After Moy-
chap's war they started floggin orf their old steam-boats and buildin
brand new moty-boats. Now, in the later twenties more and more
moty-boats was 'phut-phuttin' into sight, specially on the broader
busier Cuts like the Grand Junction.

Then comed the Grand Union [*see p. 223*]. 'They' joined the
Grand Junction from the Regent's right oop the Warwick to
Birnigum. 'They' was bent on gettin their wide boats from the
docks o' London to the heart of Birnigum. 'They' was out for beatin
us Number Ones with the narrow-boats out of a trade. The Grand
Junction already had broad locks all the way from London to
Branston. They could already get wide boats orf the Paddinton Arm
oop to Berkers or even Leighton Buzzid; and barges as far as
h'Uxbridge, pinchin the coal-carryin to the Lectric Light and the
Gasworks; but beyond there some bridges wasn't man enough nor
the Cut wide enough in parts to take two passin barges. You could
take a moty and a butty breasted-oop all-in-one-go through the
broad locks from London to Branston. You couldn't do that through
the narrow locks of the Warwick and the Birnigum, you had to
work each of yer boats through sep'rat, bowallin the butty by hand;
took twice the time and twice the water. The new Grand Union
Canal Comp'ny set about widenin all the locks from Branston to
Birnigum, speedin-oop the traffic.

It didn't come about overnight. For several years we was glad of
the regler orders for ferryin the thousands of concrete blocks from
the wharfs of the Longford Concrete Comp'ny on the Coventry,
'tween Ten Guinea Ackerdook and Longford Bridge, to wherever
they was buildin the new wide lock. But moty-boats *did* seem to
come about overnight. Suddenly we was seein moty-boats bustin-
out all over the Cut. We was forced to join 'em in the end but at
first none of us Number Ones ankered after a moty. A conversion
of yer 'orseboat cost yer almost as much as a new butty, and the

hinjin-'ole [*engine room*] took oop yer tonnage space. You was payin
out more for carryin less. Some of the Number Ones went into the
steam trade, buyin ex-Comp'ny steam-boats. Charley Court bought
a n'ex-Fellas' steam-boat. I think it was the old 'Earl'.

David Ambridge had a brand new moty-boat built by Mr Tooley
and his sons at Banbury [*1928*]. I remember how keen them Tooley
boys was on hinjins, specially Herbert, he was always puzzlin over
Meechanical Magazines. I reckon if Herbert 'adn't had the polio he
would of gone over to the motor-racin business. Instead, he stayed
loyal to his old Dad and limped along with the boat-craftin to the
end of his days.

Dan Doughty had his 'orseboat properly converted by Alby
Faulkner [*L. B. Faulkner, Leighton Buzzard*]. Dan drawed coals
from the Midlands to Dickinson's Paper Mills agen London. Instead
of one trip a week from mine to mill and back with his 'orseboat, he
was now doin two trips a week with his moty. It wasn't that the
moty went faster. You can't go fast on the Cut, it's too narrow. The
more power you put on, the more 'floosh' [*wash*] you builds oop on
both sides of the boat, it pulls yer forend down and yer soon gets
yer deck awash. You was still bound by lor to the pace of the 'orse.
Anythin faster creates a floosh that's bad for the Cut, wearin away
the banks and towpaths and wastin precious water. The moty could
keep goin longer than the 'orse, day and night in some cases—
providin the locks stayed open. The Captains was drove to keep
goin longer and longer hours to compete and pay orf their new
moty-boats.

It was terrible 'ard for their Best-Mate on the butty. Nell Canvin
was Dan Doughty's second wife and a good bit older than 'im.
'Never 'ave a moty-boat, Rose', Nell used to say to me. 'At least old
Charley and Cobber gives yer a night's rest. A moty needs no
stable. You just keeps steerin till yer 'ead 'its the chimney, and
that's yer night's rest.'

As long as our old Cobber and Charley kep goin we couldn't see
no need for a moty but Alby and Moycle never let oop, kep pesterin
us for a ride on a 'put-put'. Jack Monk was only a young man then.
He was workin for Mikey Ward's brother, Rose Ward's uncle,
steerin this moty-boat. Rose's Grampy Ward, Old Two Tots, had it
converted when they was Alby Faulknerin [*working under contract
for L. B. Faulkner*]. Their butty was the 'Percy Veruns', same as

ourn. It wasn't often you knowed two workin boats with the same name. I knowed a 'Friendship', built at Branston before Moy-chap's war, was still workin when Joe and Rose Skinner had their 'Friendship' built at Sephton's; and I knowed two 'Forget-me-Not's, but there wasn't many 'twins' and we was all self-registered with our own numbers.

All his life Jack Monk loved children. Children was always drawed to him. He was always teasin 'em, makin 'em laugh. He'd come to the rescue of any kiddie if he could. He offered to give Alby and Moycle a ride. Alby were over the moon. Our Rose had gone to her Auntie Arryut's with her Auntie Lizer else she might of gone with her little brothers to keep 'em in order. Jack already had Rose Ward and her little cousin Phoebe aboard. Rose Ward must of been about nine or ten. It was a beautiful summer's day. Alby were *that* h'excited—I think the moty-boat were the 'Trust to Me'—his little face were beamin with trust as Jack lifted him aboard to show him the hinjin.

Accordin to Rose [*Ward*], after a short spell with Jack oop top, the kiddies had all settled down in the cabin to play 'Appy-go-Lucky' [*jack-stones*]. Jack was leanin out over the side copin with a tricky bit of steerin when Alby, just for devilment, scoops oop one of the jacks and makes orf chucklin with Moycle chasin after him, oop the steps and headlong into the hatches. They'd forgot they was on a moty-boat. There's no hatches on a moty-boat, just a short flat counter with the 'pellers' churnin underneath.

Alby ran straight orf the counter into the Cut and was drawed into the pellers.

If Jack Monk hadn't had the presence of mind to grab Moycle by the seat of his braces Moycle could of drownded too.

'Cross me 'Eart and 'Ope to Die'

THEY blamed me at the h'inquest.

'No child should be allowed on a motor-boat', they said.

As if I didn't blame myself. Over and over.

Jack blamed his-self. He couldn't understand how the little chap could forget he was on a 'motor'. He'd showed him the hinjin. He'd held him while he steered. He'd sat on the cabin top for quite a while enjoyin the ride. The older ones had soon lost h'interest, ankerin after playin in the cabin. Boat-children are often tied to their own comp'ny for days. It's a treat to play with others. In a while Alby wanted to go down and play too. One minute he were chucklin, 'at 'ome' with the others in the cabin, the next he were in the Cut, little limbs flailin in blood.

Poor Moycle blamed his-self, for chasin Alby oop the steps. He was only eight. He'd seed the 'ole terrible h'accident, the water churnin red with Alby's blood, the black box that took his remains away. Night after night I were oop with him in the cabin, burdened with my own grief, and battlin with his nightmares.

'BIG BLACK 'OLE, Mum. Big black man comed to take me away.'

'Wot does the man look like, Moycle?'

'I can't see his face. He's dressed all in black and he's got this black box to take me away. Don't give me to him, Mum. Don't give me away.' He'd cling to me, sobbin.

'We shall never give you away, Moycle. *Never.*'

'Promise?'

'*Cross me 'eart and 'ope to die.*'

That's wot we always used to say on the boats when we made a solemn promise, and we used to make the sign of the cross on our left breast to show we'd rather be struck down dead than break that promise. To comfort him I told him wot you'd never of told a child in them days.

'Remember when I was oop in that 'orspital in Coventry? When I nearly died? They told me I couldn't 'ave no more babies. We've only got you and Rose now. You're our *only* son. We're lucky to 'ave yer, Moycle. We shall *never* give yer away. *Never!*' He'd go back to sleep then. He trusted me.

He'd have to move out of our cabin soon. The Boat h'Inspector had been on at us. Moycle didn't have to move out by lor until he was twelve but he was growin oop fast. I didn't want to move him yet while he was still so oopset. He was too big to go in with Lizer and Rose. It would mean convertin the forend of 'Britannia' into a deck cabin. We already had a section of stowage taken oop by the 'orse fodder. A deck cabin would cost us money, space, orders, we'd have to hire a change-boat or be laid-oop in dock earnin nothin. We ought to convert to a moty while he was at it, but none of us could bear to think of a moty-boat.

Moy-chap was still very bitter about Alby's death. He didn't blame Jack, he blamed the Grand Union, 'They'm killin the Cut, drovin us all to moty-boats.' He blamed the Grand Union for most of our troubles ever after, specially when they took over the other Arms, the Leicester, the Loughbrer, the Erewash. 'Grabbin more and more Cut, makin the trade faster, more cut-throat.'

He'd lie there in the cabin in the middle of the night, woken oop by a n'injin chuggin past, rockin our boat, 'Bloody Grand Union! Them's the ones wot killed our Alby.'

'Shhh! You'll wake Moycle.' But it was as much as I could do to keep my own sobs quoyet. I could only give way to them at night. By day I had to be strong to cheer oop the others, and to brave oop

[112]

to every passin moty-boat, achin to hear that clear little laughin voice on the cabin top, 'Put-put! Put-put!'

None of us laughed at a moty-boat now. None of us called it a 'put-put' no more.

'*No child should be allowed on a motor boat.*' Huh! They should try stoppin 'em! Already we was seein young lads steerin the moty-boats, 'andlin the controls, being told orf by their Dad for 'openin-oop' [*increasing speed*]. There was no lor against it. Some of them youngsters picked oop hinjin knowledge faster than their Dad but, in the main, most children of the Number Ones still stayed on the butty within safety of the 'atches.

The winter after Alby was drownded we heard cries for help. It was Jack Monk *again*, flat on his stummick, hangin over the counter of the same moty-boat, clingin on to Rose Ward with one hand and her sister, Lucy, in the other, both in the Cut. The h'injin was just tickin over so Jack was able to hold 'em clear of the pellers but it was a bitter cold November day. Rose was about ten, Lucy was three years younger. They couldn't swim, Jack couldn't let go. They was stuck.

They girls was limp and blue all over when we hauled 'em out. We had to work fast, cut their clothes orf, chaffin 'em, rubbin 'em, wrappin 'em oop in 'ot water bottles, makin 'em drink 'ot drinks. They couldn't drink for their hands shakin and their teeth chatterin. It seemed hours before they could stop shudderin and their colour started to turn back. They hadn't been in the Cut long but the shock of the icy cold had tooked their senses away and very nearly their life too. They say that even good swimmers can lose their life that way, from the first shock of fallin in. This time it was Lucy wot forgot which boat she were on, and Rose had tried to save her. Jack had grabbed them both. He were still shiverin with shock for ages after. It was touch-n-go-go. A *very* near do.

After that Moy-chap were more down on moty-boats than ever.

The next mornin Rose found Cobber dead in his stable. He'd had a heart attack.

''Owever will old Charley manage? Shall us 'ave to 'ave a moty-boat, Dad?'

'He'll manage,' Moy-chap vowed, grim, 'we ent 'avin no moty-boat!'

I 'ates to think wot Mrs Susan Ward would of done without her

Rose [*later Rose Whitlock*]. Rose done her duty by her mother all
her life. Susan had only the two girls, Rose and Lucy, she'd lost a
son at birth. She was left too long. They couldn't find no help.
There wasn't the 'cautions against the 'emridge [*precautions against
haemorrhage*]. It took her nerves a long long time to get over it.
For weeks she couldn't walk. For months she couldn't make the
locks. For years she couldn't face the shoppin. Shoppin was always
a woman's work. You'd never catch a boatman doin the shoppin.
Years later, young Alf Bodley was the first boatman I ever seed
comin past the moored boats with his wife's shoppin. Took some
courage that did. I've never forgotten it. His wife was poorly,
expectin their first baby. I poked my head out of the cabin as Alf
and the shoppin bags walked past, and just gawped. Oop popped
another boatwoman's head from the next cabin, and the next, and
the next. Alf and his shoppin walked bravely on. None of us said a
word, flappergast.

From a n'early age Rose Ward done all the shoppin for her Mum.
Her Dad, Mikey Ward, was never very robust. He had some kind
of nervous complaint, always shakin his head as if in pain, and havin
to go inside the cabin to have a lie-down. The other chaps said he
had water on the brain. I used to think they was foolin but, lookin
back, I reckon poor Mikey must of suffered some sort of pressure
like that. Rose had to be mother and man as well in that family.

'Take over, Rose,' her Dad would say, 'andin over the hanimal or
wotever else he was workin, 'I'll 'ave to go inside and 'ave a lie-
down.'

When eventually they had their 'orseboat converted to a moty
down Branston, the man wot showed Mikey how to look after the
hinjin, start it, clean it, wot-av-yer, said, 'You'd better watch as
well, Rose, you'll probably be the chap wot has to run it.'

Most of us 'Roses' had to brave the controls of a moty-boat in the
end but in the main we was glad to leave the runnin of the hinjin to
our chap. Rose Ward done the lot.

Rose had a miserable childhood while her family worked the
'orseboat for her Grampy Ward. He was down on 'em all and this
made Mikey down on Rose. Rose walked miles with that 'orse.
When she wasn't walkin the 'orse she was tied to the steerin. On
the top of the cabin you have a hole where you fix the big stud to
ease the rope when yer long-linin [*on a long tow*]. Rose was tied to

that stud with only just enough slack to allow her to shove the tiller over.

'You undo that rope, I'll give yer a blinkin good hidin!'

The threat was enough, but Rose hated being tied that tight, specially through tunnels. In them days they was often carryin great tree trunks from Buckby to Booburne to be made into lock gates. Trees are even riskier than wheat to steer. Rose was always terrified the boat might capsize in the tunnel in the dark and she'd be trussed underneath.

Grampy Ward were a sour old booger. We called him 'Grumpy' Ward, or 'Old Charley Two Tots', I don't know why. He *did* help his sons to set oop in boatin. He had three sons and three daughters. He called one of his boats the 'Three Brothers' and another the 'Three Sisters'. Mikey was the youngest and worked with his Dad. Mikey and his family worked the 'orseboat and Old Two Tots lived on the butty. He were yooge, had the dropsy, never left the boat, liked to think he 'knowed it all'—'News-o'-the-World' were another of his nicknames—and nobody else were to know nothin, do nothin, have nothin, without his consent. He begrudged anythin light-hearted, even a smile, let alone a 'Bunfight'. On the Cut any public jollification was dubbed a 'Bunfight'. He held the purse strings and Mikey and Susan and their two young daughters was tied to him. He never liked 'em to do anythin orf their own paddle, not even a whistle, not even a song. Not that we done much singin in them days.

The boatmen had their few songs they kep alive in the pubs, 'Ten Green Bottels', 'Keep yer 'ands orf, she's mine!', 'Wot is a man but the Leaves on the Tree?' and wot-av-yer; and snatches of songs brought back from the trenches, 'Inky-pinky parly-voo?' But us women had little chance of pickin oop songs. Minnie Littlemore's 'Home Sweet Home' lasted us for years until the comin of the wireless. Not that many of us in them days had the money to buy a wireless. Me and Moy-chap had no money for a wireless, not until we splashed out on a second-'and 'cumulated' for the Queen's Coronation.

Mikey Ward, strangely enough, were the first chap I knowed to have a wireless. It was a darin do-it-yerself-without-'*im*-knowin sort of job. A chap from Hillmorton helped him to fix it oop. They had to wait till dark, when Old Two Tots was out of sight in his cabin on

the butty, to smuggle the bits-n-pieces on board. It took oop quite
a bit of room in their cubby-'ole at the end of the sidebed where
Rose and Lucy slept. They had to trail a wire out of the cabin
and all along the plank and keep twiddlin a knob to pick oop any
wisp of sound at all. It were a very comin-and-goin affair. They only
hoped the old man wouldn't spot the copper wire. They was
perfickly safe while the butty kep behind but in Long Buckby stop
lock, where they measures yer cargo by yer depth in the water and
you pays yer toll for the Leicester Cut, the butty comes alongside.

Old Know-it-All spots it. 'Rose! Wot's that wire along yer Dad's
plank?'

'I dunno,' sez Rose, knowin perfickly well, 'decoration, I think.'

'I'll 'ave that later to mend the 'orses' muzzle.'

'Wot's 'e chobblin-on about?' Mikey whispers to Rose.

'He's got his eye on that wireless wire, Dad, to mend the 'orses'
muzzle.'

'We'll see about *that*!' As soon as the old chap ducks into his
cabin out of sight Mikey whips orf the wire and bundles it into the
air-'ole box. From then on they had to wind it round and round a
windmill-thing, stick the windmill outside whenever the old chap
wasn't about, and bring it in every time they finished listenin. They
kep that wireless secret for months till one day they was comin
along by 'Willerboy' on the North h'Oxford when little Lucy,
knowin the 'windmill' was safe inside and there'd be hardly a sound,
twiddles the knob.

A full brass band blares back along the Cut to Rose and Old
Know-it-All on the butty.

'Wotever's that?' cries Rose in a whittle [*panic*], knowin perfickly
well.

'A Bunfight at Willerboy', sez Know-it-All, peerin acraws to
Willerboy to see if he could 'ave a grumble about wot was goin on.

'Of *course*!' Rose sighs with relief as somebody turns down the
volumes and they glides on towards Hillmorton masts. Those
wireless masts had suddenly boosted that band out of the blue.
When they first said they was goin to charge yer for listenin to the
wireless Rose honestly thought they was goin to have chaps with
telescopes perched at the top of them masts holdin out their 'and
for every time you twiddled the knob.

Hillmorton, Rugby, Daventry, masts was bustin out all over in those early years of wireless. Lorries was bustin out all over too. More and more roads was spannin the Cut, sweepin away old lockside pubs and cottages to widen the bridges and build new ones. Wharfs was fallin into disuse as more and more people and factries turned their backs on the Cut and took delivery of their coal by road.

When their little wharf becomed derelick Aunt Tovey and Dad decided it was time to sell oop their little cottage on the bank and shift to Branston where all the Stowell boat people was havin to move when their cottages was pulled down to make the main road. In them days Branston was choc-a-bloc with boat people's cottages where all those Council estates are now. Ramlins, Littlemores, Mellas, Carters, Dawsons, Kents, James and many more of the old well-knowed boatin names. All buried now, like Dad and Aunt Tovey, within shade of the crocketty spire of Branston church, some with 'stones', some without, all 'at home' overlookin the peaceful Cut windin along in the valley below to the little stone-arched bridge in the distance. 'Bathin' bridge we always used to call it on account of the villagers swimmin there in summer. That spire of Branston church oop on the hill is a proper h'eyecatcher [*landmark*]. You can see it for miles as you travel along the Cut. It always brung back mem'ries of my Dad.

'Yer Grampy Mella's buried within shade of that crocketty spire', I used to tell the children, 'and yer Granny Mella's buried at h'Oxford within sound of the little bell of St Barnabas.'

I wished I'd asked *my* Mum and Dad about *their* Granny and Gramp. It's a job to garner the 'leaves on the [*family*] tree' when you've no picture fota albums, no letters, no schoolin, and yer spreaded away from yer roots at eight to go and work for Granny Statham. I don't blame my Mum and Dad. There was so many of us, we had to part before we should of went. I tried hard to explain to the children that my Mum and Dad was their Granny and Grampy. I hadn't the heart to tell Moycle that they wasn't his. It might of stirred oop, 'Who was *my* Granny?' 'Who was *my* Gramp?' 'Where did *I* sprung from?'

I often wondered at night, lookin at his peaceful face asleep in the lamplight, who his mother sprunged from. Where was she borned? How long had Granny Gore lived in that tumbledown farm'ouse? We never went down there no more after we had

[117]

Moycle. We got our fresh vegetables from Mr Bloomfield. After that terrible winter when we lost our little Syer and the Bloomfields was so good to us we never could pass Claydon Top Lock without our Rose nippin orf to see 'my' Mrs Bloomfield.

Mrs Bloomfield had been blessed with a little girl of her own by then, Doris, her 'gift o' God' as she called her. As the years went by Rose would play with Doris and her 'guardian angel' little dog, Tiny, who, ever since Doris was a toddler, always put his-self between her and danger, never allowin her to walk between him and the Cut. Even if we couldn't spare the time to stop and tie-oop there, we'd at least h'inquire after everybody as we went through the lock. You *did* in them days, *h'inquire*, it was only manners, that's how we all kep in touch.

I could never understand Granny Gore not even h'inquirin after Moycle. Hardly a day went past when I didn't dwell on *my* little lost ones, even the ones I'd lost before they was borned, the little boy I lost with the rope in Birnigum, the little girl I lost in Coventry 'Orspital. Our little Syer with the red-gold curls . . . Our little Alby . . . *My poor little Alby!*

'Don't cry, Mum. Me and Rose is still 'ere. You've still got me and Rose.' Moycle was a real prop to us now. He was at last growin out of his nightmares. He was even playin with Alby's cigarette cards.

Boat-children cadged cigarette cards from all the chaps they met on the wharfs along the Cut. They was one of the few 'toys' they had. Moy-chap gave each of the boys their own bacca-tin to keep theirn in. When Alby was alive they was always pinchin each other's cards for devilment, but after Alby drownded Moycle never touched Alby's tin. It was as if them cards was sacred.

'You might as well 'ave 'em, Moycle', his dad sez.

'You 'ave 'em, Moycle', I sez. 'If Alby knowed, he'd want yer to 'ave 'em, that's for sure.' Rose cadged every card she could to give to Moycle. Aunty Lizer would always bring some from his Uncle Appy and Aunty Arryut. He'd be over the moon when they made a set. Them sets was like the Crown Jools. Moycle loved them cigarette cards. He'd spread 'em out on the table-flap in the cabin and study 'em for miles, the pictures on one side, the readin on the other, puzzlin wot that readin was 'talkin' about. He was gettin like me, ankerin more and more after the schoolin. He still didn't like goin without Rose, he loved helpin her with the locks and all the other boatin she was learnin him to master, but I made him go, even if it was for only half a day. He'd started goin on his own to the Foxford School when he was drawrin the concrete blocks regler from Longford for the new Grand Union locks. The Kid Catcher [*Attendance Officer*] was very strict along that Coventry Arm. He patrolled the towpath on a motorbike.

'They've gone to school', I used to tell him when he came nosin round. It were only half a lie, our Moycle had gone but our Rose would shoot orf and hide as soon as she heard his motorbike. I'd given oop with our Rose. Her Dad wasn't keen, he were another Granny Statham.

'All schoolin learns yer is DIS-CON-TENT!'

The Boatman's Welfare had just done oop an old barge from West Drayton in the Grand Union's boatyard at Hayes and moored it across the way at Bulls Bridge to make a proper schoolroom for the boat-children. I'd made Moycle go when he was last tied-oop there. I had a battle with Moy-chap, he hated anythin to do with the Grand Union. I were determined *my* only son was gonna tend that school, get every bit of schoolin wot I never got. Syer were determined *his* only son were gonna take after *him*, be a Number One.

'*Some*body's gotta stand oop to this bloody Grand Union!'

'I will, Dad,' sez Rose, she was about ten then, 'I'm gonna be a Number One.'

'You can't without the schoolin,' her Auntie Lizer sez, 'they sez from now on it's gonna be all fishal-papers on the Grand Union,' [*official forms*].

'We'll manage,' Rose sez, 'me and Moycle between us.'

We was tied-oop waitin to be let in to this big black 'ole wot led to the private wharf under a mill in the middle of Birnigum. We called this Cut the Bottom Road. We 'ated the Bottom Road. It was the devil's own stinkin stagnant ditch under the buildins, bridges, and railways of the city. Heavy traffic dropped smuts and muck from the bridges on top of us, the towpath was never cleansed by rain and was filthy with soot and horsemuck. It was so dark the 'street' lamps was left on all day and 'vag'runs' slumped in the shadows. Everybody chucked their waste and their dead dogs into it. The moty-boats was findin it a nuisance gettin their pellers caught on rubbish, more and more of these dirty trips was being foisted on to us old 'orseboat Number Ones. It made us and our boats filthy dirty. We laid sacks over the 'atches so we wouldn't traipse the muck back into our cabins every time we worked the locks, but they wasn't much cop.

Every so often the towpath went oop over a n'orse bridge and the Cut branched orf under the bridge into a black 'ole guarded by a big iron-railed gate to stop yer boat goin any further 'cept on business. There was oondreds of these private wharfs hidden away under the factries and foundries of Birnigum. It was a job to know some of 'em was there, tucked away in dark channels, if yer didn't know yer wouldn't know. We used to bring inkits and billets of metal to the foundries, sand to the glass factries, and wheat to the mills. Right oop to 'Er 'Itler's war there was still mills grindin corn in the bowels o' Birnigum.

Moy-chap walked through the little side-gate and into the mill to remind 'em we was still waitin to be let in. There was only room for one boat at a time at this place so it meant 'nooverin' and the ropes was filthy with fat from towin earlier through a thick crust floatin on the Cut from a soap factry.

We worked hard to unload. We wanted to get away as soon as we could out towards Tammerth where we could have a go at cleanin down the boats and us-selfs before nightfall.

The last factry we passed as we left the Bottom Road were a printin works. As we drawed level a great spurt of red stuff came surgin out of their sluice, splashin our paintwork, drippin down our 'atches like blood.

'Mum!' Moycle threw his-self at me, buryin his face in my apron. He were shudderin all over.

'It's all right, Moycle,' I sez, tryin to comfort him and steer at the same time, 'it's only reddle, it's not blood.'

That night we was back to the nightmares again.

'Big black man, Mum. Big black box to take me away. Don't give me to 'im, Mum. Don't let him take me away.'

'We shall never give yer away, Moycle', I took his hand in the darkness and 'crossed' my breast, '*Cross my 'eart and 'ope to die.*'

When we next tied-oop at Sutton Stop the 'bobby' was waitin. Moy-chap was wanted in Mr Veater's h'office. 'You'd better come too', he said to Moycle.

I guessed we was oop before the Boat h'Inspector. We still hadn't put Moycle into a cabin of his own, we was meanin to do somethin about it when he'd grown out of his nightmares. We all trekked after the bobby along the towpath, Moy-chap, me, Moycle, Lizer, and Rose, and all the other boat people wot happened to be tied-oop there. That's how we was on the boats. If one was goin to be in trouble we was all goin to be in it together. Moycle clung to me tight. It wasn't the Boat h'Inspector, it was a tall thin city-chap in a long black overcoat. He had a face as long as a funeral.

'I have reason to believe that this child is Wilfred Woodall', he sez to Moy-chap.

Moycle clung to me, terrified, no idea wot he was on about. Neither had we. Proper dolesome this chap was, readin out a fishal-paper on and on, 'Wilfred' this and 'Wilfred' that. I looked to Mr Veaters. I trusted Mr Veaters.

Mr Veaters came over and put his arm around my shoulders.

'Rose, this gentleman is a solicitor . . .'

Granny Gore was dead. Our Moycle was her only child. He was worth a lot of money. The man was goin to take him away to be schooled and brung oop proper.

Moycle began to cry, clingin to me. Moy-chap put his-self in front of Moycle, standin oop for him, 'Where's yer *proofs*? Where's yer *'thorities?*'

The funeral-chap holds oop this posh black box with a brass 'andle.

'All Wilfred's papers are in here. This black box holds proof of everything.'

Mr Veaters asked Moy-chap if we had any fishal-papers.

We had no fishal-papers, no black box to stand on.

Moycle clung to me sobbin, 'Don't let him take me away, Mum!'

They wouldn't even let me take him back to the boat to talk to him and clean him oop. The bobby was tuggin at him. Moycle were like a wild animal kickin and screamin, 'Mum! You promised!'

The boat people was all for blockin the way but Mr Veaters told us there was nothing we could do, the lor was on their side. I had to stand there watchin as the bobby carried him screamin away, 'Mum! You promised!' His hands reachin out to me, his face streamin with tears, 'Mum! You *promised!*' . . . past the 'Grey-hound' . . . 'You *promised!*' . . . past the cottages to the big black 'erst [*hearse*] of a car, 'MUM!'

I suddenly noticed Rose dashin from the 'Britannia' after them, leapin the lock, and gettin to the car just in time to hand somethin in to Moycle. They druv away. Rose was left cryin and wavin at nothin. He was gone.

For weeks after, I had nightmares, wakin in the night to his sobbin. No Moycle. I wished I was dead.

Poor Moycle! At least, thanks to Rose, 'e'd got 'is cigarette cards.

Weatherin-On

ME and Moy-chap couldn't talk about Moycle. I'd try but I'd just
clamp-oop. It's hard to fathom yer feelins when you hasn't the
words. Syer bottled his-self oop, just like he did when he came
back from the war. I'd wake in the night with a nightmare, to find
his place in the bed cold and empty, the moon streamin through
the open slide, and him sittin outside in the hatches havin a quiet
smoke. I'd know by the glint of his tears he were pinin for all his
sons, for Moycle, for Alby, for little Syer. All gone now. *'For what
is a man but the leaves on the tree?'* You just has to weather on.

Some months later Mr Veaters wanted us again in his office. The
'funeral-chap' had sent Mr Veaters a piece of paper for oondred
pounds to pay Moy-chap for raisin Moycle. Moy-chap were *that*
airyated [*irate, angry*]! Talk about song-n-dance! Talk about blue
murders?—Wouldn't touch it with a boat-shaft!

Mr Veaters tried to get him to accept it, he knowed we was
always hard-oop, owin a bit, payin a bit. *Oondred pounds!* Moy-
chap wouldn't 'ave it. He would *not* 'ave it.

"Im and 'is black box! Yer can send it straight back!"

'All right. All *right*! I'll send it back.' Mr Veaters nodded at a big package in the middle of the floor. 'But I'm not sending *that* back.'

It was for me. It was one of them little rubber-roller mangles like wot our Arryut's was. There was no message with it but I knowed *that* were from our Moycle. '*When I'm a Number One, Mum, with me own put-put, I'm gonna treat yer to one of them rollers.*' He knowed now he would never be a Number One but he'd kep his promise. I only hoped that one day he would forgive me for breakin mine.

For several years I were the only boatwoman doin my washin with a rubber roller fixed to my dolly-tub. I were the envy of the other women all along the towpath. It saved me a lot of wringin and dryin out. Every time I fetched it out of the laid-'ole I'd think of 'Little Booger' clamped oop by his petticuts in Granny Gore's old iron mangle, and wondered where he were prisoned now in his gilded cage being brung-oop proper.

'I wonder wot our Moycle's oop to, Lizer? I wonder where our Moycle is, ay?'

'We mustn't think of 'im as our Moycle no more, Rose. He's Wilfred now. At least he's got 'is schoolin. You was always ankerin after 'is schoolin.'

I had a job to think of him as Wilfred. I only knowed one Wilfred, Granny Keys' grandson at the 'Pigeons' 'gen h'Oxford. We knowed him ever since he was a little chap visitin his Gran with his Mum and his little sister. He used to love to 'help' us make the lock. He growed oop clever, won a place from the village school at Kirtlinton to one of they posh schools in h'Oxford. Since then his mother, Mrs Wickson, Granny Keys' pretty daughter, Lil, had taken over the 'Pigeons'. Her husband, Mr Wickson, was h'injineer oop at the new Cement Works, and Wilfred was now a growed-oop schoolboy wavin to us in the mornin as we set orf along the Cut and he set orf on his bike along the towpath to Bletchington Station to catch the train to h'Oxford. I tried to picture our Moy—*our Wilfred*, settin orf to his posh school with all his books and pannerfernalia. I only 'oped, no matter how clever he growed oop, he'd never forget his Mum and Dad on the boats, his Aunty Lizer, and his big sister, Rose.

Our Rose never forgived that 'funeral-chap' for creepin-away her little Booger. We was lucky to have our Rose. She were now only-daughter and only-son rolled into one. She was as good as any chap on the boats, yet she were thin and wiry like her Aunty Lizer but with more bloom in her cheeks and very pretty 'air, dark and curly like her Dad's used to be. She were always older than her years. Her Aunty Arryut had gived her a pretty nightgown, growed-oop, celanese with real poofed sleeves. 'That's for me bottom draw', she sez to our Lizer. She was only about thirteen. Lizer didn't like to hear her talkin growed-oop like that, she still liked to think of her as a child. She was still a child at heart, her old Suzy-doll was always on her bed, but she were one of the nippiest youngsters I ever knowed with the boats. She was all for gettin forward, gettin 'em ahead. It was as if havin had all her little brothers one by one snatched away from her she wasn't gonna let life ever again steal a lock in front of her. I was always tryin to make her steady-oop. If there'd been a 'Lympics for lock-wheelin, our Rose would of beat the lot.

It was the same with the sheetin-oop, tyin-oop, washin-oop. All done proper, mind yer! Nothin slap-dash about our Rose, just top-speed. Same with the shoppin, no sooner nipped orf on her bike, she was back to the cabin with the goods. Lizer dubbed her 'Biff-bat'.

The biff-bat craze was all the rage on the bank. It was a small wooden bat with a rubber ball fixed to the middle by a string of 'lastic. They had to see how long they could keep biftin the ball without missin it. We was goin along the North h'Oxford for Wyken one hot summer's morn, that peaceful quoyet stretch after Hillmorton. All we could hear was the call of the swifts, the quack of the dooks, and the clop of Charley and Moy-chap ploddin the towpath. All of a sudden one of them stunt-jobs [*stunt aeroplane*] flies over low, trailin a banner, blazin some 'warnin' like a huge black shadow over us. Could of been 'End of the World about to come' for all *we* knowed.

A farm lad on one of them little russet [*red-brick*] bridges 'gen Clifton told us it said, 'BIFF-BAT COMPT. RUGBY'. As we neared Ruckby we could see all these 'biff-bats', oondreds of 'em, hurryin along to the Compt with kiddies and growed-oops attached, as if drawed by 'lastic. People was glad of a craze like that to help them forget their troubles in them miserable years of no work in the early thirties.

We was glad to be still in work but a lot of the old wharfs and mills we used to draw to was goin out of business. I mind [*remember*] deliverin one of the last loads of stone to the old Wolvercote wharf, and one of the last loads of wheat from London docks to Meads's flour mill on the Wendover Arm. The Wendover was sposed to be a broad Cut, it was built at the same time as the Grand Junction, but it was that silted-oop and low in water. They used to say it leaked into Lord Roofchild's dinin-room. When we got to the mill we seed the owner proppin oop his doorway. Granny Statham always used to say, 'When the master props oop his door trade must be bad.'

'The mill can't grind with water that's past' were another of Granny's sayins. Some of them old mill wheels, like the one at h'Oxford [*Castle Mill*], down below Louse Bridge, the iron 'orse-bridge near Hythe road-bridge, had been turnin since the days of William the Conker. Now they'd altered the road-bridge for traffic the Cut finished at Juxon Street, we couldn't get down to the mill no more nor through to the h'Oxford Basin. All them big merchants, the bewry, the builders, the coal merchants, wot used to have tons and tons delivered to their wharfs all round Worcester Street Basin and New Road Basin, was forced to move their deliveries else-where. Some went over to the lorries and some to the wharfs at Juxon, Walton, or Hayfield, where Thomas 'Ambridge had 'is coal mountains. My Mum could remember when she was a little girl there were heaps of coal, stone, grain, pipes, along Hayfield wharf, with rows and rows of 'orses-n-carts as far as the h'eye could see, and *her* Granny tellin her, 'When *I* was a little girl this were all plowed fields.'

Bertha 'Boshum', Rosie Beauchamp's mother-in-lor, still lived in that little ferry-'ouse and worked the penny-ferry at Juxon Street— (it were a flat raft wot she pushed out and pulled back. We used to put the 'orse on sometimes to save goin over the 'orsebridge to get on the river towpath)—but the Motor King [*Lord Nuffield*] and his motor-cars was takin over the Basin. [*Nuffield College is on part of the site, the rest is a car park.*] That's the motor-car for yer! It took away a lot of work from the Cut, but it brought us a lot too. Tons of stone we carried for road makin, from Artshul [*Hartshill*] 'gen Nuneaton, and the Rowley Rags from agen Rowley Regis. Massive lumps of stone was handed into the boats and we dumped 'em out at no end of sites and Council wharfs, mostly on the h'Oxford Cut, not only at big town wharfs like Ruckby and Banbury, but little country wharfs like Aynho, Heyford, Enslow. We carried it 'as dug'. Council chaps with big 'ommocks [*sledge-hammers*] would have to split them, and boys with little 'ommocks [*stone hammers*] would finish the job, breakin big stones into littler stones for road fillin. I knowed two old chaps, blinded by the job when they was boys, doin it for the rest of their days.

We carried buildin materials, sand, ballast, stone, cement, to the new factries like the new Courtaulds on the Coventry, the 'Allymin-yum' on the h'Oxford, the 'Yoover' and the 'Ovaltine' on the Grand Union. We carried coal to the 'Ovaltine' too when it was first started, then they growed into their own posh fleet, seven pairs of narrer-boats, decked-out as 'Ovalteenies', carryin their own coal constant from the Midlands. Toovey's Mill was agen the 'Ovaltine' at Kings Langley. We took coal there too. They had their own two boats for carryin grain. The grain was shooted-in loose at the docks and sucked-out loose at the mill. Wide boats, Toovey's was, spotless. One was the 'Golden Spray' with all her writin pict-out in gold. I've forgot wot the other was called but it were equal spruce. The Pearsalls and the Smiths worked 'em with cart'orses. I were very friendly with Carrie Smith when she were a girl.

Some of the new factries was very clean and perticler but others was more-n-more p'lutin the Cut. We was beginnin to see 'foamin-oop' all along the banks, cloggin the condits and sluices. It's bad enough on a river but at least the river's always on the move flushin out with a spring at one end and the tide at the other. The Cut never gets flushed-out; it shifts in the locks and it gets topped-oop with rain—if yer lucky. The first time we seed the foam and smelled the chemical from the waste tip at 'Awkesbury comin to meet us right oop by Bedderth, I sez to Moy-chap, '*That* can't be right-n-proper!'

But there was nothin we could do about it, we wasn't the 'thorities; and the new factries was bringin work. They was now startin to turn out the ready-mades cheaper than you could make 'em yerself. All our married life I'd made Moy-chap's trousers, 'spairs' we called 'em. The whole of the front, the 'falls', flapped down to open, and buttoned oop to a bilston to close. The bilston was a strong band of extrer material stitched well down to carry yer side pockets, and shaped into a deep band to fasten at the front. This front band carried yer eight tin buttons, two for yer waist band, two for yer falls, and four for yer braces. The bottom of the leg was flared to channel orf the worst of the rain from the top of yer boots or to roll oop if yer were forced to do a bit of tunnel-leggin. I made 'em in cord for everyday and black broadcloth for best. They was fully lined, lasted for years, and took no end of washin and dryin. For years Mrs Thomas had been at the Buckby Bottom lock, on the Grand Junction, makin the uniform shirtses and undervests for Fellas Morton, with 'Fellas' writed on their tin buttons. In the thirties Mrs Clarke at Buckby Top lock began sellin the ready-made workin spairs. They was cheaper than I could buy the stuff and make 'em and they weared well. Syer would call in her little front-room-shop at the lock on our way to London and she'd order them ready for us to pick oop on our way back.

Most of the London boatmen and the bargees had their stuff made at Pennintons at Brentford. For those who travelled to Banbury, Foster's the tailors was another good shop for boatmen's gear. Rose Skinner of the 'Friendship' would often 'oblige' by leavin yer order at Fosters, pickin it oop on her way back, and handin it over to yer at Sutton Stop.

Later we bought our ready-mades and boots from Mr Aymus' [Amos] shop at Stoke Bruin. He'd had the parafeen store and rope chandlery for years but in the early Grand Union days he was branchin out into the ready-mades and wot-av-yer. He done the proper h'Oxford shirtses, front gusset, warm folds, an all, and the boatee-blue stockins as well. The only trouble with his ready-made cords was, they stinked. It was summat to do with the dye. I couldn't stummick 'em in the cabin until I'd washed 'em and given 'em a good blowin along the Cut. Even flappin on the line they whifted to 'igh 'eavens. Even the chaps in the Snug at the pub— and the Snug was no bed o' roses—wouldn't stummick Moy-chap in his new cords till he'd weared orf a bit.

The comin of the ready-mades brung them on the bank h'oop into the fashions, and us on the boats h'oop into their second-'and market. We picked oop some beautiful cast-orfs from the Salvation Army. We wasn't bothered about being miles behind the times, all we was worried about was keepin out the weather. Folk studyin fotas of us taken on the boats makes the mistake of thinkin some of those fotas is earlier than wot they are.

'Look at that hat!' they sez. 'That's '20's style, this fota must have been taken in the '20's.'

We had our own style. I weared a gent's skirted coat [*frockcoat*] right oop to the king's Silver Jubilee, and a warm closh-'at all through the war with 'Er 'Itler. Them deep-crowned 'ats suited me well. I still carried my long thick 'air. When our Arryut had her hair docked she persuaded our Lizer to have ern shorn too. I were tempted. Moy-chap wouldn't 'ave it. He would *not* 'ave it. Threatened divorce. *Divorce!* Divorce was for fast 'uns on the bank. You never heard of divorce on the boats. Not until after the war. There was some wot wasn't married, mostly dirty old Rodney-boaters, women who'd pick oop with anybody, hangin loose around tunnels to jump on with men-crews, or sluttin from boat to boat with her kiddies from one old boatchap to the next; but you never heard of divorce.

There wasn't much 'goins-on' neither. It's a job to have 'gentlemen callers' when yer family's clustered round yer all day and yer home's all open and above board. There's no 'back door' on a boat, and yer front door's always on the move. Even when we caught oop with another chap I would never have a say-so [*pass comment*] unless Moy-chap drawed me in.

Moy-chap never had much chance to dally after another woman. By the time he'd trudged miles along the towpath with Charley, hauled ropes, or shifted tons of stone or coal by the barrer all day, he'd had enough. It was as much as he could manage—if we was moored near enough to 'the public'—to swing the string at bar skittles. More often than not we was moored for the night in the middle of nowheres, miles from yuman 'abitation, and he'd catch oop on a bit of a shave or a bit of harness-mendin or a bit of ropework before havin a quiet smoke outside in the 'atches and then turnin in. He never smoked in the cabin and he always slept on the outside of the bed because he was usually the last to get in and the first to get out to see to the 'orse in the mornin. He liked his little 'abits, did Syer, wasn't 'appy with change, *no* moty-boat, *no* bobbed 'air-do.

So I weared my 'air in wirelesses [*earphones*], two plaits crossed over the top of my head and wound round and round in circles round my ears; and I weared the big 'duchess' second-hand, good as ever, wide-brimmed straws to shade the beatin sun, and deep-closhed fee-lors [*velours*] wot stayed on well in the wind and channelled orf the beatin rain.

You was used to battlin-on in all weathers. At least you knowed, when you was soaked through it couldn't soak no further. We always said, 'A drop of rain won't hurt'. As long as you was well-shod you was all right. We all wore boots on the 'orseboats. Us women weared the high-laced leather boots. I always made sure ourn had plenty of good sole between the feets and the towpath. In the '30's, every time we passed through Stoke Bruin, I used to leave a bit of money, wotever I could scrimp together, with Mr Aymus towards the next pair of boots. He used to send away to the boot factry in Northamton, and get them cheap for us. When he was gettin too old to tend the shop his daughter, Mary, came home with her husband Charley Ward and took over. Mary was about fifty by then. I'd leave the money with Mary, and Charley would get the boots for us.

Some towpaths was proper-kep', cambered away from the edge, but once the moty-boats was come about, many paths was let to go into broken banks and boulders in winter, and overgrowed with swans' nests and snake-bites in the summer. That's why we weared boots, winter and summer.

In summer we battled on without much shade, in the blazin sun. Some parts of the Cut are wooded-over and give a welcome shade, but for the most part trees wasn't encouraged and hedges was planted well back to stop the fallin leaves from siltin-oop the Cut. You just had to plod on in a dazzle. The sun blazin on the water and on the shiny cabin top could make yer eyes burn if you was on the steerin. We'd rig oop the big trap umbrella and lay sacks over the burnin 'ot paintwork but the sun would still blaze down, scorchin 'ot. We'd take turns walkin the 'orse, flappin one of them giant 'rhubarb' leaves to waft away the flies, makin sure Charley weared his earcaps to keep out the hordes of flies his tail kep' swishin oop out of the overgrowed verge. *I* croshered them earcaps, and at the end of every day Moy-chap would clean out Charley's ears with a parafeen rag to make sure that they stayed out of trouble.

In winter life was a different 'game'. The iron paddles of the locks

wot burned us with heat in the summer burned us with frostbite in
the winter. Yer breath would freeze on yer eyebrows, yer wet skirt
would freeze like a sharp board to yer legs. I used to get chapped
legs, chapped cheeks, cracked hands, cracks so deep on the top of
my thumbs you could lose a thrippenny bit down 'em. *Agony*, tyin
wet ropes or battlin in a blizzard with a metal winluss to free frozen-
oop ratchets.

In all weathers yer first perpriety [*priority*] was the boat. As long
as you knowed how yer craft was goin to be'ave you was all right.
You knowed in winter her timbers would break if you didn't break
the pressure of the h'ice around the hull. You knowed in summer
her timbers would open oop and she'd let in the water if you didn't
keep sluicin her down in the heat. The sun plays oop no end with
them wooden-hulled boats, fetches the tar out somethin chronic.
They always needs docktorin. You has to caulk 'em with tar and
oakum. Tooley's always done our'uns. You knowed how well yer
boat would be'ave with different cargoes. You knowed how she
'andled empty, but you never knowed how she'd 'andle in *wind*.

WIND was yer worst booger on the Cut. You never knowed how
yer craft would be'ave from one gust to the next, stemmin the Cut
broadside at one whoosh, with yer forend in the rads of one bank
and yer starn in the rhubarb of the other. It was easier if you was
loaded, yer boat swimmed deeper in the water, but yer planks was
set high, bowed like a bendy-bridge over the top of yer cargo. You
could be blowed orf the top, battlin with a shaft to keep yer footin
and to free the forend. If she was empty she floated higher on the
surface of the water catchin every gust, willy-nilly, like a leaf. You
shafted and stroved, stroved and shafted to set her aright. No
sooner was she freed and straightened oop, the next gust would
blow yer broadside into the rhubarb. The rhubarb was this great
big umbrella-leaf plant growin all along the bank. No end of them
'seven-quoyners', big boulders with at least seven sharp corners,
would be lurkin underneath to unship yer rudder or lodge yer boat.
Poor Syer would be strugglin with Charley and the wind to tug us
orf, the wet tow-rope searin through his hands like a red-'ot poker.
If we shortened the tow we pulled in the bow, the wind would
swing out the starn, and we'd stem Lizer and Rose battlin on the
'Percy Veruns'. If we let the tow out we blowed broadside into the
side of a bridge and nearly broke 'Britannia's' back.

It was no good givin oop, tyin oop till the wind 'bated. Sometimes it blowed for a whole week, you just had to keep weatherin on. The only consolation was lookin back and seein another pair o' Number Ones strovin in our wake. All over the Cut we was all in the same boat, boogerin the wind, strovin to get 'em ahead. You never gives in. If yer gives in yer goes under.

Our Rose would not *never* give in, not even if it killed her.

It did kill her at the finish. She were only fourteen.

I were terrible fond of our Rose.

There was a serious drought that year on the h'Oxford. All the pools [*reservoirs*] for toppin oop the Cut was empty. Clavercote Pool was empty, Wormyleighton Pool was empty. We was barely into June, all the summer to go, and they was already havin to lock oop the locks. This means you can only travel between certain times. You had to work faster than ever to beat the locks, else we was losin money. We was already earnin less by havin to carry less because of the draught [*depth of the boat in the low water*]. We'd a load of stone from Nuneaton for Banbury Council wharf.

It had been the loveliest May, fluffy dabchicks and dooklins galore, lambs a-gamblin in the fields, banks thick with wild flowers. Most of all I remember the mayblossom, foamin all along the towpath, frothin oop and oop over the hedgerows, thick and creamy along the boughs. The weather had been so dry and still the blossom had laden like that for weeks, as if it were goin to last for ever. I had never seen the may as it were that year. Ever after, whenever I smell the may I'm back at Napp'n Summit and the day we lost our Rose.

It was early afternoon. We was aimin to make the summit on the h'Oxford—that's 'The Thick' [*Napton six locks*] and 'Arryboy's' [*Green Lock*] and the two top at Marston Doles—before they put the padlock on for the night. In the summer they was often locked to save water from six o'clock at night to eight in the mornin, but that year the drought was so bad they was lockin-on the padlocks from four in the afternoon till eleven o'clock the next mornin. We was havin a job to make a livin, there was no distance in the days.

There's only so much water in the Cut. It can only be topped oop by yer side-ponds and sluices. If there's no rain there's no toppin oop of yer main, and every movement on the Cut sloshes more away over the bank. All that trip we'd been savin water by sharin the locks, waitin for others to use the same lock water. It had been a long-drawn-out trip. Rose was cha'fin to get to the top lock before it was locked, then we had the 'Level' or 'the Leven Mile Pound' as we called it, eleven miles without locks to Claydon and 'her Mrs Bloomfield'.

Thunder had been rumblin round us all day, and by noon as we climbed the Napp'n Six, big black clouds was crowdin at the summit, yet all around us the sun was still blazin down, burnin the beams and the ratchets, makin 'em too hot to handle without usin yer apron. All along past Arryboy's and comin along the Mile Pound to the last two locks the air was gettin more and more suffocatin with the scent of the may and the hot cindery smell as if we was headin for a dark furnace.

I cleared everythin orf the cabin top, I could see we was headin for a downpour. We was gaspin for rain, if only it would hold orf till we'd cleared that last lock. Rain makes iron very slippy, dangerous when crossin the lockgates in nailed boots with wet 'andles [*handrails*]. By the time we was comin oop to the bridge before the top lock it was black as night. 'SPLAT!' a huge drop of rain scattered all over the cabin top. We wasn't gonna make it.

'Leave that last lock, Rose! We'll tie-oop! Bide till it's over!'

She flit on with her winluss, regardless.

Great drops like stones began to bomb the Cut.

'Stay under the bridge, Rose! You'll get soaked!'

'—Drop of rain won't hurt!'

I glanced back at the strange twilit landscape, only the lock beams and the may stood out. Napp'n on the Hill were in darkness. In them days Napp'n Windmill were on the tumbly-side [*a ruin*]. It suddenly lit oop in a blindin flash. There was a terrible scream and a BANG! from the top lock. I swung round just in time to see Rose's winluss twistin high in the gloom, dancin with blue light. Charley bolted. The tow 'went'. Thunder crashed. Rain sheeted down, battenin me to the tiller. I longed to go to our Rose, but I were adrift, 'elpless.

At last it stopped. The sun blazed forth. Everywhere, everythin, the boat, the bridge, the towpath, the hedgerows, steamed in the tremendous heat.

When they found her winluss it were twisted and moltened

beyond belief. When we found our Rose only her hand was burned, the lightnin had hardly marked her, all the hurt were within. She were floatin in the Cut covered in may-petals.

Not a blossom was left on the boughs, they was all went.

Three-'Anded

MR TAYLOR, the lock-keeper at Marston Doles, was very kind, offered us his hut so our Rose could be laid at rest while we made arrangements.

In them days the Comp'ny lock cottage were at the first Marston lock and at the top lock were this little brick-built hut where the keeper and the lengthsman kep their work-junk, stop-planks, wot-av-yer. There was two farm cottages by the top lock. The lady from the cottages offered to make the hut clean and fit and put in some flowers from her gardin. But I couldn't bear for our Rose to be laid somewheres strange. I wanted her to be made laid-at-rest on her own bed and carry her back to where she was christened, Banbury Big Church. It seemed only meet and right.

The lady knowed how to go on. She helped me and Lizer to lay out our Rose. We washed her and arrayed her in the pretty nightgown her Aunty Arryut gived her. We gived her her Suzy-doll. We done her 'air real nice.

The Granthams, Old Lou and May and family, had been followin in our wake oop the locks on their way to Banbury. Old Lou comed from Banbury way. His people had a house in Factry Street, top of where the old drawbridge used to be. Nearly all the families in Factry Street, Smiths, Kenches, Ownses, Granthams, Tooleys, was boat-connected in them days. All 'sinked' now [*shopping precinct*]. He'd helped to bowall our boats through the top lock and helped us to tie-oop. Then he'd gone with Syer to search for Charley. Charley was still scarpered. Without Charley we was goin nowheres.

They found him tremblin in a field beside a runaway farm 'orse wot was in a terrible state. He'd bolted with a mowin machine attached and were all cut about. Charley still had his swingletree, the 'tow-bar' for towin the boat. Some calls it a 'spreader' but we always called it the swingletree. It had a hook in the middle for the tow-string and a hook at each end for the traces. The traces was threaded through the bobbins to stop 'em from rubbin. His bobbins was all intact and his earcaps and his omes [*hames*], but he were all of a lather with fright. We had to tie-oop there and stable him for the night.

Old Lou and May had to get ahead with the 'Franklin'. They was still 'orseboaters then, Number Ones, strugglin on like we. They wanted to make top-o'-Claydon that night so's they'd be quick through the locks as soon as they was unlocked the next mornin. They was goin to break the sad news to the Bloomfields and get Mr Gilkes to make the coffin ready. Our Rose would of wanted her coffin to be carried back o' the mast, she were like her Dad, proud of her boatin past, all for clingin to the old 'orse-boatin ways; but we couldn't cos we was loaded. The Granthams was old boatin stock, true-'earted boaters, stoppin to help us in our dire need even though they was losin precious journey-time. Little did we know then that in years to come we'd be doin the same for May at this self-same lock when Old Lou met his death with a heart attack.

The lengthsman from top o' Napp'n carried the sad news down to Mrs Taylor at the pub at the bottom bridge. Mrs Taylor knowed somebody with a tellyfone in the village, there wasn't a lot of fones about in them days. They'd tellyfone Mr Veaters at Sutton Stop and he'd break the news to Appy Youet and our Arryut. Only that mornin our Rose had 'put oop' her hair because she was so hot. It made her look much older. Mrs Taylor had watched her, fancyin herself growed-oop, carryin herself proud, swingin her winluss along the towpath. 'You'll have to watch out, Mrs Ramlin!' she'd called across to me from the bank, 'She'll be havin a beau before long!' Mrs Taylor was always helpful and interested in the boat people, always teasin our Rose about havin a beau. So was our Arryut. No more beau now. No more teasin.

Our Arryut were 'eart-broken. She and Lizer was closer than Aunties to our Rose. They was best chums. Rose were her Dad's best chum too, his 'little Mate', always handin him his cup of tea before she had her own, always havin the lock ready for when he got there with Charley. Now we was only three-'anded we had to take the 'orse and boats nearly to the lock before we could get started, workin the paddles. We was lucky that Charley *would* keep walkin if Moy-chap left him and went on ahead. Some hanimals got h'artful. When you wasn't walkin with 'em they'd stop and graze,

1. (see p. 29) **Minni Littlemore** (née Gill) and her family taken on the canalside at Roberts' Foundry, Deanshanger on the Old Stratford Arm of the Grand Junction Canal *c*.1910. Minnie in her traditional boatwoman's bonnet stands at the back holding baby Charley in bonnet and 'petticuts'. Minnie married her husband Peter when she was only 16 and bore him fifteen children. Peter sits third from *R* (all the other men are foundrymen). Ada's husband-to-be, Dick, sits on his father's *L*, his sister Annie on the other side. On the ground sit his other sisters (*L* to *R*) Nell, Sarah, and little Alice. Note the girls' clean white pinafores in contrast with the dirty foundry surroundings, Alice's smart hat on the ground in front of her, Minnie's washing on the line (*top L*), and the mooring stump (*bottom R*).

2. (see p. 58) **Suey Beechey** (née Dorset). Suey's family originated from West Drayton where they worked for L. B. Faulkner of Leighton Buzzard. When she married Albert they worked the horse-boats for the 'Blue Lias', the cement works at Long Itchington. Later they worked the tar-boats for Thomas Clayton of Oldbury, carrying between the Leamington and the Oxford Gasworks to the Banbury Tar Distillery. Here she is on the butty *Leam* in the late 1950s. She and Albert later retired 'on the bank' at Long Itchington.

3. (see p. 64) **Boatwomen** of 1913 on the L. B. Faulkner horse-boat *Elaine* celebrate the christening of a new-born boat-child. The traditional boat bonnet, with its long 'curtains' down the back of the neck and its low brim for shading the eyes from the glare of the sun on the water and the painted cabin top, was very practical. Originally made in printed cotton they were made in black to mourn the passing of Queen Victoria in 1901, and many of the older women retained the mourning black for the rest of their lives.

4. (see p. 65) **Ada Skinner** (née Monk) in the cabin of her change-boat while her regular boat was being used to make the famous film *Painted Boats* towards the end of the war. Ada married Jack Skinner, brother of Joe Skinner, the famous Number One who had the *Friendship* on the Oxford Canal. Ada's son, Jack Skinner Junior, married Rose Hone, daughter of Alfred Hone Junior, son of Alfred Hone of Banbury, the famous Number One featured in L. T. C. Rolt's well-known book *Narrow Boat*. This book and the film *Painted Boats* did much to arouse the national concern for the preservation of our canal heritage.

5. (see p. 87) **Rose Skinner** (née Bromage) and her husband Joe in their latter years; the last of the Number Ones to work their horse-boat, the *Friendship*, pulled by Dolly on the Oxford Canal until they retired in 1959. The *Friendship* is now housed at the Ellesmere Port Boat Museum.

6. (see p. 95) **Wedding of Betty Hone**, daughter of Alfred Hone Senior of Banbury, *c.*1930. *L* to *R* back row: Sarah Grantham, ?, Sarah Hone, Gladys Ducket. *L* to *R* middle row: ?, Elijah Ducket, Frank Ducket, Betty Hone, Alfred Hone, Amelia Hone. *L* to *R* front: Evelyn King, Rose Hone (Alfred's grand-daughter, later Mrs Jack Skinner). Taken outside Tooley's dockyard, Banbury.

7. (see p. 114) **Rose Ward** (Mrs Bill Whitlock) Rose's mother and father both suffered from ill-health and Rose bore the brunt of family responsibility from a very young age. It is good to see much happier photos of Rose in later life when she has the confidence of knowing her worth as a skilled boatwoman and the love of her family and friends. Note the nose-tin (nostern) she is carrying, and the horse's elaborately tasselled and crocheted ear-caps.

8. (see p. 118) **Mrs Bloomfield** (R) of Claydon Top Lock with little Doris in her arms (c.1930), typical of many of the kind women 'on the bank' who were a support to the boatwomen in times of trouble. The young boatwoman with her is Annie Wilson (see also Pl. 15, taken many years later).

9. (see p. 140) **Sar'anne Carter** (née Ward), Laura's mother, in her neat white apron with several of her twelve well-cared-for children. When she died all who were still very young were given homes among the boat people. Laura went to live with her aunt, Mrs Susan Ward, and became a tower of strength in that family, crewing with her cousin Rose (Mrs Bill Whitlock) to the end of their working days (1970) on the Grand Union.

10. (see p. 152) **Emma Russon** on her butty *Bascote c.*1935. Emma raised four sons on the boats. Working for Fellows, Morton and Clayton she and her husband travelled great distances all over the Navigation and carried many different cargoes. Note her elaborate hairstyle, and the sack over the 'starn' to keep the paintwork clean.

11. (see p. 154) **'Sister' Mary Ward** (née Amos) of Stoke Bruerne. Though unqualified, she had years of nursing experience during her earlier married life at Earls Barton. When she returned with her husband to Stoke Bruerne to care for her father in his old age she turned the front room of their cottage on the lockside into a surgery with free treatment for the boat people. She was eventually awarded the OBE for her years of devoted service to the community and starred in a 'This is Your Life' programme on the television. She is holding a traditional drinking water can presented to her as a tribute from the boat families (*c.*1961).

12. (see p. 155) **Susan Ward**, who lost her husband *c*.1938, sold out to Barlows just before the war. She is seen here with (*L* to *R*) her niece Laura Carter and her daughters Rose and Lucy. With only this young female crew these two Barlow boats were kept carrying tons of vital coal and materials between London and the Midlands all through the war.

13. (see p. 178) **The Trainees** (*c*.1944). Some of the educated women 'off the bank' who bravely volunteered to learn to work the boats for the war effort during the last two years of the war. Kit Gayford (*L*) with windlass was trained by Charlie Lane, Laura Carter's brother-in-law, to be one of the 'officers' to train the recruits. The famous Canal Travelling Theatre Company Mikron based their highly successful 1992 production of *Imogen's War* on the experiences of these women. The season was launched with a gallant reunion of the few remaining trainees and some now in their eighties made the effort to attend.

14. (see p. 181) **Boat Girls** helping to ferry horses at Sandford-on-Thames. This well-known photograph has long been wrongly captioned 'Oxford Number One John Humphries poles the boat while the horses are held by his *nieces* (i.e. 'Cowboy' Mary and her sister Eliza Humphries)'; but Mary assures me that the girls are her cousins, Rose and Olive, Uncle 'Jack's *daughters*, though Mary and 'Lizer' have many a time ferried horses on this precarious raft across to the stables at Cannon and Clapperton's papermill on the opposite bank.

15. (see p. 181) **Annie Wilson** (née Humphries) and her husband Number One John 'Jack' Wilson who, though they had four children of their own, 'adopted' Mary Humphries and her sisters when they were orphaned. Note the fine lettering and decoration of the Wilson boats.

16. (see p. 187–188) **Rose Skinner** (née Hone) with her little daughter Joyce in the late 1940s. Little Joyce had been playing with the coal. Rose never knew this famous photo had been taken until she saw it printed 'over and over' on a pile of plates at a boat rally in the 1980s. 'He might of tipped me the wink to spruce her oop and put a ribbin on her!'

17. (see p. 189) **Ada Littlemore** (née Mellor) being attended by Sister Ward in her little front-room surgery at Stoke Bruerne, 1946. Jenny is in her arms. Two of her children, Rose and Sylvia, are standing nearby.

wouldn't work towards the lock. Some was *that* tricky, when they seed you comin back to fetch 'em they'd turn tail and start runnin back along the 'road'. This could be dangerous, the tow-string could come orf the looby or break with such force it could badly injure or kill somebody.

A pair of 'orseboats is really a four-'anded job, two to steer, one on the 'orse, and one on the locks. You can enjoy yer work, have a change round, turn and turn about. Without Rose we had to work flat out. Three-'anded isn't so bad when yer unloaded, you can work both boats together in some places, tied side by side, wot we calls 'breasted-oop'. With the tillers tied as one, one pair of hands can steer both boats. That leaves another to lead the 'orse, and the other to get ahead on the bike, lock-wheelin. If there's no locks one of yer can have a 'rest', gettin the others summat to eat, splicin the ropes, cleanin the brasses, wot-av-yer. But when yer loaded you misses that fourth pair of 'ands.

A rope can sometimes act as another pair of 'ands. Even a child can stay a 70 ft boat with only a rope, the 'strap' as we call it. Hitched round a moorin stump ropes will hold a boat to the lockside while you work on yer own. You have to have yer wits about yer to slacken orf the ropes as the water level drops else yer boat will be left "angin on the wall' like 'Ten Green Bottels' h'accidentally fallin crocks, cans, wot-av-yer into the mud at the bottom of the lock.

A 'log' can sometimes act as another pair of 'ands. Gloster Alice always called ern the 'pig'. Gloster Alice comed from out Severn way. The 'log' was a thick rope, wot we called the 'log-string', with a heavy iron weight on the end. Some people had a chain on their'un instead of a rope. We had my Dad's log. It were very old. It were two convick balls with rings in the top. We kep it in the laid-'ole. When we was being loaded under a chute and we didn't want to keep climbin out, untyin a moorin rope, draggin the boat further along, and tyin it oop again, we'd tie the log-string to the big iron moorin ring on the side of the wharf and let the heavy cannon balls hang down inside the hold. That log would hang taut holdin the boat in close under the chute. We'd load a bit, lift the log out and ease the boat along by workin our hand along the wall, let the log hang close again, and load a bit more.

Balancin the cargo was always Moy-chap's say-so [*decision, responsibility*]. He was the Captain, the safety of us all lay in his

[137]

knowledgeable 'ands. Loose coal, stone, sacks of corn, wheat, sugar; inkits of copper or allyminyum; boxes of tinned goods; sheets of buildin material, pipes, timber—all weighed and stowed different. Yer narrer-boat hull isn't shaped regler like a box or a barge, it wendy-bows and dwindles down to keel. If Moy-chap didn't make the most of every curvy niche of stowage, we carried less tonnage and earned less money. He never trusted the chaps on the wharf to do it. Some of 'em was 'casuals', had no idea wot a strain on a boat's back or wot a risk to the crew was a nun-balance load. One dimwit once tried to load us with hot coke straight from the gas'ouse, he thought all narrer-boats was iron-hulled. We could of been roasted on our own timbers. They used to hose that hot coke down when it came out of the gas'ouse. WHOOSH!SH!SH! Talk about steam! Our kiddies used to be terrified of it when they was little.

Mixed timber was the ockerdest load to stow. Each piece had to be fitted in by hand. Syer was a prize-puzzler at that job. He'd glance at a space, say zackly which-wood which-size he wanted, and me and Lizer would pass it to him orf the wharf. If the bargemen was loadin it to him straight from their barge they'd sometimes get impatient. It was all right for them, they barges was easy, flat-bottomed, loaded by crane straight from the big ships in the docks. They wasn't Number Ones, didn't have to study their craft like we done our 'Britannia' and 'Percy Veruns'. Me and Lizer passed Syer zackly wot he wanted, long, short, thick, thin, some light as matchwood, others heavy as oak, and all the time he had to keep his weather eye on the 'trim', the level of the boat on the water. By the time we was fully loaded there wasn't a gap to spare, and the 'sparrers would be drinkin from the gunnles'.

Us boatwomen always weared a nessun [*hessian*] apron for that job. Some planks was that heavy we'd rest 'em on our knees for him to take, even through the thick nessun our knees would get bruised and sore, and our rooff 'ands even rooffer with splinters. I 'ated mixed timber.

I 'ated loadin mixed timber even more than shovellin coal and stone, and *they* was bad enough, specially when we was only three-'anded. Not that I ever let Rose do the really heavy work, but it's surprisin wot a help she used to be fillin bookits for her Dad to empty into his barrer. Now he worked alone while me and Lizer filled another barrer. We could of paid chaps orf the wharf to do it but that would of sapped any profit. We'd fix three planks together across the boat, me and Lizer, and have our barrer on the top between us. We'd fix another long plank from the middle to the wharf. Sometimes the Cut would be so low with drought or so silted-oop at the sides we couldn't get the loaded boat in close enough to the wharf. We'd have to walk the plank, twenty feets of it at some wharfs, pushin a n'iron-wheeled barrer full of stone or coal. Over the years many a barrer-load of coal has ended oop in the Cut, addin to the siltin-oop, and they'd dock yer chap's pay because we hadn't delivered a full load. In the bad times like 'the Strikes' we'd trawl for free coal and get our own back.

Workin' three-'anded was 'ard. There was plenty of other three-'anded crews about but they was mostly chaps and they had a moty-boat. I knowed we'd have to move over to a moty-boat before long, but we couldn't afford our own. It would mean sellin out to one of the big Fellas, workin for a firm, ceasin to be Number Ones. Syer couldn't bear to think of that. Not that he wasn't h'interested in hinjins. Like most chaps, if we was held oop at Banbury or Branston or 'Ricky', anywheres where there was a boatyard, he'd be drawed to any group of chaps porin over a hinjin. No end of chaps invited him to "av-a-go' on their moty-boats and he enjoyed it, but the minute I said anythin about *us* havin one he'd just clamp-oop.

We couldn't afford to take on somebody else, we wasn't makin enough. Even if Lizer was to marry, they'd want a pair of boats of their own. I couldn't see her marryin. Dick Littlemore were now married to his Ada; and Dick were the only chap I'd ever catched our Lizer blushin over. Me and Lizer was strong, we'd been boatin all our lives, we was born-n-bred to it. We had stamina, we was used to stickin at a job longer than most chaps, but we hadn't a chap's strength in our shoulders. Boatin's hard on yer shoulders, workin that big heavy rudder against the flow of the water, haulin heavy wet ropes, bowallin boats, shaftin boats orf mud, shovellin coals, and pushin barrers. We wasn't old by today's standards, Lizer was twenty-four and I was close on thirty-five, a n'old thirty-five, I'd beared five babies, I'd had no end of docktorin and repairs, and I were wore out with loss, the loss of all my true and only wealth, my children.

Me and Syer would of tooked to another boat-child if we could of found one needin a n'ome, but there was gettin less and less kiddies

on the boats, more and more was stoppin with relations on the bank
to get the schoolin. When Sar'anne Carter died, leavin all them
kiddies, they was all snapped oop by relations. You never heard of
a boat-child being put into a n'Ome.

Sar'anne were one of Old Two Tots' three daughters of 'Three
Sisters' fame. Her husband, Ernest Carter, were one of the first
Number Ones to go over to a moty-boat. It was Sar'anne wot first
showed me and Lizer how to work the controls. Sar'anne was kind
enough to help anybody. Old Two Tots was a misery yet his three
girls all growed oop to be good sorts, dauntless and hardworkin.
Rose later in life becomed Rose Bray, Voylet married Jo Beechey
of the Coventry Cut, Sar'anne married Ernie and had twelve
children. Sar'anne was a good carin mother and loved every one of
them children. They was always well 'turned out'. Her eldest, Rose,
married Walter James. The Jameses was a Northern boatin family.
Rose was expectin her first baby and her legs was bad. Sar'anne
loaned young Billy to be a little runnerboat to his big sister, Rose.
You couldn't help but be drawed to young Billy Carter, snub nose,
cheeky grin, willin and cheerful. Billy drownded in 'Salisbury
Three' [*Soulbury Locks, Stoke Hammond*], workin the lock for his
sister. Sar'anne died soon after. They said it were broken-'eart. No
matter how many children you has you never gets over the ones
you lost.

I'd of welcomed any of the young Carter-kiddies with open arms,
specially little Laura, but her Auntie, Susan Ward, Mikey's wife,
straightway took to her. Mikey were Sar'anne's youngest brother.
Their Rose took to Laura like a sister. They two was hardly ever
parted for the rest of their lives, and when, years later, Rose
married Bill Whitlock, Auntie Laura helped to bring oop their
children. They two women made a powerful team on the boats.
Rose used to boast, 'There's nothin me and Laura can't tackle, 'cept
drive a car and pen a letter.' They'd of shined at them too if they'd
been given the chance. Rose Whitlock and Laura Carter was the
last two true workin boatwomen on the Grand Union until the
Comp'ny packed-oop and made 'em redund'uns. Even then they
made the boats their home for a further six years until arthur'itis
set in, 'due', as Rose said, 'to us slackin-orf after a life-time of
bloody 'ard work'.

Life on the boats *was* 'ard but we never minded as long as we had a good 'road'. Even when we was workin three-'anded we was content with little reward when most of the travellin was so pleasant. When our Rose was alive we used to laugh, 'T'ent the money you earns, it's the sights yer sees.' And many of the sights, the scenery and wildlife, was peaceful and healin to us after Rose died, specially as we was still 'orsedrawed. For most of the 'road' we was at one with the flower-strewn banks, the myriads of butterflies, the birds, the water-varmints, the fluffy young dooklins, and shools of fish. We glided along that quoyet and proyvit the fish hardly bothered to move out of our way. In the thirties there was still long stretches, 'pounds' as we call 'em, of unp'luted water, specially on the less busy Arms like the Slough and the more 'orsedrawed h'Oxford. You could see clear to the roach and goojin [gudgeon] dartin about on the bottom. Loads of 'em would build-oop, silver and pale gold, in front of the boat. Time and again the lanky grey mollerns [herons], head and scrawny neck held high above the rads, would snatch their 'bite' and flap orf, limp as a bit of old grey blanket, into the fields to enjoy it.

On the busier town pounds and junctions the p'lution from the moty-boats, the oil and diesel, the churned-oop mud, was castin a spreadin cloud on the Cut. Everythin was gearin oop to the moty-boat. The towpaths was being let to go, the 'floosh' was crumblin the banks in some places. We was havin to pick our way more and more watchful with Charley. Us Number Ones on the 'orseboats was bein made to feel redund'uns. All those new broad locks we'd helped to build all the way to Birnigum was a help in speedin us oop Hatton two boats at a time but they'd missed out all those old graded brick-levels and setts wot had gived us such good purchase and foot'old on the old locksides. They'd made the new locksides in smooth concrete, 'opeless for blakey-boots and 'orses' 'oofs. Moty-boaters was all they was thinkin about. Moty-boaters don't have no 'orses. Moty-boaters don't need no blakey-boots, they was beginnin to swan about in the new-fangled 'poomps' and wellytons. They wasn't bothered about us and Charley, slippin and strugglin to get a foot'old, battlin to keep goin along broken footpaths.

Syer becomed more and more brusk [brusque] towards me. I knowed it was because he was afeared of havin to give oop being a Number One. For years he knowed where he stood in life, Captain Syer Ramlin of the 'Britannia' and the 'Percy Veruns', now he were feelin more and more at sea in his-self. I wished and wished I could bear him another child. We missed havin a youngster with us. A youngster's always makin yer see life afresh, sayin things wrong-way-rounded, raisin a laugh between yer. It was nearly a year since we'd lost our Rose and yet Moy-chap still hadn't picked oop his pecker [*appetite*]. I were often afeared that he missed Rose more than he loved me. He were ne'er a one to show me a lot of fuss. I never realized 'ow 'ighly Moy-chap thought of me until that proud never-to-be-forgotten day when he stuck-oop for me against that Joey-fella at Saltley. This tough Joey-fella were a joey, a day-boater. He lived on the bank in Birnigum and worked the 'orseboats along the dirty Bottom Road. Every day he took a n'empty boat from the coal merchant's wharf to the mine and fetched a loaded boat back. He wasn't same as we, he never took no pride, the boats and 'orses wasn't belongin to him. He had it all his way [*easy*]. He never lost money waitin to be loaded or unloaded, the boats was always there ready; he had a proper wage, and he got home to his wife every night.

Syer had just taken Charley through the next lock with 'Britannia' and come back to make the lock ready again for me. We was on our way back empty to Fazeley after deliverin a load of steel billets in Birnigum. We was goin to turn orf at Fazeley and go oop to the mines at Atherstone. They was still the old single locks along the Bottom Road. I was bowallin the 'Percy Veruns' with Lizer on the steerin. It was 'ard work comin down there, there are about seven or eight locks at Saltley, all greasy and mucky, too close to keep bringin Charley back, but Syer would come back and take the string from me as soon as he could. This Joey-fella could see I were bowallin flat-out. He were a big strappin fella, belts-n-buckles all over his-self. He were followin me close astarn, bearin down on me. He tried to shove past me, steal my lock. I wouldn't 'ave it. I would *not* 'ave it. I 'eld sway. He gave me such a mouthful.

'*Charmin!*' I sez.

Moy-chap came back, 'Wot's amiss?'

'Bloody woman! Won't shift out of my way.'

'Why should she? It's '*er* lock.'

'She don't count. She's only a woman. Bloody women! No rights to be on the Cut.'

—Should of seed Moy-chap's face! Talk about song-n-dance! Talk

about blue murders! He marches straight oop to this great big
Joey.

'That "woman" is my Best-Mate. She's a better boatman than
you'll ever be, with yer filthy boat and yer knackered 'orse. She's
stroved with boats all her life. She's *stroved* with boats all through
the bloody war. She's *stroved*—'

I couldn't believe my ears. I were flappergast'. Never in all my
boat-borned days had I heard a boatman spake like that. Most of
'em reckoned *they* done all the work on the Cut. They forgets when
they're boastin in the pub after a long day's trip, *so* many milestumps, *so* many locks, their women have done it all too. They
forgets while they'm sittin back at their ease quaffin their ale, their
woman has started work all over again, strovin to catch oop on her
cabin chores before the next day's hard boatin. Nobody had ever
stuck oop for us like Moy-chap did on that never-to-be-forgotten
day on that dirty old Bottom Road. I were *that* chuffed, never
knowed Syer 'ad it in 'im. Me and Lizer just gawped, 'arkin at 'im
still pitchin into this fella—

'If it wasn't for the strovin of these women, and the women
before *them*, and the women before that, *their* grandmother and
great-grandmother, *my* grandmother and great-grandmother, all
unpaid labour, the canals would of died out years ago; there'd *be*
no bloody Cut, and you'd be out of a job, *Mate!*'

I was expectin a stack-oop. The big fella were ploomped right
oop like a red balloon. Not a spit. Not a punch. Just stood there,
dumbfund.

Moy-chap calmly took the oily towstring from me.

'I'll take the boat through, Rose,' he sez to me, gen'leman-like,
'you go ahead.'

My 'ands was black, my apron was filthy, my boots was caked
with 'orses' muck but I walked along that stinkin towpath with my
'ead 'eld 'igh. I were Moy-chap's Number One Best-Mate. I were
worth all the tea in chiner.

'Petter-Petter!'

JUBILEE Year we sold out to Essy [S. E. Barlow].

The minute I woke that cold dark mornin, early in Jubilee Year, I knowed summat *omen*dous was goin to 'appen, one of my golden oops was missin. I lit the candle. That oop lay broken on the bolston [*bolster*]. It had wore right through. Strangely enough we was tied-oop zackly the same spot in Banbury Basin where I was tied-oop the night Syer first bought 'em for me at Banbury Fair. I'd sported them oops, night and day, for better for worse, for nineteen years. Nineteen years of constant wear through all the changin weathers of life for only two-and-thrippence! No oops would ever mean the same to me again. Even though our Arryut and Appy kindly treated me to a far posher pair I always treasured they little wore-ones. I kep 'em safe, rapt in waddin, at the back of the ticket draw along with Suey's seaside fota, her Pines address, and our marriage soostificut.

As I packed away the bed into the bed-'ole cupboard and lit the range I sensed in my 'eart that a new scene were about to open in our married life. It were bitterly cold. Syer had gone already to fetch Charley to be shod. Mr Plester had offered to do him early before the bewry 'orses. The bewry 'orses sposed to come first, he had their contract, and they'd all need frost nails put in their shoes that mornin to stop them slippin-oop on their deliveries.

The day before, Charley had started stumblin along the Tunnel Straight at Fenny. Though we called it 'the Tunnel' it were no longer covered-in. My Grandma Fisher at h'Oxford had well remembered it being opened out. My Mother had remembered it when the high wall of the tunnel was still standin between the towpath and the railway. In our day the high wall were gradually gettin lower as the heavy steam trains thundered past on the other side tumblin the rocks orf the top down on to the towpath or into the Cut. Charley always picked his way careful along there, we called it 'the Rockins'.

Charley would usually bacca along the Rockins. We'd loose the tow from the mast and he'd take his-self up and over the turnover bridge to the towpath on the other side. This turnover bridge was built special for 'orses to change towpaths, and there was a little 'public' there with a trough outside for the 'orses to 'ave a drink too. We'd slip the tow back on the mast and he'd take his-self along the towpath to Banbury. He'd stumbled again on his way to Banbury. Mr Plester couldn't shod him that evenin, he'd got his hands full, shoddin a bunch of wild Irish 'orses for Jesse Smith. He promised he'd do him first thing the next mornin. He were married to Margaret by then, they rented a little house in Middleton Cheney and he travelled back and forth to his old forge in Tooley's dockyard in his motorbike and side-car.

He kep his promise. He and Syer managed to coax Charley out of the stable and across a path of ashes they'd strewed for him across the yard to the smithy. At the smithy door Charley sinked down and were gone, *just like that*! Wot he caught, wot he lacked, nobody knowed. They found nothin untoward at the knacker's yard. Us Number Ones done all our own vettin, but Charley were gone before we could try to doctor him. He'd had a useful steady life on the Cut. He'd had the best of care, never flayed with the whip, never galled from rooff gear, nor driven to eatin his stall, nor scratchin his-self raw under bridges. He were close on thirty, not old for a boat-'orse. Some were still ploddin along at fifty. 'Old Billy' notched-oop 62! But he were down the Northern Navigation.

The moment somebody learned Essy we had lost old Charley he were turnin the startin 'andle of his motor at Glascote, and he stood

waitin for us at Banbury Basin that afternoon as we came back to
our boats oopset from seekin in vain for another good boat-'orse.
Essy knowed Moy-chap ever since they'd comed out of the h'army
after the 'Fourteen war. He'd been chasin Moy-chap for years to
work for him.

'How about it then, Syer?' he sez.

Syer were right down low. He knowed he'd never find another
Charley. He couldn't afford a moty. He was at the end of his
Number One tether.

'You'd best come aboard, Mr Barlow.'

Essy were a big chapel-man, stood no 'igher than six pennerth o'
coppers. His real name were Samuel after his grandad, but we
always called him Essy, not to his face, of course, to his face he
were always *Mister* Barlow. He were a chip orf his grandad's old
firm, the 'Limited' [*Samuel Barlow Ltd*], and had his own boat-
buildin business at Glascote. In them days Glascote was the little
town on the end of the big town of Tammerth. He had about
fourteen pairs of coal-carryin narrer-boats registered at Tammerth.
We used to call the Limited boats 'Old Sam's', and Essy's boats
'Young Sam's'. I were worried that Moy-chap would be right low in
the dumps after sellin-out to Essy but, though he were no longer
his own marster and the boats would have to be registered under
Essy's name at Tammerth, no money changed hands. Essy wasn't
after old boats, he was after good crews, specially the old family
crews, the Number Ones. Number Ones knowed best how to tackle
every crack and cranny of the Cut, they took a pride in their craft
and gettin 'em ahead. Syer stuck out for workin his same boats. The
'Percy Veruns' hadn't long been docked. We'd paid Tooleys for
that. She were older than 'Britannia' but both boats had been regler
docked at Tooleys' and old Mr Tooley reckoned they was both good
for another twenty years. Essy agreed to convert 'Britannia' to a
moty for Moy-chap, take over his regler runs, and get all further
orders. Syer agreed to work the orders and pick-oop backloads
whenever he could. He'd be paid only when he delivered the goods
but he were used to that. I can't remember how much he was paid
at the beginnin—we worked for Essy for so many years—but it
were half-a-crown a ton at the finish. Essy would hold back twelve-
n-six a week towards dockin, and sixpence a week 'Orspital Fund.

Some reckoned we was paying twelve-n-six a week rent for our own boats but it were a wonderful relief, after all them years of stintin, to have the dockin taken orf our shoulders. The 'Orspital Fund were even more wonderful. It 'cleared' [*insured*] me and Moy-chap 'and any children until they are sixteen'. As we hadn't got no children left we was allowed to clear Lizer. That 'Orspital Fund were the first ever perk for me and Lizer. We called it 'the B'novalent'.

We trusted Essy, he trusted us. No fishal-papers, just face to face, shakin 'ands, 'Gen'lemen's Greemens' they dubbed it.

Troubles always come in threes; a broken oop, a dead 'orse, and 'Jubilee'.

'Jubilee' was the name of the old change-boat Essy loaned us while 'Britannia' were being converted to a moty at Glascote. '*Oo*'s Jubilee, the Lord only knows. They said it were Queen Victoria's, I reckon it were Noah's. The hinjin were a good'un, 'Petter-eighteen-'orse', but it was too powerful for the boat. Talk about shiver-yer-timbers! If you had a cup of tea on board you needed it in a bookit! That hinjin were bolted down with great big cold-screws yet it kep workin loose from its mountins. We had to keep puttin on the belts-pump to pump out the water seepin in through the seams. Good for tonnage, bad for tolls; but we didn't have to pay no more tolls, and no more 'orse-fodder, we just showed a ticket, 'Essy Barlow', at the different toll h'offices and fuel depots and 'they' and Essy sorted it out between 'em.

Essy left us free to work the boats in our own way. It were oop to us how many trips we managed in a week, how many hours a day we worked. That hinjin 'petter-pettered' all the hours God sent. Once Moy-chap had got it thuddin-over he never wanted it to stop. It was such a palaver to start, hottin-oop, pumpin-oop, blow-lamp, meths, h'oils, wot-av-yer. The rim of that flywheel was seven inches wide, seven and a 'alf 'oondredweight to turn over. Me and Lizer never managed to sprung that old hinjin to life, we hadn't the strength. We could shine-er-oop with 'Bluebell' and sandpaper, we could bunk-er-oop with diesel, and feed-er-oop with h'oils, we could work the rods [*controls*] and handle that skinny iron tiller, but we couldn't turn over that heavy flywheel.

Handlin the tiller *and* workin the rods was muddlin at first. Sometimes you needed three hands for stoppin and 'nooverin, you'd forget and loose yer tiller. The water would surge, the tiller would fly across. It was nothin like the bulk of the old wooden 'orseboat tiller we still had on the 'Percy Veruns' but it could fetch yer a tidy old tonk [*blow*]. Moy-chap fashioned a handy tiller-strap, a plaited noose, and fixed it just to hand, above the steerin place to hook the tiller handle. The handle had a special notch just before the tip which held the noose. The tip was smooth wood, let into the iron, to save yer hands from frostbite in the winter. Just as we could set the old 'orseboat tiller 'at rest' by oop-endin it on its cradle for the night, so we could put the metal moty-boat tiller right out of the way, either by takin it orf in sections or by fixin it out to the side to act as a handrail across from the boat to the path or across to the butty breasted-oop at night.

On the broad Cuts like the Grand Union we could work breasted-oop a lot of the time when we was goin back empty to the coalfields, specially where there was a lot of locks. One of us could take the both boats into the lock while the others worked the locks at top speed without one of us havin to have the butty on the checkin-strap. On the longer pounds Syer would steer, towin the butty oop close on crossed-snubbers while me and Lizer got on with our cabin chores.

Though the entrance to the wide locks was narrow we prided ourselves on steerin into the lock smooth without a brush to the bank. We prided ourselves on not a brush with *anythin*, not even a rat's whisker. You can't always avoid it, specially in wind, but you has pride in yer judgement, a respect for yer craft, a respect for the Cut, and a care for each other. It's surprisin how the slightest bump at one end of a boat can fling a body unawares orf the other.

On the narrow Cuts like the h'Oxford we travelled the longer pounds on a long snubber so the butty was well out of the floosh and the racket of the moty-boat. When we was 'orse-drawed we took the peace and quoyet for nat'ral. Now silence were bliss, golden. We took the cleanliness for granted too. Now we had to wash down the paintwork several times a day when the wind blowed that dirty exhaust over my clean cabin-top. At first we was all red-eyed, choked-oop, black as sweeps from that exhaust. If we put on the h'extrer chimney to carry away the spumes [*smoke and fumes*] the hinjin hotted-oop. In the end Moy-chap got Mr Tooley to fashion a cutter to fit inside the top of the chimney and cut the smoke. The thud of that hinjin numbed yer ears, you couldn't hear a thing 'cept thoomp!-thoomp! petter!-petter! It was dangerous at blind bridge-'oles, specially on the narrow Cuts with growed-oop verges. You could never hear the hinjin or the smackin-whip of another boat comin the other way. You had to look back and rely on Lizer or whoever was steerin the butty to let yer know if another boat was comin. It was easier to hear back there at a distance. She'd beckon like mad for us to blow our brass horn. That was the year we 'had words' with the 'Pioneer' stuck in a bridge-'ole oop the Warwick. She were a Fellas Morton wide-boat, testin the wide locks from London to Birnigum. She never done it again.

The 'orse has perpriety over the hinjin. Two hinjins meetin in the one bridge-'ole had to use their manners, or their language. As trade got tighter with more and more moty-boats chasin fewer and fewer orders, men got greedier on the busier 'roads', and it was just yer bad luck to get held-oop for an hour while two chaps, wedged in the bridge-'ole, battled it out between 'em. It would start with a slangin match and end with a stack-oop. We'd have a brew-oop of tea, sit back and watch the fisticoofs, and offer 'em both a cup when they'd finished. Then we'd get out the shafts or the block and tackle and sort the boats out between us.

It was usually the scruffiest outfits wot drove themselves into such a fix. The rest of us thought more of our craft. If we seed a dirty Rodney-boat breastin the bridge-'ole we'd hang back, their bugs wasn't worth catchin. Terrible catchin is bugs. They love warm damp dirty places. At least the old 'Jubilee' had no bugs. You had to watch that when you took to a change-boat. *Some* of us I could mention wasn't so perticler as the rest of us. Me and Lizer waged constant war, keepin a store of goose quills to dip into a bottle of Condey's Fluid and poke into all the cracks and crannies, always boilin our washin and scaldin our crocks. I *always* likes to scald my crocks. When we was h'iced-oop for weeks at Ruckby in '29 I took a job at the 'Orspital, washin-oop. Piles o' crocks! Clouds o' steam! 'Rose!' Sister calls through the hatch, 'Are you washing up? Or are you *sterilizing!*' I can't 'elp it, I'm a very *perticler* Rose.

Every spring I'd get Moy-chap to set oop the bricks and build me a good fire on the towpath to heat the water in the zinc bath for my dolly-tub. We'd get everythin move-able out of the cabin, all the draws, all the beddin, wot-av-yer, on to the grass and give them a good wash and scrub. In the evenin we'd wait for the range in the empty cabin to die down to a good red h'ember, seal all the cracks and crannies on the outside, take the chimney orf, plug the chimney-'ole, the doors, the air-'ole box with wet sacks, and we'd sprinkle Jeyes 'Sanity' Powder on the h'embers and close everythin. That powder would fumycate with sulphur and brimstone all night long. Sometimes we'd use the big flat Jeyes Sulphur Candle on a plate of water instead. Whether you used the powder or the candle it made my beautiful black and brass polished range all red and roosty, but it had to be done. It was the only way you could be sure you had no bugs.

The sulphur smell was terrible when you first opened it oop in the mornin. You had to wait a good hour before you dare go in. *Then* wot a spring-clean! Washin the cabin with Oodson's Soap, shinin the range with the Zebo and the Bluebell, puttin back my clean scrubbed draws, my fresh beddin, my starched crosher, my sparklin ribbin-plates, and all my brass knobs and h'ornamentals. I'd have a good wash—I do *love* a good wash!—wash my 'air, my 'underneaths', and braid my 'wirelesses'. With my clean white apron and my beautiful fresh cabin I were Queen of the Castles.

On Jubilee Day we was Queen of the Cut with our new Essy Barlow painted pair, the moty 'Britannia' and the butty 'Percy Veruns'. With our old Charley's white tail flowin down the back of the butty rams'ead, union jacks buntin all along the washin lines, the holds swept clean, and the plank-seats rigged across, we was takin two loads of h'orfanites for their Jubilee treat to Opus Woods [*orphans; Hopwas Woods*]. It was one of the many treats Essy gave to the children of Tammerth,—h'orfanites, cripples, Sunday Schools, wot-av-yer—over the years. We was sad yet glad on that Jubilee Day, there was we, longin for a kiddy, and there was two boatloads nobody wanted. Still, we enjoyed givin 'em a treat, and it *was* a treat in them days for town kiddies to get away from their own backyards out into the open country. We always took 'em to Opus Woods. It wasn't all that far, just a few miles along the Cut. Beautiful it was there, just the mill, Opus paper mill, and a few cottages clustered in their own rooky-nook, with the woods and the fields to rove in all day long. Over the years many a Tammerth kiddy owed their happy day at Opus Woods to Essy Barlow. That Jubilee Day we brought our boats back to Glascote loaded with tired-out kiddies and floppy bluebells.

The next day we was down to earth with a boomp, a load of steamcoal from Pooley 'All mine for 'the Trout', the stinkin hanimal food factry down the Slough Arm. We hadn't been there since me and my Mum and Dad and three sisters used to went there with the posh roobish orf the Paddinton Arm. The steamcoal was fed to their yooge boilers and vats. The men used to work in their wooden clogs and long leather aprons, stirrin oop these cauldrons with great long-'andled iron ladles. Though it stinked all round the factry, the waters of their Cut was crystal clear. Shools of fish came for the food and cleared oop everythin else. It was always very clear and very cold along that Slough Arm because no factries used it for suckin-in nor spewin-out.

Now we had taken oop more space on the 'Britannia' with the hinjin-'ole and the fuel tank we was down to carryin forty-six ton and less than that when there was a drought and we was low in the water. We had to do longer hours to fit in more journeys. 'Britannia's' new hinjin was a 'Petter-twelve-'orse', less powerful than the old 'Jubilee' but still me and Lizer couldn't start it, we wasn't allowed. That hinjin was Syer's pride and joy. It kep goin and so did we, steerin on and on, till my head hit the chimney, and I'd hear Nell Canvin's words, 'Never have a moty-boat, Rose; at least Charley and Cobber gives yer a night's rest.' Charley and Cobber be both gone to glory now, we had no choice.

We was lucky to fit in two round trips from the Midland coalfields every three weeks, down to London and back, or down to h'Oxford and back. Moy-chap was paid about five pounds ten a trip. Out of that Mr Barlow kep back the weekly dockin and the B'novalent. The boats was covered for dockin but not for ropes, and ropes had gone oop a lot, from twelve-n-six when we was married, to thirty bob by then. We was often held-oop waitin to be loaded or orf-loaded. If they hadn't room on their wharf for the load they'd ordered they'd keep yer waitin outside so suit their conveniuns. Some of the factries paid Barlows compensation for that but Moy-chap was never paid nothin for waitin time, only for tonnage. Me and Lizer was paid nothin at all, but all us boatwomen was used to that.

Moy-chap always handed his money over to me, straight from the clirk in the toll h'office. I'd hand back to Syer his 'baccy and beer'. I never begrudged him goin to the 'public', he needed men's

comp'ny, he needed the cheer, he'd been knocked-oop enough
with losin our kiddies. Me and Lizer never made it our business to
go in to the 'public'. Our Mother never made no practice of it,
there were always too much to be done, all yer cabin chores to
catch oop on. Syer would bring us out a glass of stout sometimes;
liquors I never did crave, but a glass of stout on a summer's evenin
were very acceptable.

Our 'public' were the towpath, tied oop along of the other family
boats, doin our washin, keepin an eye on the kiddies while their
mother had a proyvit wash-down in her cabin, or went to the shops.
That's where we'd catch oop on the news with the Wards, the
Beauchamps, the Ownses, the Russons, the Littlemores; mark how
their kiddies had grown, and try to fathom out 'ow the outside
world was blowin on somebody's cumulated wireless.

The year the old king died—I can't remember zackly which year
it was, but I know I was tied-oop along of Ada Littlemore—when
Emma Russon called us along the towpath to listen to the new king
givin oop, 'andin his kingship over to his brother.

'Blimey, Ada!' I sez. 'Three kings in one year. That's a bit much,
ain't it?'

'A *dee-vor-cee*!' sez Ada.

'*Twice over*!' sez Emma.

Me and Emma and Ada couldn't fathom out *that* sort of goins-on,
sport o' kings and wot-av-yer.

We didn't see so much of Emma, they worked for Fellas Morton,
and didn't often travel our h'Oxford 'road' but we was beginnin to
see more and more of Ada and Dick Littlemore and their kiddies
'cos they was carryin for Essy too. They had the old 'Hood' at that
time with our old 'Jubilee' hinjin as their moty-boat, and the
'Captain Cook' as their butty. The 'Hood' was old but her timbers
wasn't so ropey as the 'Jubilee' and stood oop well at first to the
'Petter-eighteen-'orse'. Dick called it 'the h'Admiral' and was at its
beck and call from morn to night. Ada was taller and stronger than
me yet even she couldn't turn that great flywheel.

The 'Captain Cook' had a fore-cabin, built into the little deck at
the front of the boat, but Ada never used it as a cabin after Suey
Beechey's daughter died in the fore-cabin of Suey's boat. Only the
evenin before, me and Ada had been chattin, watchin Suey's girls,
Agnes and Clara, laughin and callin across to Rose Beauchamp's

daughters as they passed by on their boat, the four girls was all about the same age and the best of chums, Agnes, full of life, promisin, 'See yer at Banbury Fair!' and wavin till she were out of sight. Suey's two boys usually slept in the fore-cabin but they had to get oop early the next mornin to take another boat so they swapped cabins that night with their sisters. The fore-cabin was very small, just held a bed and a stove. It was a very cold night, Agnes must of closed the slide right oop, blockin the air-'ole without realizing the stove was still in. When Suey went to wake them in the mornin Agnes and the dog were dead and Clara was unconscious. Suey's screams soon brought help and Clara was saved. Ada never used the fore-cabin on the 'Cook' after that. Dick had the bed and the stove taken out and they used the space for stowage.

Dick were one of Minnie Littlemore's sons from Stowell. Ada's father, Ernest, was one of the Stowell Mellas [*Mellor*] but her mother, Jemimah Dawson, was born at h'Oxford. They worked the 'Severn' and the 'Princess Mary' for years for John Griffiths of Bedderth. They carried coals from Atherstone to the glass-bottle blowers at Alperton and Hayes on the Grand Junction. Ada was the third child of their large family and were borned agen 'Arecastle Tunnel. She came oop to fame as being one of the few boatgirls to be sent out to service. She picked oop a smatterin of schoolin and bettered herself at a big house agen 'Awkesbury 'All. She looked after their four children. The family thought the world of her—was even goin to learn her to drive their big motor car—wanted her to stop with them on the bank for always, but Dick comes along just in time and woos her back to the Cut.

She was then a tall handsome woman with dark hair, braided like mine, in 'wirelesses'. She had four kiddies. They was made to be'ave, pull their weight with the boats and the locks. Her eldest, Gladys, was younger than my Rose but she was just like her, not in looks, Gladys was fair, but in her trim figure and neat handlin of the boats. Charley comed next, he was about eight and knowed almost as much about hinjins as his dad. Rose and Sylvie was like two little fair-haired dolls, and Gladys, like my Rose, was a proper big-sister to them.

There was a quoyet strength about Ada that made you feel she knowed wot's best. It was to Ada I turned when my arm swelled black and blue with poison. She worked out that a tiny bit of Zebo polish must of got into the sore crack of my thumb when I was black-leadin my range. That lead travelled to a big lump under my arm. Ada drawed the poison by poulticin my thumb with bread and boiled sugar, over and over. Agony it was, but she made me bear it. It done the trick, saved my arm. She made me go to Mary Ward's when we got to Stoke Bruin, just to make sure it was all cured. Mary said Ada had probably saved my life.

Mary had come home to nurse her father, Mr Aymus, now he was goin blind. She wasn't 'lettered' a nurse [*qualified*] but she'd had a lot of esperience. Her Dad wasn't a lot of trouble, her husband was copin well with her Dad's shop, and her daughter was growed oop. Mary, bein used to havin her 'ands full of nursin, wanted more to do.

'The boat people are always turnin to you for help', her Dad sez. 'You said yourself that the shop was full of wounded this morning. Why don't you turn the shop into a surgery and be a proper nurse to the boat people?' And that's just wot Mary did. Her husband moved the shop down to just below Top Lock and they turned their front room into a spotless surgery where we could go to her for free and have treatment. For years she looked after us out of her own pocket. Later the Grand Union made her 'Sister' Mary and helped out with the cost of materials, but to the end of our boatworkin days she gave us all unstintin' of her time and comfort. Many a boat-child owed its survival to Sister Mary.

I tried not to envy other boatwomen their children but I couldn't help it. I envied Ada her four kiddies. I envied Mrs Russon her four fine sons. I envied Mrs Own her Rose and Bet. I envied Rosie Beauchamp her Rose and Phyllis. I remember goin through Thrupp one Good Friday and seein Rose and Phyllis, standin outside 'Number 6' in their clean pinafores all ready to go to the 'Bulford Bunfight'. I burst into tears. Many a time in the past my Rose had been with them. The Bulfords were the family at the big house at Thrupp and every year Mr Bulford used to give a Hot-Cross-Bun Party in Thrupp Chapel for the children of Thrupp and any of the boat-children who happened to be passin through. For some it was the first time in their lives that they'd been to a party or had a hot-cross bun. In the grim thirties a Hot-Cross-Bun Party with boat-children welcome was a rare treat.

You think you've got over yer loss till you seed two little girls in clean pinafores, and it all comes rushin back. If only we could of adopted another child. I envied Susan Ward her adopted Laura. Rosy, cheerful, dark-haired Laura had growed into such a godsend to her Auntie Susan. When Mikey Ward died, Susan sold out to Barlows, the Limited. The Ownses and the Granthams too were to sell out to Barlows in the end.

Essy still let us use Tooleys for some of our dockin. I well remember about this time, just before the war, seein 'Cressy' bein converted at Tooley's dock. We'd never knowed nothin like it, a workin boat bein turned all over into a n'ouse. We thought it a terrible waste of 'aulage use, and 'Mr Rolt', her Captain, were not quite the ticket. But he was always very civil in passin, and 'she' were very pleasant too.

By that time we was well set into our regler Barlow runs, down the Grand Union with the 'beans', the small coal, for the paper mills at Home Park, or down the h'Oxford with great lumps of steamcoal for the paper mills at Wolvercote. I was always terrified of goin down to Wolvercote on the h'Oxford. You're on the full spate of the river there. The trouble was there was no room down at the mill to wind the boats. You had to wind before you went, on the mainstream of the river, and go down with the current backwards. In the old 'orse days we used to stable the 'orse at Duke's Cut, and the lock-keeper would help my Dad or Moy-chap to turn the boat with ropes from the bank before we went down to the mill. Lizer never seemed to turn a hair about goin down relyin only on the moty, but I think every boatwoman who had to face oop to goin down there was afeared of it in her 'eart of 'earts. You just had to face it. If yer gived in at Wolvercote you'd certainly go under. It was the Littlemores wot first learned us the 'noover. You 'noover'd the moty a little way past the junction and then reversed to come alongside the butty, and pull the ropes to tie the boats stem to starn. Breasted-oop the two boats are carried down on the force of the millstream with the moty travellin starn first and the butty doin the steerin. Years later it was the Littlemores what took the last load of all down to Wolvercote.

You could go down to the mill breasted-oop because yer boats was loaded and low in the water and could fit under the low trees on both banks. Once yer unloaded at the mill, the moty is already facin oop-stream to use the full force of yer hinjin to travel back

against the current, but you has to tow the butty because now yer
boats are empty and ridin high on the water you can't fit under the
trees, you has to hog mid-stream. You always had to warn the chaps
at the mill you was comin so they could close the sluices and weirs
so we wasn't dashed about. In windy weather they'd turn out with
extrer ropes to steady us. Flood was yer biggest worry. I always
had the say-so in flood [*casting vote*]. Moy-chap and Lizer always
used to turn to me.

"Ow about it then, Rose? Shall us risk it?"

I'd eye that line of rads along the towpath. If I could still see the
rads showin at least two feets above the flooded towpath I was willin
to risk it. You had to risk it, otherwise you might be held oop for
weeks, earnin nothin, waitin for wind and water to drop. When I
was a little girl with my Dad and we had only the one boat held by
ropes to the bank with Mother steerin, I felt much safer, maybe as a
child I didn't realize the danger. I was always worried when I was
older, I knowed only too well if that old 'Petter!-Petter!' stopped in
'mid-'noover', we'd be swept away down river and over a weir.

At Shipton Weir Lock there used to be a lovely little cottage,
'Tommy Orner's' we used to call it after the lock-keeper wot lived
there [*Mr Tom Horne*]. He saved me from a swan when I was about
fifteen. I was leadin the hanimal, I think it was Troy, along the
towpath, the Cut on one side, the river on the other, and the verge
was so overgrowed I walked straight into a swan's nest. If Tommy
hadn't of been comin along with a boat-'ook I'd of been battered to
bits. Ever after I always walked extrer careful along there and if
there was any sign of a swan my Dad would take over with a boat-
'ook and a lump of bread to fend 'em orf.

Now we had the moty we had other dangers to face oop to. The
main trouble was attractin the 'tention of Syer when he was steerin
the moty and we was way-back on the butty. Chaps on the bank
used to take advantage, peltin us with stones, pot-shottin at us with
air-guns, or flarin their proyvits [*exposing themselves*].

Most chaps only flared the once but there was one 'orrible chap
who always did it at the open window of a dingy oopstairs room,
backin on to the Cut at Nuneaton. We was travellin back and forth
drawrin stone to build airydromes at that time. He'd wait until Syer
had 'Petter!-Pettered' past, then he'd stand at this open window
and flare his-self at me and Lizer. I told Syer about him and he told

the chaps at the 'public', but it was a job to tell which house, they was all in a long boondle [*terrace*].

Me and Lizer looked away, but he still did it. He really annoyed me.

'Next time, Lizer,' I sez, 'I shall take a *good eyeful!*'

And I did. I seed he was standin next to a broke washstand jug without a n'andle. 'Stick it oop in the air and use it as a n'andle!' I shouted at him.

He were *that* shocked. We never seed him again.

Another chap had a spate of appearin stark naked tween 'Bakers' and 'Pigeons' [*locks*] on the h'Oxford. It's really lonely and pictur-skew along there with the reeded banks and the water ripplin in the sunlight.

'*It ent the money you earns, it's the sights yer sees*', Lizer would say to me under her breath, and there he'd be, white and skinny, without a stitch, travellin barefoot, noiseless, alongside us, starin straight along the towpath, his face full of sufferin, like Jesus. When we next glanced sideways, he'd be gone, vanished, as silent as he came.

We told Mrs Wickson when we next tied-oop at the 'Pigeons' but she had no idea who he might be. Nobody did find out. He went away and was never seed again. We was lucky to still have Mrs Wickson at the 'Pigeons'. So many of the old publics where we used to stable our 'orses was goin out of business. Some, set at the old 'orse-travel distances, like the 'Old Victoria' at Fenny turnover bridge, was by-passed by the moty-boats. Others like the little old 'Globe' at Stowell, and the 'Runnin 'Orse' and the 'Nag's 'Ead' at h'Oxford were bein pulled down out of the way to make room for new motor-roads and bridges. We missed so many of our old friends of 'orse-drawed days, the saddlers, the blacksmiths, the corn chandlers. Mr Pratton Aines, the corn chandler at Aynho, had been Charley's friend for years [*Pratt and Haines, corn merchants, Oxford, had a wharf at Aynho*]. He'd cut oop chaff and mix a feed to Charley's personal requiremuns. He always got a bumper truss of hay from Mr Pratton Aines.

Friends we still had on the bank, like Mrs Wickson, becomed even more valued. She still welcomed us with oil lamps and candles in her parlour at the 'Pigeons', and let us fill our water cans from the pump at her kitchen sink. Her Wilfred was a man now, gone to join the Royal Air Force. It didn't seem all that many years since he'd been a little lad first visitin his Granny Keys, thrilled to help with the lock and have a ride on a boat. Every time I thinked of Wilfred I'd think of Moycle. He'd be a young gentleman now. We never heard words of him. I didn't hope to any more but I often wondered where he was. Wot he'd turned out like.

There was talk of war. We was kep on the go carryin stone for another big airydrome oop the Leicester Cut; pickin oop cement from the Clifton Arm on the North h'Oxford to bring to Napton and Fenny Compton to build wot they called 'pill-boxes'; carryin inkits from the docks to the works at Samson Road in Birnigum, and, in between, the steamcoal, as usual, down to Wolvercote.

That's where we were goin when we came acraws May Grantham of the 'Franklyn', top o' Napp'n, where we lost our Rose. Old Lou had died of an 'eart attack. She couldn't carry him on her boats, they was loaded. The lock-keeper allowed her to 'rest' him in his hut. Just as she and Lou had stopped to help us in the past so we was able to stop and help her to carry him into the hut. The fun'ral people in Banbury came out to tend him. Old Lou were a Banbury man, and were buried at Banbury.

We was at Sutton Stop when somebody comed along the towpath to tell us we was at war with 'Er 'Itler. We never knowed much about 'Er 'Itler in them days, he were nothin to do with us on the boats. We was just goin to carry on in our own little tin-pot way when our Arryut and Appy turns oop to make sure we has 'identity' [*wartime identity cards*].

'If you don't have identity, Rose, you don't exists. If you don't exists, you gets no food, no rations.'

'Name?' the identity lady sez at the Coventry h'Office.

'Mrs Syer Ramlin.'

'How do you spell it?'

I gave the lady our marriage soostificut.

Then she dropped the bombshell.

'MRS JOSIAH RAMPLING.'

'*Joe* Syer? Well I never!'

I kep the Joe, it's rather nice to 'ave the two, but I wasn't bothered about the 'Ramblin'. I were more at 'ome with me Ramlin. I've kep me Ramlin ever since.

'—Under the Trees!'

THE night they bombed Banbury Lock we was lookin forward to a bit of peace [1940]. We'd had enough bombin agen Birnigum and Coventry. Only a few nights ago we'd been tied-oop at Sutton Stop when a bomb fell in the Cut. Luckily it didn't go orf but it shot the empty boats along of us right oop out of the water and knocked the bank about. Last night we'd been tied-oop at Top o' Napton and 'ad the 'igh jinks, flares-wot-av-yer, of the planes goin over to bomb Coventry. It was a relief to get to Banbury and look forward to a nice quoyet night in the country.

We was carryin day after day and often into the night. We'd had to black-out our oil-lamp on the front of the boat to keep the beam down, but they'd repainted the arches of the bridge-'oles and the sides of the locks white so we could see 'em in the dark. Most of us on the boats has cat's eyes, we're wise to the dark, but it were still dangerous workin in the dark, specially in winter when the lock-sides and gates were slippery with frost and we had to rely only on Lizer's down-held torch to guide us into the black lock. There was no shortage of work, orders came thick and fast, the Government was even payin half the tolls to keep the canals workin all out for the war effort.

Late in the afternoon of that lovely day in August we tied-oop agen the Banbury Lock.

'I'll go and get a shave and a haircut at the barbers', Moy-chap sez, 'and we'll 'ave a nice quoyet night 'ere.'

Now we was earnin that bit more he could treat his-self to a shop-shave now and again.

I were just goin to have my beauty treatment, a good wash, when he comes straight back. 'Rose! Lizer! We're not stoppin 'ere. There's a bloody great circus tent down on the Marshes. That'll show oop like billy-o when the moon gets oop. Jerry'll bomb that tonight, mark my words!'

'Don't be so daft, Syer. Why would Jerry bomb a circus, ay?'

'He'll think it's the Allyminyum.'

The real Allyminyum factry, wot was workin non-stop for the war, was close to the Cut on the outskirts of Banbury. We'd helped to carry the materials to build that factry years before. A dummy factry had now been built further out in the fields between Bourton and 'Craperdy' to trick the 'nemeny'. We couldn't risk a raid; Essy had put oop our war-pay to three-n-thrippence a ton and we was loaded to the gunnles with steamcoal for Wolvercote, any little wave would wash right over us.

We loosed away from Banbury Lock. We was lucky that they hadn't yet locked the lock. Banbury was always locked oop every night and every weekend, from 6 o'clock Saturday evenin to 6 o'clock Monday mornin, to protect all the coal wharfs. We travelled on away from Banbury towards h'Oxford for a few miles and tied-oop along of the Littlemores' old 'Hood' and the 'Captain Cook' agen Twyford Bridge.

Next mornin a lengthsman came and told us Banbury Lock had been bombed in the night. If we'd of stayed 'put' we'd of been a gonner. 500 pounder in the lock and another in the Basin. Nobody was killed, thank the Lord. Moy-chap was relieved to hear the 'Strugglers' was still standin, even though it had been rocked on its feet. The only real casualty had been Mrs Malloy's cockerel, he'd lost every single feather but he were still crowin, and Mrs Malloy was already chargin '6d. a look' for the Spitfire Fund.

Jerry hadn't beat us yet, but we'd had a near do. So had the

Ownses [*Hones*], Alf Junior and his wife Lizer of the 'White City' and their daughters, Rose and Betty of the 'Rose and Bet'. If they hadn't of been held oop the Craperdy side of Banbury they'd of been tied-oop in that Basin. They had the coal contract from Badgeley Coalery to Banbury Co-op. They used to go through the lock and unload at the Co-op wharf, carry on down to Banbury Station, wind at the back of the Banbury Spencers' football ground, and come back through the lock to moor in the Basin ready to cast orf again, back to the coalery, first thing in the mornin. After the lock was bombed, and while Mr Bloomfield and his gang of maintenance men was re-buildin it, they had to unload at Castle Street wharf straight into the Co-op's own 'orse-n-carts. The Co-op had their own coal lorries too but they used 'orse-n-carts in wartime to save petrol.

The Littlemores, like us, was loaded with coal for Wolvercote. We knowed Essy would crop oop somewhere, or get a message to us some'ow along the bank—as he always did—to tell us 'wot next'. We decided we might as well finish the job we was doin, press on to Wolvercote, deliver our loads, and warn any boats we met on the way that they wouldn't get through Banbury.

At Aynho Weir Lock we met another 'Essy' pair, the Woods' boys, Alf and Fred, comin back empty from h'Oxford Radiators, down by 'Ayfield Road drawbridge, this side of Dolly's 'Ut. Alf was only eighteen and Fred was sixteen.

'It's no good goin on to Banbury, lads, you won't get through, the lock's bombed. You'd better wind at Nell Bridge and come along of us.'

We met the 'Friendship' with Rose a-steerin and Joe and Dolly trottin along at their usual pace. They hadn't heard the lock was bombed. It made no difference, they was too clockwork in their ways to alter course, come wot may, they was set for Banbury, on they went.

We met the Beauchamps, Rose and Jo and their family, bringin their four boats through Somerton Deep. They hadn't heard about the bomb.

'If my poor old Dad hears that, he'll be worried to death about us, we was sposed to make Banbury last night. I'm glad we didn't! As yer goes through Thrupp, call at Number 6, will yer, Rose? Tell Dad I'm still 'ere, all safe, thank the Lord!'

[161]

Rose and her Dad were *that* close!

The Woods' boys tied-oop their boats and came down to help the Littlemores and us to unload at Wolvercote. The mill wharf could just take the four boats. When we all got back Essy was waitin for our six empty boats outside Wolvercote.

'The Banbury Lock will take weeks to mend. You can either tie-up this side of Banbury and wait without work, or you can go on down the Thames to London, pick up a supply of steel from the docks for the Munitions in Coventry and come back up the Grand Union. You all know the dangers. It's no picnic whichever you choose. I'm not going to persuade you what to do. You must decide for yourselves.'

Moy-chap and Lizer looks to me, "Ow about it, Rose?'

I were more frightened of goin down the river than the bombin. We'd never been down the Thames, but I thought about the 'little boats' wot had set out on the 'igh seas to save our chaps from Dunkirk. They'd faced far worse.

'Our chaps in the forces are fightin all out for us,' I sez, 'the least we can do is feed 'em the munitions.' I looked to Dick and Ada, with their four fine kiddies clustered close, they had so much more to risk than us.

'It's oop to Ada', Dick sez.

'London can't be worse than Coventry', she sez. 'I'd rather be on the move doin summat useful than tied-oop idle. I'm game.'

'We're game too', the Woods' boys sez.

Essy sends a big motor tanker to fill us oop with diesel. The driver didn't even know the Cut was *there*, never even *heard* of a narrer-boat. The message *he* got was to 'fuel ships for London'. He brought a hose fat enough to bunker the 'Queen Mary'. He were very taken with the 'Captain Cook', all fresh-painted from Glascote. 'Blimey!' he sez, 'Jerry'll spot that'un a mile orf!'

At last the six of us was fuelled and set orf in convoy for Louse Lock, wot they calls 'Isis', sharp through the Sheepwash under the railway bridge.

In them days you had to tell the man in the jacky-box [*signal box*] that you wanted to be loosed through the railway bridge, it was too low for boats to pass under. He'd make sure no trains were due, get the plate-men to lift the plates, and swing the bridge open for you. We'd all been before on to the Thames with fuel for the h'Oxford Lectric Light, and coped with the currents from the sluices and the turbines down there, but none of us had ever boated beyond, breasted-oop, out on to the Thames proper, and down the river to London [*see map on p. 223*]—

And did Jerry know we was goin! He raided us all the way.

'—Under the trees! Get under the trees!' the lock-keepers shouted at us.

'—Under the trees! Get under the trees!' we kep shoutin to each other.

They big willa-trees along the bank was a godsend, specially when we was held oop for the locks. Even in wartime they lock-keepers on the Thames was terrible proud of their locks. Us boat people was never allowed to set foot on their spick-n-span lock sides. Only the lock-keeper or his wife was allowed to work the 'meechanicals'. They were big powerful deep locks to hold back the full force of a flowin river, far bigger than the ones wot parted the still waters of the Cut, and they took four to six of us narrer-boats at a time.

The trouble was, the lock-keepers were also ARP wardens. Soon as ever the air-raid sirens went, orf came their lock-keeper's cap, on went their tin-lids and orf they went to help on the streets of their towns. If there was no lock-keeper's wife to take over—most of 'em was out at warwork makin munitions, parachutes, wot-av-yer—there was we, held oop, sittin-dooks for old Jerry, specially the 'Captain Cook'. Ada had to chuck a clawth over the cabin at night to stop her smart paint catchin the moonlight. She still kep her brasses nicely polished. 'I ent neglectin my brasses, Jerry or no Jerry!—That blighter's comin over again! Under the trees, *quick*!'

In peaceful times, ridin high on the current with empty boats breasted-oop, that trip from h'Oxford to Thames Lock, London, could of been done in just over a day, two days at the most. It took us nearly a week. It were a nightmare. We never undressed. We daren't. We put the kiddies to bed in their clothes, just took their boots orf. One lock-keeper's wife begged Ada not to take the kiddies into London. 'Leave them with me. I'll take care of them. You can pick them up again on your way back.'

'We're not comin back this way', sez Ada.

'Not if *oi* can 'elp it!' pipes oop young Charley, and we all laughs.

We got to Thames Lock—it was only one lock in them days—

course, the tide was out. We had to stay put all day waitin for the
tide to come back oop and send us into the lock. It was a good thing
we was all empty else we could of broke the boats' backs. We
waited and waited that night in the Mile Pound, between Thames
Lock and Brentford—wot we call 'the Ham'—for the barges to
come oop river under cover of darkness to load us oop but the raids
was so bad the 'thorities wouldn't allow them—said a chain of
barges chuggin oop river with metal for munitions in the moonlight
would be 'just askin for it'.

The 'Hood' was takin in water. It had done her no good to be
stuck on the bank without the tide. We persuaded Dick and Ada,
for the sake of the kiddies, not to hang about waitin for a load but
to get goin through the Brentford Toll and back oop the Grand
Union. We must of been the first ever 'Essy' boats to of done that
Thames trip. The chap in the Toll h'Office wouldn't let the empty
'Hood' and 'Captain Cook' through. He were a new whipper-
snapper, said he'd never heard of 'Essy Barlow', he were of 'no
account' at that h'office.

'Don't be so h'igorant!' Dick sez. 'Mr Barlow's grandad were on
the Cut long before you or yer Grand Union was even thought of!'

The chap wouldn't give in, wouldn't let 'em through on to the
Grand Union without fishal-tullidge.

"Ow can we pay tullidge on empty boats?'

Moy-chap pleaded with him on behalf of the four kiddies. 'It's
not their fault they can't get a load. They've had over a week of
bombin tryin to get a load. They've been through enough and their
boat needs dockin.'

The chap let 'em through. That old 'Jubilee' hinjin kept 'em goin
right back to Branston but they had to use the belts-pump all the
way.

We was still left behind, stuck by Ham Medder outside Brentford
waitin for a load for three days and nights. Those Woods' boys were
brave, takin their turn at dodgin out between raids to get rations
and water and eel-n-mash for the five of us. The stewed eel shop
were a godsend. It were in Brentford High Street not far from the
boats. You took yer own jugs and dishes. They worked *that* 'ard in
that shop. *He* were thin as a lath and done all the cookin and
skinnin. *She* were big and fat and done all the ladlin-out from the
steamin cauldrons of stew, sweat pourin down her rosy cheeks. The

liquor [*sauce*] were a feast in itself. A big jug of eel stew brimmin to the top with parsley liquor cost yer a bob [*shilling*], a big dish of mashed pertater another bob, and a big pie on the top for a tanner [*sixpence*]. For half-a-crown we had a good nourishin meal for the five of us.

We all stayed in 'Britannia's' cabin while the raids was on. We decided if one was 'goin' we was all 'goin' together. We tried the shelter the first night. They learned yer to fall on the floor, arch yer back, and scream so the blast didn't hurt yer eardrums. The *screamin* nearly burst yer eardrums. Every time we heard the WHOOSH! of a bomb it was like a syloom down there. We was far more terrified prisoned-in under the ground with all them screamin people than we was oop top in our own 'ome in the cabin with just the five of us. It weren't all that clean down there neither. Moy-chap were white and sweatin. I could see he were gettin all worked oop. He 'ated bein prisoned-in, let alone under the earth.

At last one landed that close the bulb went out and the door blew in.

'Keep calm everybody!'

'Keep calm be boogered!' Moy-chap sez, scramblin oop the steps to the 'bonfire night' above. 'If I'm a-gonna die, I'm a-gonna die on me own boat!' And we all scrambled after him.

Us and the boys got our loads in the end but not before two more nights of BIFF! BANG! WALLOP! By the time we needed to travel through on to the Grand Union Essy's usual toll-clirk had phoned through to vouch for us at Brentford. We was able to be loaded as usual from the barges at Brent Medders.

We never needed to go down the Thames again. Our boats wasn't built for rivers. We was like little wooden match-boats on them runnin waters. I spose if we'd of been iron-hulled we might of stood oop to the pressure of the waters better, but we was still the wrong shape, too sharp in the bows, the forend would cut too deep against the current and water would come over yer deck. Then again, on tidal rivers like the Thames, the River 'Thorities don't let yer rove free, you has to pay for one of their tugs. I mind my Dad once tellin me that when he was a lad workin for John Griffiths they tried to get the contract to supply coal to Fulham Light, but by the time they'd paid for the stablin at Brentford, waited for the tide to turn and the tug to arrive to take them down the Thames to Fulham, and waited again for the tide and the tug to take 'em back it wasn't worth the candle.

The Banbury Lock was soon mended. Jerry bombed Banbury again in the autumn, hit the railway yard and the gasworks and just missed the dummy Allyminyum. That bomb landed on the side of the Cut, between Claydon and Craperdy, killed two cattle and broke the bank, but it didn't hold oop the boat people. We was restin at the 'Pigeons' that night, along of Mrs Wickson's daughter-in-law and little grandson, Roger. Wilfred had brought his wife and baby son away from London for a rest from the bombin. By then I'd given oop all hope of knowin wot happened to Moycle. I was lucky to of had him when I did. There was no use maudlin for the past, we needed all our wits about us to survive the present.

We was back to our usual runs from the coalfields down to Wolvercote, from the coalfields down to London and along the Paddinton Arm to pick oop inkits, 'chubes', timber, tinned milk, wot-av-yer from the basin at Lime'us [*Limehouse*]. No trees to get under there, just a big railway arch to shelter under, with BIFF! BANG! WALLOP! goin on all round us, and Big Bertha [*an anti-aircraft gun*] trundlin and thunderin along the rails on top of us. I used to try to get my big washin, sheets, flannel-shirts, wot-av-yer done while I was waitin at Lime'us but in the end I had to giv oop, Jerry was always on the brevitt [*hunt for a target*]. In the end I used to leave my big wash with Mrs Walker, a washerwoman at Buckby Locks on my way to London, and she'd get it all done and pinned oop in a clean towel with a big safety-pin for me to pick oop on my way back. I could still get a big wash done at Wolvercote, the men always let yer have plenty of hot water there; and our Arryut would take our big wash if we was anywhere near Sutton Stop. Appy would fetch it and bring it back all clean and fresh to us. Our Arryut and Appy would help anybody. They was always very good to us.

I tried shoppin at Lime'us once. I'd never shopped much around there because of the raids, every time the siren went they shut-oop shop. You could spend yer day didgy-dodgin in and out and still get nothin. Rationin was much fairer than in Moy-chap's war when you'd queue all day for a loaf and get none. You still had to queue for most things, of course, and you had to take yer own paper bags, shops wasn't allowed to waste paper on wrappin oop. We was used to wastin *nothin* on the boats. In the war they used to say 'The squander-bug'll get yer if yer don't WATCH OUT!' Most shops put boards outside statin their wares in chalk-writin. If yer can't read you was none the wiser. If I seed a queue I just joined it. 'Join it first, ask after' were my motto. I asked after 'oonyuns' once. The shop-keeper lept at me and dragged me out to her board.

'*No* sweets! *No* chocolate! *No* bananas! *No* oranges! *No* lemons! *No* onions! CAN'T YOU READ!'

I weren't goin to let on to the likes of 'er I couldn't read. ''Ow was h'I to know wot sez h'oonyuns!' I flounced, and took me last thrippeny bit orf h'elsewhere.

In another shop there was a portly ARP lady with a plummy voice layin down the lor to everybody that they must keep buckets of water handy outside every room to fight their own 'cinderies' [*incendiary bombs*]. The Fire Service was gettin too wore-out to cope. 'I have buckets of water outside every bedroom in my house', she sez, all 'lardy-dar', 'I hope *you* do.'

I suddenly twiggs she's 'dressin *me*. 'Pardon?'

'I hope *you* keep buckets of water outside *your* bedroom?'

'Oo, yes!' I sez, '*bookits*-n-*bookits*!'

I gets back to Lime'us Quay, wore out. The tide's gone out. The boat's dropped oompteen feets, and I'm stuck-oop in the air with the week's shoppin. I peeps over the edge, plenty of boats down there but not a soul to be seen, all of 'em in their cabins, catchin oop on their sleep or havin a chin-wag. In my younger days when I was skinny and lithesome I thought nothin of droppin through space to land on a folded sack on the cabin roof or shinnin oop and down steep lock ladders, but since havin my children I'd becomed buxom, and I can't stand hithes [*heights*], I go all of a wobble.

A young tug-captain was walkin along the quay.

''Ow's the likes of me supposed to get down there?' I sez.

We got talkin and I discovered he was Alf Bodley, the little lad Nell Canvin brung oop. To think when he were borned, Mrs Bodley's twenty-secund child, we didn't expect him to last the Blizzerth Tunnel, yet here he was, one of the youngest tug-captains facin the blitz in the London docks. Ent Nature wonderful! Nell Canvin were pretty wonderful too to raise that weak little dillun of a babe to useful man'ood.

'You'll have to shin down that ladder, Ma.'

He pointed to a narrow iron rusty ladder built sheer down the filthy slimy wall of the dock.

'Alf,' I sez, 'there's no way I'm goin down that ladder.'

'Bert! Give Mrs Ramlin a lift, will yer?'

I looks oop to see this Samson wot's goin to bear me down this ladder. It was a little chap way oop the top of a n'oyist [*a 'hoist', crane*]. It had a big flat board swayin on chains at each corner. They used it for loadin the boats from the barges.

'I'm not ridin on *that!*' I were petrified.

'Go on, Ma!'

A crowd seemed to come from nowheres, gatherin on the quayside.

'Go on, MA!'

'Come on, Rose! I'll catch yer!'

I looked over and looked back quick. Syer were raisin his arms from a sea of faces on the boats below.

'COME ON, ROSE!'

'GO ON, MA!'

I braved it. Sittin in the middle of this board with me shoppin and me eyes tight shut. As I swung out over the dock they all cheered, and when me and the shoppin were safely orf-loaded into the arms of Syer and Lizer on 'Britannia', they all clapped. Somebody struck oop 'Rule, Britannia!', and they all joined in.

We stood there chuffed on the counter of 'Britannia', me, Syer, and Lizer. We felt they was singin to us, bravin the war.

We'd a lot more war to brave yet.

'Holdin-Out'

'ITLER sent his butty-boy [*Rudolph Hess*] to make us give in, but we was still 'oldin-out.

Jerry kep playin us oop all over the docks, but we was still 'oldin-out.

'Itler named the date he and his crew was goin to land. Syer patrolled all night while me and Lizer waited oop with the poker and the rollin pin, but they never turned oop. We'd been told that as soon as they landed we was to wreck the Cut, crash the locks, sink our boats.

I prayed and prayed it would never come to that. I couldn't, I could *not* wreck the Cut. All our lives we'd been brung oop to respect the tunnels and ackerdooks, the bridges and locks built by them clever chaps of the past. I couldn't, I could *not* damage the locks. I could *never* sink a boat. A boat's yer 'OLE world. It's always a deep shock to a boatman to lose his boat.

We was agen New Warwick wharf in Birnigum the night Sam Beechey's boats was bombed. Sam was Suey Beechey's brother-in-lor. Poor Sam! He were a daycent, proyvit sort of chap yet he were found dazed, wanderin with no trousers in the bitter November cold, 'My boats?. . . My boats? . . .'

There was another old-fashion' Birnigum Number One in a rickety old 'orseboat moored along of us one night. He were very deaf, said he never took no notice of raids, never heard 'em, he'd 'go' when his time came. He always undressed, donned a proper nightshirt, and got tucked oop in bed as if he were moored way-out in the peace of the countryside.

'If I'm gonna "go",' he sez, calm as yer like, 'I'm gonna "go" in me own bed.'

It were a lively night. Whenever that old waily-waily air-raid siren used to went my stummick would always clench-oop tight with terror, yet, once the raid was on I felt it was oop to Fate. I'd tell myself, 'If that bomb 'as *your* number on, Rose, there's nothin you can do about it.' Course, we took cover from the scrapnel and them tin-lights they kep trailin over our heads, but it wasn't till the dawn was breakin and the 'All Clear' WHOO!'d out at last that you realized you was shakin all over. Then me and Lizer would set to and brew tea for everybody pickin their way out of their cubby-'oles. That night we was lucky, though there was quite a bit of damage around the wharf, we was all alive and we had a free gas supply to heat the water. Some chap lit the end of a broken gas pipe on the wharf, Moy-chap built bricks all round it, I fetched the tin bath out of the lumber-'ole and everybody around fetched wot bit of ration, tea, sugar, tinned milk they could spare.

I was glad to see in the daylight the old deaf chap's boat were still afloat. We hadn't seed nothin of him all night, and his 'atches [*cabin doors*] was still closed. It's manners on the boats never to disturb folks when their 'atches are closed. But as the sun rose and he still hadn't opened oop, I picked my way through the scrapnel along the towpath and took him a cup of tea. I banged on the side of his cabin.

'Cup of tea, Mister?' I shouts.

'You all right in there, Mister?' I shouts.

I got Moy-chap and Lizer to open oop with me. There was a terrible smell. The old chap were still in bed. We could tell he were dead. He looked just like a wise old yellowed waxwork, eyes half-closed, a half-smile, two old yellowed hands restin, just so, on top of a n'old army greatcoat. He looked so peaceful from the front it was a terrible shock to discover he were a stinkin bloody mess behind. A stray piece of scrapnel had splintered straight through the flimsy bulkhead into his scrawny back. I only hoped the poor old chap had died in shock and not in agony.

That was the mornin Essy turned oop and asked us to take on another boat, work *three* boats between us. It was the same old story, plenty of orders, too many spare boats, not enough crews to work 'em. We was to take coal to Appleton [*Alperton*] Glassworks on the Paddinton Arm, go on to Lime'us and pick oop a backload of special timber for Coventry. There was to be another mass-funeral in Coventry that day.

We unloaded at Appleton. When our kiddies was alive they used to love watchin the men blowin the glass at Appleton and at 'Ayes [*Hayes*]. Bottels and bottels, all shapes and sizes, you never knowed wot was goin to turn oop on the end of that blow-stick. It was just like a conjurin show for the boat kiddies, they'd stand watchin, bounden, and the men would play oop to them. Whenever we delivered to those old places I'd see other boat-children, still fastenated, and the lack of my own kiddies would come rushin back.

Early next mornin we was travellin empty to Lime'us to pick oop this special load of timber. No strings of barges comin through the tunnel at Maida nor at the City Road. That was a bad sign, the raids had stopped 'em workin again. When we got to Lime'us the Littlemores was there with the old 'Hood' and the butty 'Hardy'. The 'Hardy' was already sheeted-oop with h'inkits for Tydesley but the old 'Hood' was only half-loaded when they'd been held oop by another raid. The weight was puttin pressure on 'Hood's' weakest timbers and they was havin to keep the hinjin goin to pump out the water. I was shocked to see how grey Ada's dark hair was goin, the strain of keepin four kiddies safe and the old 'Hood' afloat was takin its toll. One of the kiddies was not very well. They decided not to hang about in the smoke and heat for the rest of their load but to sheet-oop them shinin h'inkits and get under way.

That night was a real bad'un. When we came out in the mornin after the 'All Clear' we heard it had been one of the worst nights so far, seven London 'orspitals hit, and bombs dropped right out to Hayes and Southall. I wondered how far Ada and Dick had got and whether the old ''Ood' was still chuggin-on. There was a beautiful mornin somewhere oop above us but we couldn't see it for a sickly-sweet pall of smoke. They said the ware'ouses down river had been bombed and the water were ablaze from shore to shore with burnin rubber and sugar. (Soon after, the sugar ration was halved and you couldn't get knicker-larstic for love nor money.)

'They've sunk the "Hood"!' Somebody shouted down the quay. My 'eart stopped.

'Wot about *Ada*?' I shouted back. 'Wot about *Dick*, and the *kiddies*?'

It wasn't Ada's ''Ood'. It was the h'HMS ''Ood'. I know I didn't oughter say it—after all, every man lost is some poor mother's son—but I were *that* relieved.

Our special load of timber turned out to be coffins for Coventry, flat-packed efforts, do-it-yerself like. We'd hardly got goin back

[171]

along the Regent's, done the first six locks, when Jerry started playin oop again. We had to went into the shelter at City Road Basin with the 'paper-dashers'. The paper-dashers belonged to John Dickinson's, the paper mills at Apsley. They had two pairs of narrer-boats dashin constant to-n-fro the ware'ouses at City Road Basin with all the paper, envelopes, ledgers, wot-av-yer for the city h'offices. They had their own wide-boats as well to bring the great big rolls of foreign grasses from the docks to make the paper at the mills. One pair of narrer-boats was worked by three men, the other pair by a daycent famly, Mum, Dad, and their growed-oop daughter, I forget their name, we just called 'em the Paper-Dashers, and they squashed into this shelter along of us. We all survived that time, thank the Lord! The shelter wasn't much cop, just a buildin on the quay where the ARP wardens made us all congregate. They wardens liked yer all under the one roof at the start so they could count who was missin afterwards. Not like in poor old Coventry where so many was killed, blasted, or buried without trace.

Every time we came within sight of Coventry there seemed to be less of it. Ever since I could remember, whenever we came through Withybrook on the North h'Oxford we'd always look out for the three 'cathedrals' [*spires*] down in the valley, the big one in the middle [*Coventry Cathedral*], and the two smaller ones on

either side [*Coventry churches*], and knowed we was drawrin
nearer and nearer to the city. Now the big one was missin.

When I was a little runnerboat for Granny Statham I used to get
orf the 'Victoria' as soon as we came through Withybrook Bridge,
and walk back over the bridge to Withybrook Post h'Office to
collect Granny's pension. Then I used to run back along the towpath
and get back on again at Jack Langford's cottage. It was a very
pretty little cottage, some distance along the towpath, with two
stables but ne'er a public. Jack's parents kept a public, 'The Duke'
at Duke's Lock on the South h'Oxford. All along the towpath to
Jack's cottage in the old days you could keep yer eye on the three
'cathedrals' down in the valley. The post lady from Withybrook
always used to clomp over Withybrook Bridge in her heavy GPO
boots and big black GPO cape and walk along the towpath to
deliver letters to Jack. I mind once seein a whirlwind WHOOSHin-
oop from the 'Opsford Valley ackerdook, catchin under the post
lady's cape, whirlin her high into the air and into the Cut. For one
moment, seein them 'cathedrals' below her in the valley, it looked
as if she were bein tossed over Coventry Cathedral. Me and Old
Man Statham fished her out with a boat-'ook. She were still clutchin
Jack's letter—it were only a postcard—and were determined to
finish her GPO duty, clompin on, soppin wet, to Jack's cottage—
wot isn't there now—over 'Olly 'Ill bridge, and back along the
railway—wot isn't there now—to Withybrook post h'Office.

As soon as we tied oop at Coventry with our 'special load of
timber' they started to unload us. They was desprat for our cargo.
They'd had another big raid the night before and were expectin
another. It were goin to be full-moon and all the oil-drums with
their 'chimleys' were set out on the windward side ready to make a
big smoke-screen. Moy-chap were anxious to get the three boats
orf-loaded, winded, and back out along the Cut beyond the city
before evenin. There was no locks to be worked along there.

I had to go to the Food h'Office for new ration books and clothin
coupons. We was startin clothes-rationin from then on. I arranged
to meet our Lizer at our Arryut's. Appy hadn't been called oop, he
was doin valuble warwork, keepin the Lectric Light still goin and
fillin-in with ARP work, and Arryut was workin flat out at the
Munitions. We was hopin to press 'em both to come out of the city
with us on the boats for a night's rest. They still had no children,

they was spare Aunt-n-Uncle to everybody in the Row. They was still 'oldin-out in the same little 'ouse at the end of the Row. They'd moved their bed down into the cellar. It was snug and dry down there. Appy had rigged oop the lectric light, decorated the walls with a string of little Union Jacks, and stuck oop a big poster of 'Er 'Itler to practise his darts on.

The Food h'Office were gone, only a doorpost and a fireplace still standin. I were all at sea. It were a job to get yer bearins, where the streets used to went. The stench of sewage and gas were terrible. It took me ages to sought a way round the rubble and dusty rescue workers to our Arryut's. The whole Row were gone. Where our Arryut's had been were a great big hole full of water, big enough to of drownded one of Robinson Powers' waggon-n-'orses. A bobby told me it had happened two nights ago. He knowed Arryut and Appy, 'ad a cup o' tea and a laugh with 'em many a time. Nothin had been found of either of 'em. He took my arm and helped me over to the Relief Centre where he'd taken our Lizer. My poor sister just looked at me and held out her arms. We clung to each other. No words would come. They made us have a cup of tea. They said death would of come instant. There was nothin to be done. The lady said there was to be a special funeral service soon for all those who had perished without trace. She promised she would let Mr Veaters know, and that from now on our new ration books would be at Sutton Stop, and boat people was to have extrer tea and cheese rations, a regler supply of matches, and extrer boot coupons because we was doin valuble warwork.

Me and Lizer helped each other back for one last look together at our Arryut's. We stood quoyet payin our respects. Our Arryut had been borned only a few streets away at Coventry Basin. I minded that day, all those years ago, when me and Alby was called out from school by Miss Sticks to find Granny Statham's 'Girls' come to fetch us, 'You've got a new little l'Arryut.'

I minded how good Arryut had been to all our kiddies, specially our Rose. Now there was only me and our Lizer left of our family, and we had no 'ome on the bank to turn to. It had been a daycent little 'ome. Arryut and Appy had always made us welcome. Now there was nothin left among the rubble 'cept a tatter of Union Jack and a shred of 'Itler's poster. Wot 'arm had they and thousands of others he had killed done to 'Er 'Itler? I grounded that shred of poster down and down into the dust with the heel of my boot. If me and Lizer could of got our 'ands on the real 'Itler at that moment we'd of teared every evil wicked bit of 'im into bloody shreds.

I laid that little bit of Union Jack in the ticket draw along with our other treasures. If 'Itler thought he were goin to b'reave us into givin in, he'd another think comin. That little tatter of Union Jack made us more set than ever on *'oldin-out*.

Winnin Through

MOY-CHAP agreed with Essy to carry on workin the three boats on the Wolvercote run but not down to Lime'us. It wasn't worth it, all them locks; and it was far safer nippin in and out between raids gettin away with two boats loaded, than riskin the lot, waitin for three. Us Barlow boats wasn't never sposed to be reglers down there, we was gap-stoppin, coverin for Grand Union boats, but they hadn't the crews.

It was tricky enough at Wolvercote with the three loaded boats, specially when the river was in flood; windin the loaded moty to go down backwards, starn first, on the current, towin the two loaded butties, breasted-oop. There was many a n'airy moment when you felt the river racin yer along out of control. You just had to trust the chaps at the Mill to work fast to lift their rollers over the weir to loose the pent-oop waters, lift the boards to ease the mill-race, and grab our ropes to steady us oop.

The Littlemores had taken on the three boats to work the Wolvercote run as well. They was braver than we in their old 'Hood'. It was still petterin along—*just*—but Essy was buildin them a brand-new 'Hood' at Glascote. None of us realized then that it was to be the last workin boat to be built there. Though there was plenty of work the Cuts was gettin more and more neglected. The mud-'oppers and maintenance teams was scattered away at the war, the narrow Cuts was siltin oop and oop, broken banks was left untended, losin water, and the water levels wasn't bein topped oop.

It wasn't so bad on the main Grand Union. Though they had the Maffer's flight at one end and the Cowroast at the other drawrin the water orf the summit, they 'ad a string of pumpin-'ouses to drawr water from the rivers and streams around and keep pumpin it back into the Cut. How I *loved* peekin into them pumpin-'ouses when I was a kiddy. They 'ad 'igh churchy windows, and the light would come floodin-in on all this SHINE, the floors, the steel, the brass. Like a shrine they was, them pumpin-'ouses. My kiddies had loved 'em too. You could run and get yer lock ready, then, while you was waitin for the boats to come, you could run and take a worship in the door of the pumpin-'ouse. You never went in, you wasn't sposed, but the man would always nod and grin at yer over the noise. Great big steel rods pumpin oop-n-down, oop-n-down, and a big wheel goin round and round, and a big shiny 'andrail all round so the men was preventioned from fallin into the machinery. Spotless, them pumpin-'ouses was kep. *Spotless!*

When I was a kiddy we used to take steamcoal regler to the ones at Ivano. There was plenty of room for two boatloads there and they'd fetch it away by 'orse-n-cart to their other pumpin-'ouses as they needed. The two *my* kiddies used to love best was the one at Northchurch and the one at the Cowroast. They'd stand there regler in the doorway, chatterin away to the men as kiddies do, stoppin every now and again just to gaze and gaze at all that SHINE, *fastenated.*

It was bad on the Birnigum and Coventry, more was flowin out of the Cut than was bein put back, specially in the war. In big cities like Birnigum and Coventry the Fire Service had always had a right to certain points where they was allowed to pick oop water from the Cut. In some parts of Birnigum the Cut was so built-over, a little red fire-door in the wall of a buildin were the only clue the Cut were *there!* Durin the blitz they'd had to take out more water than they should. This meant that we had to carry less tonnage 'cos the Cut wasn't deep enough. We was paid on tonnage, we was workin just as hard as ever, riskin all on the shallow Cuts, and losin money. So when Essy asked Ada if there was anythin perticler she wanted built into the new boat, 'Yes,' she sez, 'another six h'inches on the width of the bed. If we can't carry the h'extrer coal we might as well 'ave the h'extrer comfort!'

When yer 'ome is only 7 feets by 10 every h'inch makes a world of difference. I think if Ada had asked for three chimneys like the 'Queen Mary', Essy would of done his best. He were desprat to 'ang on to us old boatin-family crews.

The Grand Union were desprat for crews too. We learned from Susan Ward that they was havin to rope in women from orf the bank, h'eddicated women, to work their boats. Susan was still battlin on with only her Rose and Lucy and young Laura. Laura's brother-in-lor, Charley Lane, were bein paid to learn two women from orf the bank, Miss Gayford and Miss French, 'ow to work the boats, and they was goin to learn all these others. *Trainees* they was called. They certainly added a bit of life to the Cut. Whenever we noticed a fresh scrape of paint on a wall or another brick knocked out of a bridge, 'Ah!' we'd say, 'The *Trainees* 'ave been at it again!'

We never really got in 'co' [*company*] with 'em, they never talked the same as we. Some of 'em was 'opeless, couldn't stick the loife. Some of 'em was downright lardy-dar, speak to yer as if yer wasn't quite the ticket; but some was real game, willin to learn, and stuck it to the finish.

They was always chuckin packets of cigarettes to each other, and some of 'em weared face-paint, and some of 'em weared trousers. Course, as time went on some of the younger boatwomen found the trousers was warm and practical, and some took to the smokin. You seldom seed boatwomen on the narrow Cuts smokin cigarettes until the Trainees came along. Me and Lizer never took to it. We never took to no powder-n-paint neither. When yer workin out in all weathers all day you haven't time to think of that. We had a block of 'Snofire' for our chapped hands and legs, where our wet skirts chafed the tops of our boots, otherwise our posh beauty-treatment were always a good wash. I do *love* a good wash! Lizer took to the trousers in time, 'slacks' they was called, but I never. Moy-chap wouldn't 'ave it, he would *not* 'ave it. 'T'ent ladyfied, Rose, women wearin trousers!'

Some of they Trainees got into a fair old pickle. We came to Wigram's once, where you turns orf the Grand Union to go oop the Warwick to Birnigum, to find two Trainees, with a pair of Grand Union boats loaded low with h'inkits, headin straight for the wall of the bridge with a dead hinjin.

'How does one stop?' 'one' wailed to Moy-chap.

'Don't worry!' Moy-chap sez, noddin at the fresh scrapins of paint all along the wall, 'All Trainee's boats is made to stop *some'ow!'*

Mind you, if you wasn't ready for it you could easy stall yer hinjin there where the deep of the Grand Union meets the shallow of the h'Oxford and you'd 'ave a job, as these had, to make the bridge-'ole.

We picked oop another cryin, adrift in her butty in the dark of the Blizzerth Tunnel. Her mate on the moty 'ad'nt a clue she'd lost a seventy feets butty till she came out the other end and turned to see—'Oo, *deah!'* A boater would know the second that tow 'went', he'd sense the 'drag' *before* it went. They was 'amachers', usin only one rope in a figure of eight. You *could* tow like that but you keeps dartin about and works loose. Dangerous. Moy-chap showed 'em how to fix a pair of craws-straps, and how to make a boater's knot, a 'yooz' knot we always called it because you was always 'yoozin' it. It was a simple bowallin noose [*bowline*], non-slip.

Some of 'em had the manners to nod 'Ah, do!' or to loose yer by if they could see they was holdin yer oop. Some seemed bent on throwin their weight about with needless shows of puntin and shuntin. Moy-chap let rip at one of 'em windin her boats at Longford.

'Everybody has to learn!' she flung at him.

'Everybody en't paid by the Government with paid leave every five minutes!' he flings back.

She was puntin about windin both craft in the one tight 'ole. It's a very tight windy-'ole at Longford. We always used to wind the butty at Sutton Stop and tow it along starn-first to Longford, then you had only the moty to wind for towin back. She was a game-'un, marstered it neat as yer like at the finish. Me and Moy-chap doffed our 'ats to her. She 'ad to laugh. She 'ad a lovely laugh. We all laughed. You was always glad of a laugh. A laugh's better than a stack-oop.

Those Grand Union boats was a bit bigger than our'uns. 'Rickys' we called 'em, cos some of them was built special at Rickmansworth. When the Grand Union took over the Cut their plan was to carry bigger cargoes with less boats and crews all the way from the London docks right oop into Birnigum. They widened the 'road' in many places and rebuilt all those locks oop to Birnigum but the money ran out before they could afford to do the dredgin. We was always towin the Trainees orf the mud. It wasn't always their fault, their craft was too deep for the draught.

We had them Trainees to thank for the new lock, top o' Napp'n, where we lost our Rose. We was always havin trouble with that lock. The walls wasn't true. After they got wedged in it durin the war and blocked the Cut, the Comp'ny had to pinch a bit orf the farm'ouse gardin and rebuild the lock. That wasn't the only thing we had the Trainees to thank for. It was them wot kicked-oop about the Bottom Road. When you travelled loaded oop the Warwick to Birnigum you wasn't allowed to wind at Camp'ills and come back down the same way to go back round to the Coventry coalfields, you had to go along the Bottom Road. I think it was to save water on the Warwick. The Bottom Road was shorter but it took a lot longer because it was such a dirty drag, all single locks, a lotta locks, and a lotta bowallin. They Trainees wasn't gonna make donkeys of 'emselves! They wouldn't 'ave it. They would *not* 'ave it! We seed 'em swannin back down the Warwick, breasted-oop, *empty*! From then on we all done it, travelled back the same way. It was a much longer distance but faster, because of the double locks.

There was one more bonus we owed to them Trainees. I reckon it was due to them 'avin regler leave that Essy started offerin us a paid holiday towards the end of the war, first two weeks in August while the mines was closed.

'Two weeks, six pounds a week', he offered Moy-chap. 'Where would you like to end up?'

We chose Banbury, and he'd plan our trip accordin. Usually a load of coal to Wolvercote. We could call on our friends the Bloomfields, the Stanleys, Mrs Atkins at Craperdy, Mrs Butler and all the other lock-keepers on our way to h'Oxford; stop at the Wicksons', see her little grandson, Roger, if he was down for a visit; see the Beauchamps, the Coleses, and the Johnsons as we came back through Thrupp, and then tie-oop in Banbury where most of the other boatin families was moored or had a room or a n'ouse down Factry Street.

Whenever we tied-oop at Banbury I'd always make the h'effort to visit Mary Humphries, 'Cowboy' Mary. Years before, when their Mum and Dad died, Mary and her sister Eliza had been adopted by their Uncle and Auntie Wilson. After Eliza had married they kept on at Mary, 'We would like to see you married and settled down, Mary. Can't you find a good chap?'

Mary could of had any amount of chaps but she loved her Uncle's old 'orse, Bill, wot had drawed the 'Mabel' for many years. Mary did everythin for him.

'I'm sellin Old Bill and convertin the "Mabel" to a moty, Mary', her Uncle sez one day. They was Number Ones and beginnin to feel their age by then. Mary had to say a sad farewell to her last 'orse. By then Alf Hartree who worked on the wharf at Banbury was chasin her, turnin oop all over the Navigation, bumpin along the towpath on his BSA and pillion.

'Here he comes again, Mary!' her Auntie Annie would cry, pleased as punch.

But Mary loved the peace and freedom of her life on the Cut, didn't want to marry and settle down in a n'ouse in Banbury, never slept in a n'ouse in her life. I found her cryin once.

'I wonder 'ow they goes on in a n'ouse, Rose? 'Ow on earth do they *manage*?'

'You'll manage all right, Sport. Do yer *love* 'im?'

'I *do* love 'im, but I don't want to live in a n'ouse.'

'He's crazy over yer, gallyvantin after yer all over the Cut. Love like that's worth puttin oop with a n'ouse.'

'Promise you'll come and see me, Rose, when I'm prison'd in a n'ouse?'

I felt sorry for Mary, she'd hardly married and had her little girl when Alf, like thousands of other young husbands, was snatched away to the war. In her little house oop the Warwick Road, 'gen the 'Warwick' pub, she were cut orf from the Cut and the boats. She had a bad time havin little Margaret, and her own mother wasn't alive to turn to. Alf's mother did wot she could but I know 'ow much I'd missed *my* Mum when our Rose was borned. At least I had Moy-chap and was amongst my own boat people. Whenever I got the chance I'd walk along Factry Street and oop Castle

Street—it was only a narrow cobbled lane in those days—and out the top between the "Orseshoes' and the 'Pigeons' and along the Warwick Road to visit Mary. She was that pleased to see me. We'd chatter-chatter shovel-n-tongs, all about the old days on the boats, and the 'orses, and the boat people.

She took in several little evacuee kiddies during the war. I used to take them these little wooden toys the prisoners of war used to sell us. There was several of these prisoners workin the farms around Stoke Bruin. I don't know if they was 'Jerries' [*Germans*] or 'Eye-tyes' [*Italians*], they had big round red patches stitched on their blue uniforms. They used to love to help work the lock for us at Bottom Stoke, and they'd trade these beautiful wooden toys they'd made, countin frames with wooden beads, little 'orses on wheels, wot-av-yer. We didn't understand their jabber and they didn't understand ourn but we'd smile and trade between us. They rarely wanted more than half-a-crown, just to give them a bit of pocket-money.

I loved to watch how Mary's Margaret was growin oop and learnin to share with the others. When she was little she'd sit on my lap and my heart would ache to have my arms around a child again. She had so many pretty little ways and was such a comfort to her Mum, she brought back many memories of my Rose. I watched Margaret through her infant years, through her first schoolin, makin her letters and drawrin her name, and by the time she was seven, towards the end of the war, she was showin me how easy she could read. There was me, a growed woman of forty-four, not knowin me letters, and there was she, a little mite of seven, knowin full books. I'd of given *anythin* that last Christmas of the war to 'ave a little girl like Margaret wot knowed her schoolin.

When I got back to the cabin I burst into tears.

'Wot's oop *now*, Rose?'

'It's Mary's little girl, she reads beautiful.'

'That's nothin to *cry* about!'

I couldn't stop. The war had got me right down, I was beginnin to cry for the least little thing, then my nose would start to bleed. Real bad I was gettin. Moy-chap fetched Lizer.

'You can't keep havin these nose-bleeds and gettin down in the doomps like this, Rose', she sez. 'You'll 'ave to see the doctor. P'raps it's yer 'anky-panky?' She knowed I were goin through 'the change'.

'It's not *that*. It's them *doodle-boogers*.'

Since the summer we'd been dodgin these new bombs 'Itler was flingin at the London end of the Cut. Flew by themselves out of the blue. We called 'em doodle-boogers. They had a n'orange light on the end wot cast a glow on yer and a hinjin wot cut out just before it dropped. As long as it were still throbbin over yer, shakin yer boat in its glowin light, you was all right—some other poor booger was gonna cop it. You'd strain to hear 'ow much further it would keep goin then—Deafenin silence. BANG!

Now we was havin to face oop to a n'even worser doodle-booger. Just before Christmas 'Itler had started sendin rocket-bombs, no light, no throbbin, no warnin at all. BANG! I'd had nearly six years of air raids. At least with the raids we knowed how to carry on, but these new wicked 'boogers' got me right down. I couldn't sleep. I was livin on me nerves.

After Christmas we kep hearin on other people's wireless how we was winnin the war, we needn't bother about black-out no more, 'Itler was on the run. Yet all through January and February in the cold and the snow he was still flingin these evil 'boogers'.

Towards the end of March the skies was full of *our* chaps goin to bomb Germany. Now and again the old doodle-booger still sneaked through, but by then our clever chaps on the gunsites had somethin to spot 'em comin and they'd sound the sirens to warn us. One mornin we was moored in Lime'us Lock, along of no end of other boat families and their kiddies. It was broad daylight, spring sunshine sparklin on the water, a job to realize we was still at war. I couldn't think wot was wrong with me. I was *that* tired, couldn't even raise my arms to braid my 'air. I stood on 'Britannia's' counter, my arms restin, heavy as lead on the cabin top. I'd had a good night's rest yet I was that exhaustered I was almost asleep on my feet. The sirens went. I stood there watchin everybody scurryin orf the boats, passin the kiddies acraws, hurryin to the shelter. They'd all got orf 'cept me. I were rooted to the spot.

'Rose!'

I couldn't move. Not one little step. 'Adn't the strenth.

'ROSE!'

This doodle-booger was comin straight for me.

This is it, Rose', I thinks to meself.

It suddenly fizzles like a spent balloon, shoots straight out acraws

the water into a barge of timber on the far side of the dock. BANG!
Oop it went in a cloud of flames and smoke, showerin blazin 10 ft
planks in all directions. It were one of the last doodle-boogers of
the war.

I clung to the tossin boat.

'*Rose,*' I sez, '*Yer still 'ere.*'

The next day Lizer went with me to the doctor.

'I'm not surprised you're so tired, Mrs Ramlin,' he sez, 'you're
about four months pregnant.'

Jinny

I CAME to town with a BANG!

'Fireworks!' Nurse Cornflake sez. 'It's VJ night. The Japs have surrendered. The war's *really* over at last. *A new little baby girl.* What a lovely way to celebrate Peace. What are you going to call her?'

'Jinny.'

'Why not *Victoria* Jinny? "V.J." for VJ night?'

We kep 'Victoria' for best and 'Jinny' for everyday.

She was born in the cabin of the 'Britannia', at Tusses Bridge, 'gen the Coventry Lectric Light.

'—Should charge her up for life,' Nurse Cornflake sez, 'she's bound to be bright.'

Nurse Cornflake was like that, brusk and breezy, down to earth. Her language was a bit choice. It needed to be with some of the rough'uns she had to deliver. You got quite a few rough'uns on the boats. You get rough'uns in all walks o' loife. Nurse Cornflake gave 'em as good as she got—with bonus. She was a tough middle-aged woman from down Manchester way. She could be very down on yer if yer didn't look after yer pregnunt self. Her name was something like Cornthwaite but to us boatwomen she was always Nurse Cornflake.

It was nearly fifteen years since I'd last come to town with our Alby. The lor had been tightened oop a lot more since then. You now had to stop tied-oop in the one place for three weeks before and three weeks after havin yer babe. It still cost yer two guineas to have the nurse. Moy-chap wasn't paid while I was laid-oop. He went to work on the Coventry Lectric Light. Most of the boatmen were well-knowed from deliverin fuel there over the years and could usually get a job, shovellin coal. Tons and tons of coal was delivered out of the boats on one side of the Cut, drawn by chains on a belt-bridge [*conveyor belt*] across the Cut, to the main works on the opposite bank. There was a little footbridge alongside of the

coal-bridge for the men to walk over to the main Lectric Works.
There was great big grabs, 'Telfers' we used to call 'em, shiftin this
coal all day. Mr Pearsal and his son worked them Telfers for years
and knowed all the boatmen. In them days Mr Pearsal and chaps
like him would serve the one firm like that all their lives. Syer
never earned much there, about four pounds a week, but it were
quite a n'eye-opener, workin in company with other chaps, cheap
canteen, and the surety of workin set hours for a set wage at the
end of the week.

Nurse Cornflake made yer go to the Clinic 'gen Coventry. If yer
went to the Clinic you didn't have to keep goin to the doctor. The
doctor cost yer five shillins a time when you was examined so it
saved a lot, goin to the Clinic. I used to walk, it wasn't all that far,
and it done me good. She'd h'inspect yer boat to decide if she'd
deliver you in the cabin or make yer go to the 'orspital. She
h'inspected my cabin and then she came again, special, to bring
some 'high-oops' [*health officers*] to show them my cabin and the
special little garments me and Lizer had made ready for the baby.
I done the plain sewin and Lizer done the broiderin—our Lizer
were a dab-'and at the broiderin. They all marvelled at our old-
fashion' workmanship and my clean cabin.

'I don't mind how often I attend *this* woman', Nurse Cornflake
sez to these 'igh-oops, 'but I refuse to attend that woman on that
filthy boat next door. *She* will have to come into the hospital.'

She were one of them Rodney-boatwomen wot shed babies all
over the Cut like shellin peas.

For several years after our Jinny was born Nurse Cornflake would
still call in on me for a cup of tea and a chat. She had a little opentop car with a clawth shade and a mongrel dog. He'd guard that car
if she told him, no matter how long she was on a call, and he'd
guard her too when she went on a call at night to rougher parts of
the Cut. For years she delivered no end of boat-babies from Tusses
Bridge to Longford. She used to call all that bank along there her
'Maternity Wharf'. I mind the year Rose Whitlock had her Moycle,
Auntie Laura Carter was carryin him, comin out of Mr Veaters'
h'office at Sutton Stop—we always had to show Mr Veaters and his
'seckerty', Miss Edwards, each new baby born along there, and Mr
Veaters would cross their palm with silver—Laura was followed by
Dolly 'Ayes with baby Teddy, Phyllis Macdonald with baby Joycey,

Mrs Tom Smith with her baby daughter, and Mrs Stanley 'Ambridge with her baby. Little Dennis Wilson was watchin wide-eyed outside, then he poked his head round the door, "Ow many more babbies 'ave you got under this 'ut, Mr Veaters, cos *I* wants one!'

We was delighted with our'un. She was like a little fairy-doll, but she were a n'and-full, loved feedin the dooks. In them lean years just after the war it was a job feedin us-selves let alone dooks. The rationin was worser orf than in the war. Even bread was rationed. One summer's afternoon she were in a tantrum 'cos I wouldn't let her have no more bread for feedin the dooks. She was about two at the time and full of tantrums. I harnessed her out in the 'atches of the 'Percy Veruns' till she be'aved herself.

'You can stop out 'ere', I sez, 'and *cool orf*!'

I was busy in the cabin when I heard such a quackin and a little voice outside sayin, 'Dooks 'ave it, ay? Dooks 'ave it.'

Talk about 'coolin orf'! The little minx had taken orf all her clothes and was 'feedin' 'em to the dooks, droppin 'em one by one into the Cut. Brand new 'poomps', socks, pilches, liberty-bodice! And clothes was still on precious coupons! We'd had to find all new clothes for her since she was borned. I'd gived away all my good second-'and clothes believin I couldn't 'ave another child. I'd gived 'em all to young Mrs Bozzel [*Boswell*] when she had her five little boys quick-as-that-one-after-the-other. I kep Mum's shawl, of course—couldn't never bear to part with *that*.

We was in a very poor way again after the war. We was back to the two boats and 2/6 a ton, and the 'Strikes' at the pits and the docks. We was glad of a n'odd stockin for sixpence from Woolworths, we was glad of a n'old parachute to cut oop into petticuts, we was glad of penny cups without 'andles, 'utilities' the chap on the market called 'em.

The Cut wasn't so peaceful as it used to be. It was nearly all hinjins now, and some worked all night, chuggin past, rockin yer boat. There was still a few big cart'orses, stallion-things, drawrin the barges down London way, but on the South h'Oxford there was only the last two Number Ones, the Ownses [*Hones*] and Joe Skinner, still tradin with hanimals. That was the year, just after the war, that Rose Own married Jack Skinner, nephew to Joe wot worked the 'Friendship'. The Skinners go back a long way in boatin families. Jack Skinner always looked smart, even when he was in his workin gear. Rose were first swept orf her feet by the jaunty angle of his trilby. Jack were one of the first of the young boatmen to take to the trilby, and to the Vaseline hair cream, until it began to melt with passion on his first date in the pictures with Rose and ran down the inside of his collar.

Rose had never slept away from home until she married Jack. On the first trip after their weddin, they was comin back from Tusses Bridge with a load of coal for h'Oxford Lectric Light to find the Summit on the South h'Oxford had almost run out of water. There was just enough in the middle to float them to Claydon. They had to stop there, stable the 'orse for six weeks, and find jobs on the bank with the Co-op. Rose delivered milk and Jack delivered coal. Soon after, Alf Own, Senior, ceased to be a Number One and sold the 'Cylgate' to Barlows.

It seemed a terrible thing to us that the h'Oxford Summit had been left to run out. It just showed that the Comp'ny no longer cared about the Cut. Maintenance yards was bein closed down. Good, loyal, long-servin maintenance men like Mr Bloomfield was bein pensioned orf at eight bob a week. Others, like Mr Allbrey [*Aubrey Jones*] at Thrupp, was put in charge of longer and longer stretches. Lockside cottages like Mr Bloomfield's at Claydon and the one by Bakers' Lock was bein left to fall into rack-n-ruin. The next year 1947 were to bring the worst weather for years.

It started early in '47, just after Christmas. The evenin before the freeze set in we was unloadin at Tyseley and the Cut was wrinklin in the wind. The next mornin it was flat, still, sheet of h'ice. It was only thin, but all day long, comin down the Warwick from Birnigum, we was shaftin it away from buildin oop in front of the boats. By nightfall we'd reached the top of Hatton. It was a bitterly cold, frosty night. We could tell the locks would all be h'iced-oop by the mornin. None of us wanted to be stuck, h'iced-oop for weeks, out in the wilds at the top of Hatton. We'd had enough of being h'iced-oop out in the wilds without work that last bad winter before the war when the h'ice along Tunnel Straight at Fenny was eighteen inches thick. Eight weeks we was h'iced-oop with the Taylors at Fenny. The Taylors, two brothers and two sisters, was gettin on in years, they was workin for Essy. They had four boats and we had two. There was no work—there was only a Co-op and a gasworks at Fenny—and no money. Moy-chap and the two Taylor chaps had struggled through deep snow to Southam to be signed on the dole. Three times a week our chaps had to present 'emselves at Southam. The elderly Taylor chap couldn't manage it, he was done-in, and Moy-chap had to plead for his dole ever after. When at last we all got movin and earnin again we had to pay it all back.

In '47 we was determined to get to Sutton Stop where there would be more chance of Moy-chap, and p'raps our Lizer, gettin a job. The moon was risin. We decided to risk goin down Hatton that night. There's a big syloom [*mental hospital*] 'gen the top o' Hatton. We'd fetched coals for it many a time, the patients used to wheel it away and get oop to 'igh jinks with this coal. There's *twenty-one* locks to the bottom.

'We're barmy to even think of it,' Lizer sez; 'we might as well tie-oop to the syloom and 'ave done with it!'

Lizer was right. Hatton's bad enough in broad daylight; we was mad to go down in the freezin moonlight, but we did. We'd already put Jinny to bed in the 'Britannia'. Moy-chap steered 'Britannia' with the butty breasted-oop, usin the hinjin to hold 'em steady in the locks. Me and Lizer stayed on the frosty bank all the way, it was too dangerous in the dark to be steppin on and orf boats and along slippery gates. I stayed on one bank, she stayed on the other, callin acraws to each other now and again to make sure each was still there. You can get down both sides of Hatton, usin the bridges when necessary, but you has to watch out for those black 'oles, the old open locks and the coolvits. Each lock has four hefty ground paddles worked by wheels like a chaff-cuttin machine. Each wheel left yer breathless. Moy-chap bet at the start that we wouldn't make it before half past ten. We made it in two hours, got to Warwick Two by a quarter to ten.

'Just in time for you to 'ave a pint before closin', I sez. He certainly deserved it, h'expertly 'andlin them two boats and his precious little daughter safely down through them dark h'icy waters.

He came back from the pub with a newspaper, the *Daily Mirror*, with a big fota of Ada Littlemore and her kiddies bein tended by Sister Ward in her little front-room surgery at Stoke Bruin.

'I'll keep that for Ada,' I sez, '—give it her when we next meet.'

'*When*,' Lizer sez, 'if we're h'iced-up 'ere in the mornin we shan't see another boat for weeks.'

The next day we made slow progress, breakin a passageway

through the h'ice, and shaftin away the floes from the lock gates. In the locks there's only h'inches to spare at the best of times, if you gets wedged down by h'ice the water can come pourin in over the deck of yer boat and drownd yer.

The next day we shafted along to Long Itchinton Smoke-works [*cement works*]. The h'ice was gettin thicker by the day. In the wartime the constant traffic of boats kep the h'ice breakin. After the war there wasn't half the traffic on the Cut that there used to be but, thank God! when we got on to the main at Napton the h'iceboat was still workin and we found our passage way cleared, one boat wide, all the way to Hillmorton. *There* was Ada with the 'Hood' and the 'Grenville'.

'Yer a filmstar, Ada! Yer in the *Daily Mirror*!'

Poor Ada! She didn't feel like a filmstar. She were expectin her sixth, and their new 'Hood' had been playin oop good-n-proper. It had been built just that bit too sharp in the bows and kep ridin oop on the h'ice and priddled her timbers [*torn, holed*]. The Lapworth boys, they was Number Ones, drawrin coal from Nuneaton to Dickinsons' papermills, tied the 'Hood' and the 'Grenville' to their boats with short snubbers, and the six of us, all empty, chugged along in convoy, through a whirlin blizzard, knowin we shouldn't meet nobody. Everybody would be strovin, like us, to get to Sutton Stop before the worst of the winter set in.

Snow, snow, and more snow. Every night at Sutton Stop the boats was buried, every morn we dug ourselves out. The snow was so deep we walked straight on to it from the top of the boat. The h'ice was so thick that every day we could stand on it to break it from all round the hull. Night was as light as day because of the snow. The dazzlin white made yer eyes ache. Moy-chap went to work on the Coventry h'ice-breaker to keep the Cut open from the Coventry coalery to the Coventry Light. They had a team of nine 'orses, with a man to urge each 'orse. Moy-chap growed quite fond of his 'orse, he always did like workin with the 'orse. They had about twelve more chaps on the bar of the breaker, to rock the boat from side to side, crackin the h'ice out to the banks.

The poor dooks had a time of it. Every day I poured boilin water on the h'ice to melt them a patch of water. They skidded and skated on the h'ice, much to our Jinny's delight, and swum round and round, takin it in shifts to keep the patch of water open. Some got

very cheeky, waddlin along the plank and knockin with their beaks
on the cabin doors for food. The birds were hungry too but it didn't
do to leave food around because it drawed the rats. Moy-chap had
to keep his 'catty' on the go to keep the rats down and the rabbits
in the pot.

We had some good old 'get-togethers' in the 'Grey'ound'. Rose
Skinner's brother, George Brummidge, were a dab-'and at the
squeezebox, and several of the chaps could do the tap-dancin on
the stone flags in their cleated boots. On the boats in my day the
Skinners and the Humphries was best-known for their dancin. The
marster-chappy of all for playin, dancin, *and* singin were Alf Own
Senior. He could play the squeezebox, and dance and sing, all at
the same time. He had a clear true whistle too, and a rattle of
wooden bobbins, 'Shake them bobbins!' he used to sing. It was a
song the old boat-chaps used to sing to make their 'orses get a move
on. Old Alf were in his house at Banbury that winter of '47 and
were soon to give oop 'is 'orses for ever.

Joe Skinner could sing pleasant when he were young. Joe and
Rose was tied-oop in the 'Friendship' outside their cottage at Sutton
Stop all that winter of '47. They kep their chattels, tin bath, old
bike, wot-av-yer in the cottage and still lived in the 'Friendship'. I
didn't blame 'em, their cabin were lovely inside. Since Sephtons
had built it they'd had it docked and decked [*decorated*] several
times. Herbert Tooley at Banbury done it the last.—Should of seed
her food cupboard door! He done it a treat, full-blowed roses,
turriffed castle, flags a-flyin, standin proud above flowin waters.

[191]

Rose had a cumulated wireless lodged on a shelf in the cubby-
'ole in front of her monkey-'ole at the end of their sidebed. Many a
time that winter I took our Jinny along to see Rose. Rose loved
children. She had none of her own, she envied me no end. She'd
twiddle the knob to see if she could find 'that children's chap wot
lived on the wireless' [*Uncle Mac of Children's Hour*] for Jinny.
She wasn't even two—no idea where his voice comed from, but
she'd sit there, propped between our coats on the sidebed, little
legs straight out, *listenin*, eyes as round as port-'oles.

The Littlemores was tied-oop next to us. Jinny loved their Rose
and Sylvie. They was big enough now to go to school. The ash-
road from Sutton Stop had been cleared and all the boat-children
used to walk along together to Foxford School, Longford. It was
quite a long trek but they was used to it. They was gived a good
hot dinner at the school. Our Jinny used to throw a tantrum to see
'em all goin orf to school without her. Moy-chap had fixed oop two
special eye-'ooks on the wall behind the sidebed so I could harness
her in the cabin until they'd gone. Then she'd be perfectly content
to be harnessed on the cabin roof. She were like most boat-
children, very hardy, never seemed to feel the cold. It could be
quite warm for her with her back to the warm chimney and her
little legs covered in coats. She had a grandstand view of all wot
was goin on, the men shovellin the snow out of their holds, the
women cleanin their 'atches, the vegetable-chap comin along the
ash-road with his pony and cart. He was married to one of Rose
Skinner's nieces in Coventry and did a roarin trade at the beginnin
of the h'ice-oop, sellin fresh vegetables to the boat people. There
was quite a throng of us tied-oop there at the beginnin of the snow
but as the idle weeks turned to months, no end of families quit the
boats for ever. They moved in with relations on the bank, found
jobs in the towns, then rented a room of their own, and at last got
their names down on the Council list for a pre-fab [*prefabricated
house*].

Our Lizer was lucky enough to get some outwork. One of the
'igh-oops wot Nurse Cornflake had brought to see the work on our
baby clothes wot me and Lizer had made when our Jinny was born,
owned a posh shop, ladies' underwear. She left a box of sewin work
at Mrs Nelson's shop agen the 'Grey'ound' each week for our Lizer
to broider. It was the same over and over, fancy petticuts. Our

Lizer loved it. She got that quick at it that by the end of that winter she were earnin over thirty bob a week.

Even the longest winter has to end some time. One night at the end of March it rained and it blowed all night long. In the mornin all the snow and h'ice had gone. There was *so much* water after all that snow all the boats was adrift. We was lifted right oop, with our iron moorin rings as well. Some of the bridge-'oles was that low on the water you just had to steer for the 'ole and 'ope for the best. It made for fast travellin! And no end of 'debriss', broken branches, chicken-coops, wot-av-yer pilin oop against the bridges and the lock gates. At Lower Heyford on the South h'Oxford the Cut was as fast and muddy as a river because all the paddles at the locks were drawn. You could hear the water roarin through the bridges. It were far too dangerous to attempt to get down to Wolvercote. We had to stop moored at the 'Pigeons' for some time, until at last the waters were quiet and the Cut went down enough to see the tops of the tall rads all along where the towpath should be.

Mr and Mrs Wickson were still at the 'Pigeons'. Their little grandson, Roger, Wilfred's lad, were about seven by then. I always used to look out for him, he were just like his Dad used to be. He loved the boats and the boat people. When he was very young he longed to be a lengthsman. Mr 'Azel were the lengthsman along that stretch in them days. He always had his dinner in a knapsack and walked with a limp. Roger looked oop to Mr 'Azel. He was goin to be a lengthsman just like Mr 'Azel when he growed oop. He got his 'Auntie-Gran', as he called her, to pack *his* dinner in a knapsack, and he worked hard to limp zackly like Mr 'Azel, he thought it went with the job. He'd of made a toppin lengthsman. By the time he were seven he were that keen-eyed a youngster he'd tell just by the build-oop of water spillin over the lock and into the weir-'ole at 'Pigeons' that *somebody* were emptyin the lock a good mile away at Northbrook. He knowed all the different boats and the sound of their hinjins. He'd be at the lockside ready to greet us.

'I knew it was you coming, Mr Ramlin,' he'd say to Moy-chap as he 'helped' us with the lock, 'I could tell it was your Petter. I could hear it across the fields as you came under Old Brighton Bridge. I knew it would be "Britannia" coming round the bend.'

He'd ask his Auntie-Gran if he could ride along with us to the next lock. I loved to watch him steerin, standin on the counter beside Moy-chap. It seemed no time at all since his Dad, Wilfred, was his age, standin on the stool in the 'atches steerin the 'orseboat. Already our Jinny, though she was only two, loved to sit on the cabin top holdin the end of the butty-tiller 'helpin' me or her Aunty Lizer to do the steerin. In no time at all *she'd* be standin on the stool in the 'atches steerin all by herself. Me and Moy-chap were goin to make the most of every mite of our Jinny's growin-oop. She were our little marvel. Nobody was ever goin to creep *her* away from us.

Spare h'Admirals

AFTER the snows of '47 we had a blazin hot summer.

That was the year we was shocked by the clutter of 'bandoomed boats on the different Cuts. All them boats wot belonged to the railways with their big railway letters blazoned on their sides, all them Fellas Morton pairs, moored idle, half sunk by the weight of water and roobish in their holds. There was rumours that 'Fellas Morton' was 'goin under', that the steam trains was goin 'lectric, that the railway and canal companies was selling out to the Government.

We was beginnin to feel spare h'admirals, as if the Cut were dyin orf. Even the great trees we'd knowed from the Cut as eye-catchers all our lives was dyin orf, killed by the starvin rabbits wot had nibbled all round their barks on the high snow level of '47. Many of the old boatin families was quittin the Cut, the Beauchamps, the Wilsons, the Coleses, the Wards. Susan Ward had married David 'Ambridge by then and gorn to live on the bank at Branston. Rose Ward had becomed Rose Whitlock and Laura Carter had becomed 'Aunt' Laura and was helpin Rose and her husband, Bill Whitlock, with their boats and their first baby. They was still workin for Barlows, the Limited then.

Soon after '47 all the rumours came true. The Cut was turned over to the nation and becomed British Waterways. They done the same with the railways and the docks and the coalmines. Nobody was bothered about us, we was allowed to carry on workin for Essy in our own little tin-pot way with our 'roses-n-castles'; but all the poor old Fellas Morton boats had to become 'yeller perils' [*painted in the plain regulation yellow and blue livery of the nationalized fleet*].

We was lucky that the 'Britannia' and the 'Percy Veruns' was still fitted with side-clawths. This meant we could still pick oop all sort of backloads wot needed sheetin-oop instead of relyin only on coal and returnin empty each trip to the coalfields. Our old 'flats' [*tarpaulins*] were wore-out but in them days you could hire topsheets like the farmers hired their sacks. There was places along the Cut where they could be picked oop and returned. One of these places was agen Fenny Stratford, and that's where we first came upon the Fieldins [*Major and Mrs Fielding*].

They was a Salvation Army couple wot lived on their boat the 'Salvo'. They lived in the cabin and had converted the hold into a Sunday Schoolroom cum chapel. Major Fieldin played the squeeze-box and they learned the boat-children to sing little choruses and told them bible stories. Sometimes they tied-oop at other wharfs along the Grand Union but they was mostly tied-oop this side of Finny Lock agen the 'public' because the boat people done their shoppin there. The 'public' was a shop as well. Their name was Vaughan and they baked lovely fresh bread. There was another good shop servin the boat people on the other side of the lock, their name was Tarbox. Word would spread like wild-fire along the Cut wherever the 'Salvo' were in port and we'd try to moor alongside. We knowed our kiddies would be in for a happy evenin. Our Jinny *loved* them Fieldins, even when she were only three she'd sit and listen, good as gold, and join in all them choruses.

In the summer of '48 we came acraws the Schoolmaster [*H. R. Dunkley of Coventry*].

We didn't know he were a schoolmaster when we first seed him, we thought he were one of them 'fishal-snoopers' [*official boat inspectors*]. We often seed him on the bank of the Cut along the Coventry and the h'Oxford, always writin in his little black book, and we'd steer clear of 'im. It turns out that he were only boatspottin, collectin names and numbers and wot-av-yer because he was h'interested in the 'istry of the Cut.

That summer the Cut was low agen h'Oxford and we'd run into a scour-pud [*build-up of mud*]. We couldn't use the hinjin for fear of gettin deeper into the scour. 'Wot we needs is a n'orse!' Moy-chap sez, and we all laughs. Apart from Joe Skinner's old mule, Dolly, the 'orse had all but fizzled-out on the h'Oxford.

'*There*'s a n'orse, Dada!' Jinny shouts, pointin back from the cabin top.

Lo-an'-be-'old, comin along the Cut behind us in the far distance, there's this chap trudgin along the towpath with a n'orseboat. It was the Schoolmaster. He'd decided to try and see for his-self in his school 'olidays wot it must of been like to work a n'orseboat. Essy had hired to him the 'Lily of the Valley' and 'Old Bill', a boat'orse bought from a gypsy for ten pounds, and sent him to pick oop 22 ton of coal from the Griff to take to Morrell's Bewry wharf agen h'Oxford. He'd got his wife and two little kiddies aboard. She'd never steered in her life, but he thought she'd better steer while he coped with the 'orse. By the time he'd levered her orf the bank once or twice he swopped and let her lead the 'orse. At Bedderth Hill all the boats waitin to load at Newdigate was linin the Cut on both sides with their tillers oop in the air.

He knew she'd never cope with liftin the tow over all that lot.

'Throw me the tow!' he sez.

Old Bill, feelin the tow tooken orf, thinks it's the end of the trip and takes his-self orf towards the stables. *She* can't deal with the 'orse, *he* can't get orf the boat. He'd taken to givin a bookit o'coal to anybody as came to their rescue. By the time they'd got to Mr Thomas at the gaugin-lock at Banbury they was three ton down.

'Never mind,' sez Mr Thomas, 'we'll say those three inches were drying-out weight.'

We was in the middle of a drought but Mr Thomas were very h'understandin.

The other side of Banbury the Schoolmaster finds his-self—he didn't know 'ow—on board with his wife and nobody with the 'orse. He tries to put a plank down to the bank and nip acraws while Old Bill's grazin. The minute he sets foot on that plank Old Bill starts orf again and nearly yanks him in the Cut. He keeps doin this, grazin and yankin. No matter how stealthy the Schoolmaster sets

that plank down, Old Bill *knows*. Comin oop to Aynho there's a
'mug-n-a-maggit' [*fisherman*]. My Dad always called 'em that, he
reckoned there was a maggit on one end of the rod and a 'mug' on
the tuther. Oondreds of 'em was sittin all along the bank as far as
the h'eye could see, comed all the way from Birnigum. A 'contesty'
it was. They was always havin 'em at weekends. 'Arf of Birnigum is
a mug-n-a-maggit at weekends.

'Tap the horse, would you, Mate?' the Schoolmaster pleads to
each one. There's no way he can get to the bank his-self because of
the mud. Each 'taps-on' the 'orse until, at last, Alf and Lizzie Own
comes to the rescue with a muzzle to stop Old Bill from grazin. It
was quite a change for the Schoolmaster to come to *our* rescue. We
made friends. We was all goin to the same wharf.

'We'll see yer through to the finish', Moy-chap sez.

There was quite a rally of us at the Juxon Street wharf, us and
the Schoolmaster, the Ownses, the Littlemores, and Old Bertha
'Boshum', Rosie Beauchamp's Mother-in-lor, a little old widder-
lady in long black skirts and boatwoman's bonnet, wot still worked
the penny-ferry, pushin that raft out and pullin it back to the end
of her days.

The Schoolmaster's little girl was six the next day. 'Can they all
come to my birthday party, Daddy?'

'We're going to the theatre, dear. Tell you what! Let's *all* go to
the theatre. Have any of you ever been to the theatre?'

The Ownses had, but none of the rest of us.

"Ow much will it cost?' Moy-chap sez.

'I'll treat you.'

'No, thank you, Schoolmaster, we ent charity.'

'Which seats do you usually go in?' he asked Lizzie.

'The shillin's, right oop the top.'

We could all rise to that. We gave our shillins to the Schoolmaster
and followed him in a throng with Ada's baby and old Bertha in tow
between us. It were only a short step or so along to this posh
theatre. I can't remember much of wot we seed. 'Variety' it were
called. There was 'Charlie Coon', and a chap roller-skatin, twirlin
this doll in his teeth—at least, I *think* it were a doll, we was *that*
'igh oop! Best of all were them 'floosh-lavertries'. All in a row, they
was. *Lovely*!

From then on we always looked out for our friend the Schoolmaster. He helped no end of the last of the boat people. It was the Schoolmaster wot took me in his motor to sought out Suey's grave, and I laid some flowers there. I'd never been in a moty-car before. I'd been took in a 'red-crosser' when I had Hanoverian Sis, and I'd been on a tram, but I'd never been in a moty-car. It's funny how people wot lives on the bank gets sea-sick on a boat, and people wot lives on a boat get landsick on the bank. The whole world were going oop and down in this moty-car. I kep hangin out over the runnin board bein sick. The Schoolmaster were very kind. It wasn't until some time after that I found out he'd used no end of his precious petrol ration soughtin out our Suey's Pines address. I asked him to sought out our Moycle. He didn't think that was right.

'Michael is old enough to have sought for *you* by now, if he wanted.'

'They never wants yer once they has the schoolin', Moy-chap sez.

It was true. We knowed no end of boat-kiddies wot didn't want nothin more to do with the boats once they was schooled on the bank—didn't want nobody to know they was born on a boat. *Some* didn't even want nothin more to do with their Mum and Dad, 'shamed they couldn't read-n-rite.

By now our Jinny was three. We'd moved her out of our cabin into the butty with her Auntie Lizer. Moy-chap was always oop at the crack of dawn, primin the hinjin, startin oop, gettin 'em ahead. She always woke oop and wanted to be oop with her Dad. She stopped asleep longer in the butty.

As the years went by she was always askin us to learn her to read but none of us had the schoolin. We learned her everythin else, boatin, cleanin, crosherin. Her Auntie Lizer learned her simple broiderin. Whenever we tied-oop in Banbury she'd go orf to play with her little friend, Rosemary, wot lived at the 'Strugglers'. Rosemary's mother, Mrs Soden, had kep the 'Strugglers' goin all by herself while her husband was away, firefightin, in the war. She and Mrs Plester, the blacksmith's wife, were like Mrs Wickson, do anythin to help the boat people, read their letters, and let the boat-kiddies play with their own children on the bank. Mrs Soden had a n'oopstairs playroom where the kiddies could play while their Dads had a drink. Even when one rotten boatin family pinched all her sheets and Rosemary's clean clothes out of her airin cupboard durin the clothes rationin Mrs Soden still trusted us.

'They aren't *all* tarred with the same brush', she sez.

Her Rosemary could read well, and so could they Plesters, but they got fed oop with our Jinny pesterin 'em all the time to learn her to read, they wanted to play, they was only kiddies after all.

It was the same old problem, we was never tied-oop in one place long enough for her to go to school proper. There was still the barge school at Bulls Bridge—it had sprung a leak in '39 and they drawed it oop on to the bank and you went oop steps into it—and there was still the Mission at Brentford, where Mr Chapman had taken over from Mr Knight and were always good to us, but we hardly ever tied-oop down there after the war. We was workin the Grand Union less and less, it was mostly the 'yeller perils' workin on there, so we seed even less of the Fieldins at Finny. They Fieldins was only sposed to spread the Word-o'-God, they wasn't sposed to learn the children proper schoolin, but our Jinny loved them, she picked oop a lot from their texts and choruses, and it were better than nothin. Now we mostly tied-oop at Sutton Stop for the weekends where there was no Fieldins and the local schools was all shut.

It was the Schoolmaster, with George and Sonia Smith, wot wheedled Major and Mrs Fieldin away from Finny to the busy junction at Sutton Stop where boats orf the Grand Union, the Coventry, and the h'Oxford would tie-oop for the weekend and where they'd catch many more of the boat-children. There they not only had the 'Salvo' but was allowed to have the old Grand Union Toll'ut, wot had been closed down. They Fieldins was 'open all hours' to us boat families. They was a godsend with their bible-schoolin for the kiddies and their Joomble Sales. The boat-children always ranked *first* with the Fieldins, but sometimes, if there was room or joomble to spare, they'd allow the kiddies orf the bank to share. There was no end of kiddies in them Sutton Stop cottages along of Rose and Joe's in them days.

By the time she were eight, the year the Queen were coronationed, our Jinny knowed no end of choruses and texts and bible stories. Major Fieldin had a big fuzfelt board with cut-out felt pictures, Jesus and camels, Moses and wot-av-yer, and he'd 'picture' the story for the children as he told it. He'd ask the kiddies if any of them would like to put oop the pictures or letters as he told the story or said the texts. Our Jinny were that forward she done the pictures *and* told the story.

That year we lashed out on our first wireless, a cumulated from Tooley's for the Queen's Coronation. That wireless opened oop our world. It had pride of place in the cubby-'ole in front of the monkey-'ole at the foot of Jinny's bed in the 'Percy Veruns', with a posh polished brass chain linked acraws the front to prevention it from lurchin orf in the locks. That wireless was learnin us 'ow the other 'arf lived—in factries. We was hearin of women on the bank workin set-hours and bringin 'ome *fortunes*! We was hearin of 'latch-key kids' comin 'ome to empty 'ouses. At least we had no 'latch-key kids' on the boats, but some of us was beginnin to feel very locked-out from the rest of yumanity.

That year there was only twenty-four of us boats left out of all them oondreds wot used to work the wharfs agen h'Oxford. All that old Worcester Street Basin was now built-orf, car parks, builded blocks, wot-av-yer. All them old boatin families wot used to live along those old wharfs in the olden days, the Bossoms, the Beesleys, the Beauchamps, the Lookits, the Skinners, the Coleses, the Tustins, Granny Statham, Mum and Aunt Polly, would turn in their graves to know all those old 'ouses between the 'Nag's Head' and Tawney's Alms'ouses was pulled down, all the old 'ouses of Fisher Row gone. Many of the old canal 'publics' was finished, even the Wicksons had gone, the 'Pigeons' was standin empty and deserted. Ada and Dick in the 'Hood' and the 'Grenville' had delivered the last load of coal to Wolvercote. From then on the mill were havin it by lorry. There were gatherin rumours that they was goin to close the South h'Oxford Cut altogether.

That summer nothin was cut back along the 'Tunnel' at Fenny Compton. It was all growed-in, brushin the tops of the boats from both sides. Us and the Littlemores was havin to hack our own way through the 'joongle', fishin oop no end of roobish, rolls of old wire nettin, tar-barrels, wot-av-yer. It was as if no boat had been along there for weeks.

'They ent bothered about us no more, Ada', I sez.

'Spare h'admirals, Rose, that's wot we is, ay? Spare h'admirals!'

''Bandoomed, Ada, that's wot, ay? 'Ban-DOOMED!'

'I reckon,' Dick sez, 'if they don't tend the Cut, us boats don't need to pay no tolls.'

"Arf the tellus [*toll houses*] is closed,' I sez; 'they've shut that big one at Coventry now.'

'I reckon,' Moy-chap sez, 'if the lorries keep pinchin our trade we should pay a toll only once a year as the lorries do.'

'Don't be so daft, Syer!', Lizer snaps, 'We don't make enough of a livin as it is, 'ow could Essy get enough money to pay all our tolls at once, ay?'

I could tell our Lizer were gettin 'fidgitty'. Moy-chap was clearin six pounds a week but me and Lizer wasn't bein paid nothin. Lizer was forty-five, still quick and full of hard work. In the winter of '47 when we was h'iced-oop all that time at Sutton Stop she'd enjoyed earnin her own money from her broiderin. In the winter of '49 we'd been h'iced-oop at Banbury and she'd gone to work earnin a good wage at the sack factry, 'Gospel Brown' [*Gopsall Brown*], opposite the Police Station. In them days sacks was made of good strong 'essun' and hired out to farms and ware'ouses. They had to be returned to the factry to be cleaned, mended, and made ready in boondles to be hired out again for the next crop. Lizer needed no schoolin to clean and mend. She could show-oop the best of 'em. The manager-chap wanted to keep her, send her away to their place at Bristol to be trained as a supervisor. There was even one farmer, bachelor-chap, wot brought sacks from all the farms around, wot wanted our Lizer to be his 'ousekeeper. She liked him enough, he seemed a daycent chap, but he was about ten years older. Our Jinny were only about four at the time and Lizer didn't want to leave us short-'anded.

Now Jinny was eight, oop with the lark in the mornin and pullin her weight like the rest of us, steerin the butty or workin with Lizer makin the locks. Best of all she loved bein with her Dad, watchin him cleanin the hinjin or clearin out the mud-box, trimmin the lamp, splicin the ropes, or makin new fenders. They was right butties, them two! She was chatterchops chatterchops just like our Suey used to be at her age. Questions, questions, and 'Can I 'ave a go now, Dad, ay? Go on, Dad, ay?'

'Chops-Almighty' he used to call her when he wanted her to shut oop. He loved her chatter really, revelled in sharin with his little daughter his 'know' of the Cut, his pride in ropework, and his love of flowers. The first thing she always did when we tied-oop at Sutton Stop was to take a bunch of towpath flowers to them

Fieldins. If they wasn't in the 'Ut she'd knock on the cabin of the 'Salvo' and they'd come oop full of smiles to see her again. Then she'd run along to the h'Office to see Mr Veaters and Miss Edwards.

Miss Edwards had been Mr Veaters' seckerty in that Traffic h'Office for years. She was a middle-aged lady, a farmer's daughter, lived with her father and mother. Like Mr Veaters she knowed all the boatmen and their families and tooked a n'interest in our welfare. She remembered all my children, mourned the loss of each one almost as much as we did, was delighted when we had our Jinny.

'She's blooming more and more like your Rose every time I see her,' she used to say; 'she'll be handling the butty all on her own before long!'

Lizer was beginning to feel more and more 'spare h'admiral'. The next time we tied-oop at Banbury she took the wireless cumulator along to be charged oop at Tooley's Dock. Herbert still did boat-jobs but he was havin to turn his skilled boat-craftin 'ands to more and more other jobs to make a livin, chargin cumulators, sharpenin tools, makin hinjin parts on his lathe for all sorts of machinery. Lizer turns into his workshop—*there* were the farmer-chap wot she'd met at the sack factry a few years back, havin a spindle made by Herbert for his old Fordson tractor. The 'ousekeeper job was still open, he sez, if so be as Lizer had the courage to tackle it. Lizer made oop her mind then and there to give it a try. She brought him back to the boats to meet us and gave him a cup of tea in the cabin of the 'Percy Veruns'.

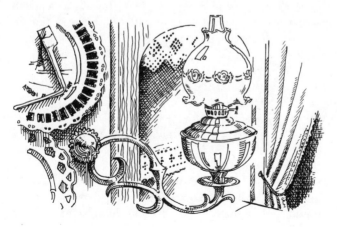

His eyes didn't arf sparkle at her little brass oil-lamp with its polished bracket, her polished brass knobs and all 'er h'ornamentals—said he hadn't seed so much brass and polish since his mother died. Syer quietly nipped orf to Herbert to find out if the farmer were all 'above-board'. He seemed such a daycent fella he woondered why he couldn't get no 'ousekeeper.

'No electricity', Herbert sez. 'They keep promising to bring the supply along there *one day*. Meanwhile, he's still waiting. He lives in a great big farmhouse a mile off the road. There's not many women today who will take on a big house like that, out in the wilds, with no electricity.'

Lizer was used to bein out in the wilds with no lectrics. Though we had the hinjin and could of charged a lectric headlamp we was content with our old parafeen headlamp and our lamps with the 'Little Princess' glass shades in the cabins.

Lizer decided to give him six weeks trial. Our Jinny were most oopset when Farmer Warren carted orf her Auntie Lizer. Within six days they was back with a little sandy puppy-dog, a special chum for our Jinny; and within six months they was married. By then 'Chummy', as she called him, were almost as big as our Jinny. He were her shadow by day and her guard by night. She never minded sleepin in the 'Percy Veruns' on her own as long as Chummy was with her. We always breasted-oop the two boats at night so her cabin lay alongside ourn. She learned him to 'Sit!' 'Fetch!' 'Bring!' and '*Stay!*'—in the hatches, or on the cabin top, or on the planks when she didn't want him to follow her along the towpath. He was so good-natured and well-be'aved the Fieldins allowed him into the Sunday School in the 'Ut with all the rest of the children.

The Fieldins kep on at me about Jinny's schoolin.

'She's a bright child. She *needs* to be with other children. She could do so well at school.'

I worried about it a lot but I couldn't see wot could be done about it. We was havin to turn round as fast as we could at the end of each trip in order to make a livin. Now Lizer was gone Jinny was a greater help than ever.

Mr Veaters and Miss Edwards kep on at me too.

'Couldn't she go and live on the farm with your married sister?'

I just looked at them. *Part with our Jinny!* Our little marvel!

Moy-chap would 'ave fifty fits if he knowed they'd even mentioned such a thing.

The Christmas of '54 we was tied-oop at Sutton Stop along with the Littlemores, the Dales, and the Atkinses. We all decorated our tillers and the tops of our cabins with evergreens. The Dales and the Atkinses we didn't know all that well, they was from down the North and had lots of kiddies. They was all playin with our Jinny and Chummy and all the rest of the children when the Dales suddenly shouted, 'The Matron! The Matron!' and scarpered with the Atkinses out of sight into their cabins. Just Ada's two youngest was left with our Jinny and Chummy on the bank. I seed a lady have a word with Ada and go into her cabin. Later she came along to see me.

It was Mrs Gunton. She was the Matron of a n'Ostel set oop by the Birnigum h'Eddyfeecation Committee for the boat-children. They was to live with her and attend the local school in Birnigum. She already had sixteen boat-children livin there. Three of the Dales was there, and the Atkinses was startin after Christmas. She wanted Mrs Littlemore's two youngest and our Jinny to come too.

'I've heard from the Fieldings what a bright child she is, and I *know* she hasn't been keeping up her school attendances. She'll be well looked after at the Hostel, and the local school is excellent. She'll be reading and writing, singing and swimming, and playing with lots of other children. You can come and visit her whenever you like and she'll be back here on the boats with you for the holidays. I know you'll be short-handed, but you mustn't think of yourselves, it's Jinny's good you must think about. She *must* have proper schooling. It's the law. I'll be at Mr Veaters' office tomorrow at two, come and see me about it.'

'Wot's Mrs Littlemore say?'

'She wants to talk it over with her husband, and I'm sure you will too.'

Talk about SONG-n-DANCE! Talk about BLUE MURDERS!

'Our Jinny is *not* goin into a n'OME!'

'T'ent a n'ome! It's a n'OSTEL!'

'Same thing. Boondled orf with a "Matron" like a n'orphanite. She's got a good 'ome 'ere!' She don't need no n'OSTEL!'

'It's the lor. She needs *schoolin*!'

[205]

'There's more to life than schoolin. *I've* managed. *You've* managed. She's as good a boat'and at nine as Rose was at fourteen. She'll make a toppin boatwoman, will our Jinny.'

'I don't want 'er bein a boatwoman, Syer, fetchin and carryin coals for other folk all 'er loife. 'Sides, there ent gonna be the work much longer. Now the petrol rationin's finished the lorries will be creepin our trade away more than ever. There ent gonna be the same need for coals neither. Accordin to that "wireless-chappie" they ent gonna let yer smoke the air with coal and smuts for much longer, the trains is bein lectrocuted, and the Lectric Lights are changin over to h'oil and new-clear h'energy.'

'That's roight! Blowin 'emselves oop! The lorries may be creepin away our trade but *nobody's* gonna creep away our Jinny!'

The day we took her to the Ostel I went with her to say goodbye to the Fieldins. They was lookin after Chummy for the day while we was gone. Jinny were heartbroken at havin to leave Chummy.

Mrs Fieldin kissed Jinny, 'Don't forget to say your prayers, Jinny.'

Mr Fieldin gave her a pretty text and asked her to read it to him. Jinny knowed it by 'eart. 'God is our hope and strength, a very present help in trouble.' They promised her that when she could *really* read, 'a whole chapter, all by yourself', they'd give her a n'Oly Bible for her very own.

Essy had come down special to say goodbye to 'his' boat-children. He was in the h'Office with Miss Edwards and Mr Veaters. Mr Veaters knowed the Ostel. He said he'd be lookin in from time to time, 'So make sure you're behaving, Jinny. I shall want to tell your Mum and Dad how well you're gettin on.'

'Where's Syer?', Essy wanted to know.

'Still sulkin,' I sez, 'but he's comin with us.'

The Schoolmaster had been down to see us specially the day before. He knowed Mr Conduct, Jinny's headmaster, 'So I shall soon know how hard you are working, Jinny.' He'd given me some special pills to take so we shouldn't be sick on the bus. It was the biggest trip we'd ever had to find all by ourselves on the bank; we'd learned it by 'eart, 'bus to Coventry, train to Birnigum, bus to Six Ways, walk to Ostel'. We managed it with Jinny cryin and Moy-chap not sayin a word.

Ada's little girls were already there. She and Dick had taken them earlier so they could stop orf in Coventry on the way back and see her sister, Sarah. The Matron showed us Jinny's bed.— Seemed like oondreds of beds in this big bare room. No castles, no roses, no pretty h'ornamentals. Moy-chap stood lost, starin out of the window. Nothin but 'ouses, fronts and backs. Suddenly his face lit oop.

'Look, Jinny! There's the Cut!'

Sure enough, in the distance, a narrer-boat glidin between the roof-tops. The Matron told us it were the Birnigum–Tammerth Cut. 'So you see, Mr Rampling, your little girl isn't so far away from home after all.'

That night Chummy began to howl in Jinny's empty cabin. I brought him in with us. Syer began to cry, terrible deep sobs, on and on. I drawed him close, and we cried each other to sleep.

On the Bank

ESSY put us on the easiest Cut of all, the Moira [*Ashby Canal*].

He knowed I'd find it hard-goin bein Best-Mate with Moy-chap down in the dumps, no Jinny, two boats to keep clean and the locks to work. I had only the two shallow locks, at Marston where you turns sharp left on to the Coventry, and at Sutton Stop where you draws through on to the h'Oxford. We drawed coals regler from Measham to Coventry Lectric Light [*see map, p. 224*].

I 'ad it easy, travellin empty to Measham on short snubbers, Moy-chap done the steerin on the moty and the butty follered of itself. I could get on with my cabin chores, until we came to the low bridges agen Measham. It were nearly all spent mines oop there and the bridges was sinkin too low to get yer boats under when you was empty. We had to put the planks out across to the bank and load oop with empty barrels and bricks wot was always left there for the purpose. We'd need as many as eight of these big barrels and armfuls of bricks before we was weighted down low enough in the water to get under the bridge. Once we was through the bridge-'ole it was out with the planks again and take 'em all back to where we found 'em, ready for the next time. It was all planks-n-snubbers oop the Moira. It was built as a broad Cut but the sides had so silted oop you could only travel single and could hardly ever tie-oop close to the bank. The bridges beyond Measham was too far sunk for boats to get any further, and the Cut beyond had died right orf.

In my young days, workin with my Dad or Granny Statham, we used to get right oop to the top of the Moira to a brickyard. There was big kilns where they baked bricks and clay drainage pipes. We carried loads of these pipes, all packed in straw, ploddin with the 'orse all the way down to different builders' wharfs all along the Grand Junction and along the h'Oxford. In them days the Moira Coalery had about six pairs of its own boats. Nearly all Rosie Beauchamp's family, the Coleses, worked for the Moira. Jack

Skinner's mother, Ada Monk as was, and her husband worked for the Moira for a time too. It was all best 'ousecoal and 'orseboats, plod, plod, all down the Moira, the Coventry, the h'Oxford, and out on to the Thames down to Readin or the Kensit [*Kennet and Avon Canal*]. Quite a trip, specially in winter when the rivers was often in flood.

There was only the one tunnel on the Moira, the Snares'un [*Snarestone*]. It was about as long as the Noble [*Newbold*] but it had no towpaths. In the old days I used to walk Dad's old mule, Ilda, over the top. The sides were too close, too sunk to leg the boat through; and the roof were too close to use yer shaft proper. You had to keep yer shaft slantin and be content with short prods along the bottom. In '55, of course, we had the hinjin.

In '55 it used to take me and Moy-chap the best part of a day to get from the Lectric Light oop to Measham. We didn't go right into the town, we stopped about a mile before, where they brought the coals by truck to the bank. We'd tie-oop there for the night and ave a n'ot meal. Through the day we had only cups of tea, on the go, but all day long my bit o' meat and potterbs would be cookin nice and slow on my range. You could only cook like that when you 'adn't many locks and when you wasn't bein loaded or unloaded, not just because of the dust but because it was dangerous havin 'ot pots on the go with yer boat bein boomped and bounced about. We'd get everythin ready for the mornin and turn in as early as we could, the men would be there on piecework to load us at first light. The coals would be 'shooted' from the trucks into the boats. Moy-hoy! Wot a dust over everythin! But, at least we didn't 'ave to load it ourselves. Moy-chap had only to trim each boat then we'd shaft along to Measham Oylit [*eyelet? islet?*] where there was a n'old-fashion' pump and we could use as much water as we liked, to damp down the dusty load, mop orf the paintwork, fill the water cans and 'ave a good wash—I do *love* a good wash!

The journey back would take all our 'cons 'nd trations', with the butty on a long snubber and each responsible for steerin our own laden craft along the narrow middle channel still deep enough to take us. Without a break—no locks to work—and no Jinny to relief us it meant a long day's standin on the one spot for both of us. No wonder so many of us suffered from the varicussed vains as we got older.

'Ow we missed our little Chatterchops! Lonely and dezlit the Moira was with just the two of us, nothin but that old 'petter-petter' to break the silence of the long snubber between us, and the big country estates stretchin away, away, on either side. All we ever seed were gamekeepers and pheasants. We done well for the pot, but we had to watch out where we let Chummy orf the plank and back on again.

We'd keep goin till dark and stop the hinjin where we felt like it, usually about half-way, agen Stoke Goldin. We'd 'ave a wash and a bite to eat, and drop into bed. We never bothered to tie-oop, just drifted. Nobody could get to us from the bank unless they swimmed, and we knowed no other craft would be comin past, not like the Grand Union, with other boats always breathin-oop behind yer.

We never drifted far, there wasn't much movement of water with the Moira bein all on the one level. The one shallow lock at Marston Junction was needed only because with so many miles on the level, all along to Measham on the Moira, all along the Coventry to Atherstone, and all along the other way to Sutton Stop, the *wind* sometimes 'drawed' the surface water from one Cut to the tuther. Sometimes you hardly needed that lock at Marston, you could just swing the gates without touchin the paddles to lengthen 'em, it just depended on the wind. Wind was always a menace, blowin the coaldust from the load back into yer face, stingin yer eyes and coatin yer cabin-top. No matter how much we dampened the load before we started we often met the wind comin back. If it blowed from behind, that could be quite a help, sendin yer along and sweepin away the surface water from yer bows.

It took us about two days to travel back. Though there was hardly any traffic on the Moira you had to travel slow because it was so shallow. As soon as you turned on to the Coventry you was back in the traffic. Even in the dyin '50's there was still quite a throng along there at times, Severn-and-Canal boats tradin with goods and timber to the ware'ouses and timberyards on the Coventry Arm; boats from down Manchester way tradin to Courtaulds; boats from the stone quarries, the coalfields, the Grendon, the Badgeley, to the Lectric Light. That Lectric Light gobbled oop no end of coal from the different pits along the Coventry. We sometimes broke our regler Measham run with a trip oop to the Grendon. Though

there was eleven locks oop there they was always kep well-oiled
and looked after and there was usually plenty of crews passin
through to lend me a n'and.

Every Friday we'd call into Mr Veaters' h'office at Sutton Stop to
'ave the news of our Jinny. The Matron wrote every week—she
knowed how 'down' Moy-chap was—and Miss Edwards would read
it to us. Poor Jinny! She spent those first few weeks catchin one
plague after another.

'I'm sorry to tell you that Jinny has measles, but she's all right.'

'I'm sorry to tell you that Jinny has mumps, but she's all right.'

All the new boat-kiddies was bein knocked back to the Sickroom
like ninepins. Mixin with all these other kiddies on the bank for the
first time in their lives they was comin oop against everythin at
once. We never got to see her once durin that first term. It was
chicken-spots at the last. Our Jinny had it real bad, worse than the
Matron had ever knowed a child to have it. Had we had it, she
wanted to know, otherwise we wasn't to come, 'it can be dangerous
for the elderly'. *Elderly*! Me and Syer looked at each other. We was
both grey and weatherbeat'. I spose as parents we was 'gettin-on'. I
was fifty-five and Syer was close on fifty-eight. *Had* we had the
chicken-spots? There was nobody alive to ask and, of course, no
recordins. I mind our Rose hatchin it that time we took our Suey
for that one never-to-be-forgotted day at the Seaside, but none of
the rest of us catched it.

By the time the Easter 'Olidays arrived Jinny was well again and
we went to fetch her back. She were *that* thin and lanky! And all
'er pretty 'air cut orf! They'd had to cut it orf to bathe her chicken-
spots.

The Matron kissed her goodbye. 'See you next term, Jinny!'

'Not if I can 'elp it, Matron', Moy-chap sez.

The Matron laughed. 'See what Jinny has to say when the time
comes. I think you'll find she will want to come back.'

She did, of course. She kep catchin her head on the cabin slide
and wantin to push 'the walls' of the boat out.

'It's all so much *smaller* than I remembered it, Mum. I can't
think how you and Dad manage. And I miss my *school*.' She was so
proud of her school. 'Birches Green my school is, Dad.'

'Seems to me ye've hardly been to school!'

She'd certainly made the most of the rare days she'd spent there.

Everything was 'sooper', the lessons was 'sooper', the teachers was 'sooper', 'specially Mrs McNaughton, she's teaching me to read, and to do Scottish dancin. I've made so many friends, it's goin to be *sooper* goin back.'

'I knowed you wouldn't want us no more.'

'I *do* want yer, Dad. I love bein back with you and Mum—and Chummy, of course. I missed you all so much when I first went there. I cried every night. My bed's nice—never been on a bouncy bed before. I was scared stiff at first to set foot outside it, all that ROOM out there! A n'OOPSTAIRS and a DOWNSTAIRS! There's a bath with taps, and there's wot she calls MEALTIMES. That's when you all sits along these big tables and eats together. She makes yer sit oop and take yer elbows orf the table, and I'm not allowed to talk. *Not allowed to talk*, Dad! *Torture!*'

He laughed. It was the first time he had laughed for ages. Our Jinny could always make him laugh.

'Do yer loike 'er?'

'She's all right; a bit down on yer. She makes yer look after the younger ones, clean their shoes, see they empties their chamber pots. "Why should I look after 'em, Matron?" I sez. "Because you're *capable*, Jinny" she sez. Mind you, there's some real rough'uns there. A lot of 'em had nits. Me and the Littlemores never 'ad no—*any*—nits. She was kind when I was poorly. She's sooper on Sundays, lets us watch her television and plays the piano for us. I *love* singin. I've learned no end of songs.'

Jinny learned us to sing with her that Easter, travellin sometimes on the moty with her Dad, sometimes on the butty with me, and sometimes walkin with Chummy along the towpath. You could sing out as fearless as yer loike on the Moira, there was only the pheasants and the dooks to hear yer. It *was* lonely for her. We hardly seed another soul, let alone another child. We sometimes seed the Littlemores in passin. The children would be *that* h'excited to see each other again. The dogs would go mad too, our big Chummy and their little Trixie, runnin to-n-fro along the planks barkin at each other, while the kiddies would keep callin across to each other till we was out of earshot, arrangin to meet at Sutton Stop at the weekend.

We'd usually tie-oop at Sutton Stop for the weekend. The children would play while we did our shoppin and spruced oop the boats ready for gettin 'em ahead at crack of dawn on Monday. The Fieldins might 'ave one of their Joombles, and there'd always be Sunday School for the kiddies. It was about this time that we noticed there was gettin less and less of us and more and more 'go boaters', folk orf the bank wot liked to 'go boating' in pleasure boats.

By the summer 'olidays they told us our Jinny's readin had come on in leaps and bounds. She read her chapter to the Fieldins on her tenth birthday and they gived her the 'Oly Bible with a picture of them and the 'Salvo' inside. By then Essy was convertin one or two workin boats to pleasure boats at Glascote. Syer began gettin orders for tiddly-ropework, fenders, tipcats, wot-av-yer, and I began gettin orders for my crosher to deck-out swanky cabins. On the long stretches without locks I could sit on my cabin top in the sun doin my crosher and steerin the butty tiller with my bare feet. I could only steer lacky-daisycal like that when the butty was travellin empty, of course. Everybody on the wireless was singin 'Ramlin Rose' that summer, and I come oop to fame among the pleasure boaters on the Cut as 'the Ramlin Rose wot steers with her toes and makes the 'orses' earcaps'.

I had no idea then it were to be our last summer on the Cut.

We tied-oop at Banbury for our two weeks 'oliday as usual. We hardly seed our Jinny, she were orf every day with her friends on the bank. There was hardly any boat-children left to play with. Our Lizer turned oop for a cup of tea while her chap Dan'll were at the Banbury Cattle Market. She was very happy on the farm.

'You and Syer ought to be lookin out for a place on the bank too, Rose. My Dan'll reads the papers. He sez there's goin to be a battle over the Cut. It's not only the h'Oxford. They say there's not the money to keep the Cuts open for the few boats left carryin. You and Syer ought to get orf before yer trapped by the stop-planks for ever.'

I never sez nothin to Syer. I daren't think how he would take to livin on the bank. On the Cut, though he were no longer a Number One, he were looked-oop-to with respect as Captain Syer Ramlin of the 'Britannia' and the 'Percy Veruns', a marster boatman, like his Dad, and his Grandad, and his Great Grandad, way way back. On the bank he would be a nobody without schoolin. It had taken me a long time to pull him oop from the doomps after our Jinny went. I still dreaded the end of the summer 'olidays when we'd 'ave to face oop to takin her back to the Ostel all over again. He didn't eat for a week when we got back the last time. If we *did* go to live on the bank Jinny wouldn't need to go away from us.

Without the boats we had no 'ome, and no h'incomins. I started keepin a n'eye out for h'empty cottages along the Cut. There was no end of 'em then. They was lonely, cut-orf, but they nearly all had a bit of gardin. A bit of gardin might be the savin of Moy-chap. I kep askin Mr Veaters 'on the quoyet' to find out about these cottages. Each one were con-dem-nated and there wasn't the money to do it oop. I could of made a good 'ome of one of them old Comp'ny cottages. In the end they just condemnated to rack-n-ruin till nobody knowed they had ever been there.

Soon after Jinny went back to the Ostel Moy-chap went even deeper in the doomps when he heard that Essy were thinkin of sellin out to the Limited. I plooked oop courage, told Syer I thought it was time we faced oop to quittin the Cut, sellin the boats, and goin to live on the bank.

No song-n-dance. No blue murders. He were even too down for that. Just silence.

'It's the only way we can keep Jinny', I said at last.

''Ow can I keep 'er with nowhere to live and no money comin in?'

'Mr Oomphris, the funeral-man at Banbury, has offered us a cottage at a peppercorn rent.'

'Wot's wrong with it?'

'It's con-dem-nated. It's oop the top of Castle Street in a yard behind the "Three Pigeons". The Council wants to make a giant crossroads oop there but they can't decide whether to pull down the "Three Pigeons" or the "Three 'Orseshoes", so there's nothin Mr Oomphris can do about it. I can go daily to clean the "Crown 'Otel", and Lizer's Dan'll can get you a job on the Council ashcart.'

'I'm not bloody ash-cartin! I'm a marster-boatman. I'm stoppin on the Cut.'

'Then you'll have to work yer own locks, Syer, 'cos me and Jinny won't be there to work 'em for yer! I want "*orf*"! I've 'ad enough! I want to share our Jinny's growin-oop. I want to enjoy 'er progress. I know I shall miss the Cut no end. I shall miss the boats, but they're gettin past it, and we're gettin past it. *This is the only way we can keep our Jinny with us.*'

Essy sold the boats and gave us two oondred pounds. Herbert Tooley said it were a fair deal for the age of the boats. We needed no removals-van. All we had was my few precious treasures from the ticket draw and my h'ornamentals. We 'ad no furniture—all our 'furniture' was built into the boats—just the little painted stool old Mr Tooley had made for the 'Britannia' when we was first married. I gived Lizer Mum's other stool from the 'Percy Veruns'. Moy-chap went on the ash-cart, and it *were* a cart, the last Council 'orse-n-cart, collectin the dustbin roobish—it were only ashes and a few tins in them careful days—from all those little back-to-backs down the bottom of Banbury, and carryin it out into the country at Crouch 'Ill. When he wasn't cartin roobish he were allowed to cart clinker from Banbury gasworks for farmers and builders to bind with rubble for drainage and driveways. He wasn't all that 'appy, he felt he were looked down on, but he were at 'ome with the 'orse and he were out in the open air wot he was used to.

I worked at the 'Crown', mostly cleanin-oop after more-n-more people from the pleasure boats wot paid to 'ave the luxury of clean white towels and a pipin-'ot bath.

Jinny went from strength to strength at the Second'ry Modern.

Mr Oomphris' cottage weren't oop to much, stuck oop this backyard, but I whitewashed it right through, run oop some curtins from the Market, polished oop the range, and decked-out my h'ornamentals. Mr Oomphris were staggered wot a n'ome I'd made of it. One day a Miss Lismore from the Council called.

'My word! You *have* made the best of it! I shall certainly put you on to our Council housing list. Mr Humphris was right to recommend you. You deserve it.'

The Banbury Council was buildin new 'ouses out in the country at a place called Bretch 'Ill. We had one of the first.

The day we moved into our new Council 'ouse we was over the moon. For the first time in our lives we had a gardin, a little one at the front and a big one at the back. That gardin were a salvation for Moy-chap. In years to come he loved to sit in that little back kitchen, it weren't much more than a cabin, with the back door open, lettin in the song of the birds and the sight of his own-growed flowers and vegetables. My front room were even more of a cabin, with my ribbin-plates on the walls, my croshered chairbacks and arm-rests, and on the mantelpiece, my Mum's polished brass knobs from the Bedstid-'Ole, my Granny Fisher's polished brass candlesticks, and Granny Statham's little Cooke's winluss.

In the beginnin we had nothin but fields in front and allotments at the back but as more and more 'ouses went oop the fields vanished. We could of seed the 'ole of Banbury it if wasn't for the 'ouses in between.

When Jinny was fourteen she winned the Essy prize.
'Not "Essy", Mum, Es*say*.'
'No need to talk posh. Wot is it anyway?'
'It's the Mayor's Prize, awarded every year. All the schools in the area compete. I shall need a clean blouse, please, Mum; I've got to read it out in the Town Hall tonight in front of the Mayor and Corporation.'
We watched her gettin ready to go, sprucin 'erself oop h'extrer special. She were out to some class or another every night, gettin far too clever for the likes of us. She scooped oop her precious Essy.
'Wot's it all about then, gal?'
'Just a piece of writing, Dad.'
'Can me and yer Mother come?'
'I'd rather you didn't. It'll put me off if you're there. Bye!'

She were gone. Me and Moy-chap sat quoyet, 'bandoomed.

'She's 'shamed of us, Syer, that's wot!'

Moy-chap suddenly stands oop.

'We're goin, Rose, and that's that!'

'We can't, Syer, not if she's 'shamed of us, we can't show 'er oop.'

'We're 'er Father and Mother, Rose. Our gal's winned a n'Essy! Put on yer best gold oops. We're goin to be in that there Town 'All, whether she likes it or not!'

The Town 'All were all lit oop. We plodded oop the wide empty stairs, Syer in his deaf'nin boots, oop, oop til we reached the top. It were packed. We was late. The goins-on had started. They squeezed us in on the back row. We got some funny looks. We was the only ones wearin 'ats. Syer had 'is best bowler wot he'd wore for years, and I had my best felt-brimmed wot I got from the Fieldins' Joomble. We could just see the Mayor with his golden corporation round his neck. He sat down and everybody clapped as our Jinny walked oop straight and tall on to the platform. Her 'air shined, she'd got her clean blouse, she looked real ladyfied in her school uniform.

'Partners!' she announced.

Me and Syer looked at each other.

'Partnership indicates the full participation and equal sharing of duties, responsibilities, and interests between two people.'

Wot on earth were she on about?

'When we were asked to write on this theme my parents immediately sprang to mind.' *She were on about US!*

'When I tell you that they were canal boat people you will understand something of what I mean. Born and bred on the boats, it was natural for them to continue living in this manner after they married. Before the advent of the motor-boat their one boat was horse-drawn. This meant miles and miles of long hard treking for my father as he walked alongside the horse, guiding him along the towpaths, while my mother steered the boat and brought up a young family . . .'

It were *all* about us, our life on the Cut, 'ow it had been a true partnership, 'ow we was a n'important part of 'istry, and 'ow our Jinny were very, very proud of us.

We was very proud of 'er too.

[217]

The clappin and the cheerin went on and on. It was still goin on as me and Moy-chap quoyetly 'slipped our moorins' from the back row and sailed orf down the Town 'All steps into the moonlight-night.

APPENDIX

Jenny's Essay

Jinny's winning essay in the story is an excerpt from this essay
written in 1959 by a boatgirl, Jenny Littlemore, aged 14
years, after only four years of state education. Jenny was the
first boatwoman who contacted me in response to my appeal
for information in the *Banbury Guardian*

PARTNERS

*Partnership indicates the full participation and equal sharing of
duties, responsibilities, and interests between two people. When we
were asked to write on this theme my parents immediately sprang
to mind. When I tell you that they were canal boat people you will
understand something of what I mean.* Born and bred on the boats
it was natural for them to continue living in this manner after they
married. They worked for Samuel Barlow of Tamworth, Staffordshire, their main cargo being coal, loaded at collieries and carried
to various power stations and wharves all over the country. Before
the advent of the motor-boat their one boat was horse-drawn. This
meant miles and miles of long hard treking [*sic*] for my father as he
walked alongside the horse, guiding him along the towpaths, while
my mother steered the boat and brought up a young family. The
horse's needs had to be tended to, of course, and a suitable shelter
headed towards for each night. Stables were provided at certain
points on or near the canal side. My father has many tales to tell of
the various horses he worked with, and of their differing natures,
but each one became a member of the family and its needs had to
be met first and foremost. My father had his first motor-boat, the
'Hood', in about 1939. After gradually getting to know and understand this new acquisition, he became skilled at working with and
on his engine, a Petter, which occupied its own position at the far
end of the cabin and became his pride and joy and kept in gleaming
condition.

[219]

The motor-boat pulled the butty-boat and enabled my parents to transport nearly twice the amount of tonnage than they had been able to with only the one boat. The boats each measured seventy-two feet in length and held thirty tons and twenty-five tons of cargo respectively. They were paid by the tonnage per trip, their main routes taking them from Longford, Coventry, to Banbury and Oxford and from the coalpits in Measham, Burton on Trent, down to the Grand Union and the London area.

Between each trip they would head back to Sutton Stop, Coventry, where their salary and new orders awaited them in the little office on the canal side. They worked incredibly hard, rising early and not stopping till late evening, their working day consisting of sixteen to eighteen hours, and for one salary. My mother prepared meals while going along, peeling vegetables, the helm under one arm, able to leave it unattended to venture down to the cabin for only a few minutes, and only then on a straight section of canal. They did not stop to eat, but my father slowed down his boat to enable the butty boat to catch up with him so my mother could pass food over to him. During the quiet, less busy times of the day, my mother's hands would be busy, working on crochet or knitted garments or articles, producing beautiful pieces of work while steering the boat.

On reaching their destination the job of unloading fifty-five tons of coal had to be tackled, and my father would take up his large heavy shovel and begin this arduous task with the men employed at the stopping place, my mother often lending a hand also. But she had other important duties to attend at these times too. She had to take full advantage of this opportunity to buy fresh provisions at nearby shops, catch up on the laundry, to bake and to clean. There is no comparison with the ease in which we are able to wash linen today and the way in which my mother had to do it. She would roll a heavy wooden tub off the boat, along a plank, on to the towpath in which to pound the clothes in soapsuds with a wooden dolly. She would then boil them in a galvanized bath standing over a fire contained within a square of bricks kept specially for this purpose. After this she would rinse them in cold water and wring them out by hand before hanging them out along the length of the boats on lines attached to the masts. The washing was always snowy-white. This task along with the handling of wet ropes, working the locks and pulling the drawbridges down, and the constant outdoor life rendered my mother's hands hard and cracked, sometimes to the extent of bleeding, and they must have been extremely painful.

They worked in summers of blistering heat, and winters of freezing temperatures, sometimes getting frozen in ice until a thaw enabled them to continue their journey. During these times my father would have to seek temporary work on the land as they were not compensated for delays. Sundays would bring a little respite as some locks and drawbridges were locked for security reasons, and then they would have to stop and tie-up. My parents lived frugal lives, their needs and wants being simple and few, but they were proud folk and experts in their particular way of life, each complementing the other by support and strength in whatever hardships came their way.

In retrospect I can hardly believe that we lived in cabins about five feet high, eight feet long, and seven feet wide in such a well-ordered fashion; that my mother tended and cared for a family of six while doing such a gigantic job of work; that she meticulously tended to such menial tasks as the polishing of all the brassware that ornamented the boat, keeping the black-leaded range in both boats gleaming, and mopped and scrubbed the paintwork and wood continually.

We were rough but clean and healthy, fit and strong, secure in the knowledge that we had parents of the best kind on whom we could always depend; truly, in every sense of the word, partners.

Canal boat life is often referred to by writers as an idyllic existence, and romanticized by people who know no better. There was little romance in the lives of my parents or their contempories [sic], but they knew a freedom beyond compare, living side by side with nature, and to their own satisfaction. Canal boating today is pleasurable and leisurely with every modern convenience that would have made real boatmen gasp in disbelief. Canal navigation and its dedicated workers have made a real mark in the history of this nation, and, although we shall never see the like again, it is good that there are those who are passionately engaged in the restoration and retention of our canal system to ensure that this important part of our heritage is not lost for ever.

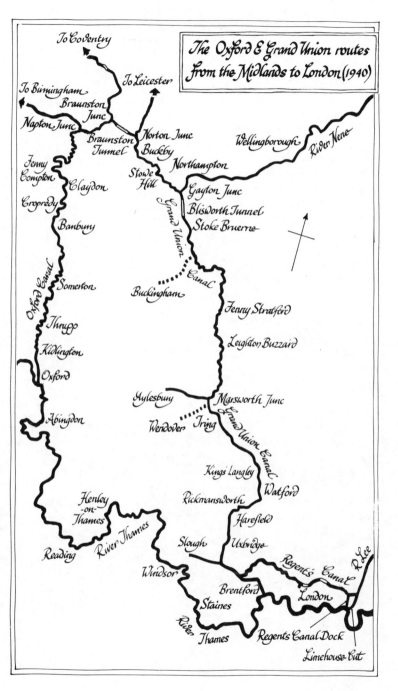

The Oxford & Grand Union routes from the Midlands to London (1940)

To Coventry

To Leicester

To Birmingham

Braunston Junc

Napton Junc

Braunston Tunnel

Norton Junc
Buckby

Wellingborough

River Nene

Jenny Compton

Claydon

Stowe Hill

Northampton

Cropredy

Gayton Junc

Banbury

Blisworth Tunnel

Stoke Bruerne

Grand Union Canal

Oxford Canal

Somerton

Buckingham

Fenny Stratford

Thrupp

Leighton Buzzard

Kidlington

Oxford

Aylesbury

Marsworth Junc

Abingdon

Wendover

Tring

Grand Union Canal

Kings Langley

Watford

Henley -on- Thames

Rickmansworth

Reading

River Thames

Harefield

Slough

Uxbridge

Regent's Canal

R. Lee

Windsor

London

Brentford

Staines

River Thames

Regents Canal Dock

Limehouse Cut

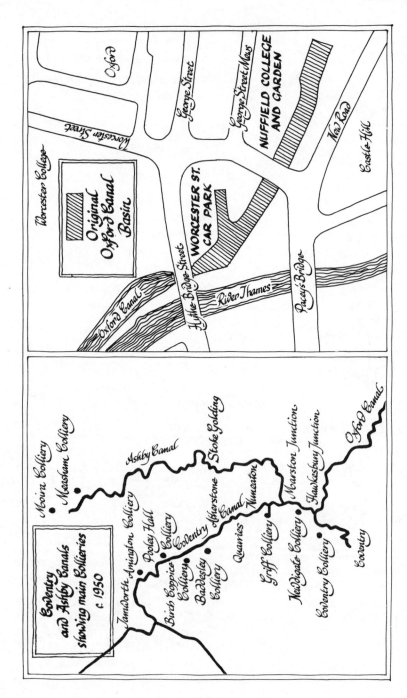

Top map labels:

Oxford

George Street

George Street Mews

NUFFIELD COLLEGE AND GARDEN

New Road

Castle Hill

Worcester Street

Worcester College

Original Oxford Canal Basin

WORCESTER ST. CAR PARK

Oxford Canal

Hythe Bridge Street

River Thames

Pacy's Bridge

Bottom map labels:

Coventry and Ashby Canals showing main Collieries c. 1950

Moira Colliery

Measham Colliery

Ashby Canal

Stoke Golding

Mowston Junction

Hawkesbury Junction

Oxford Canal

Tamworth

Amington Colliery

Pooley Hall

Coventry Colliery

Nuneaton

Atherstone

Coventry Canal

Birch Coppice Colliery

Baddesley Colliery

Quarries

Griff Colliery

Newdigate Colliery

Coventry Colliery

Coventry

[224]

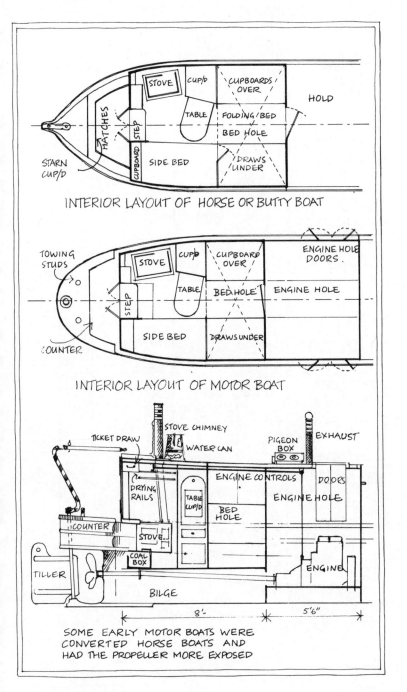

INTERIOR LAYOUT OF HORSE OR BUTTY BOAT

INTERIOR LAYOUT OF MOTOR BOAT

SOME EARLY MOTOR BOATS WERE
CONVERTED HORSE BOATS AND
HAD THE PROPELLER MORE EXPOSED

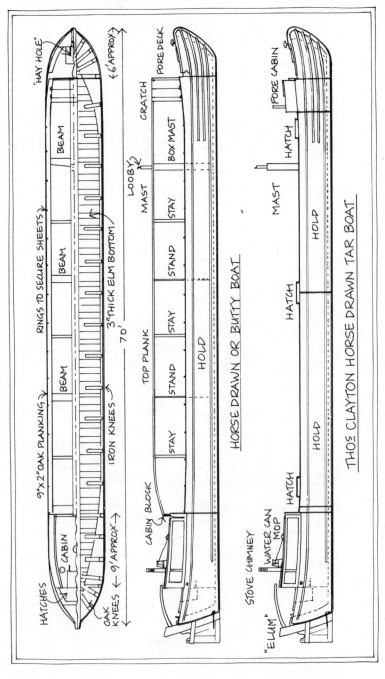

HATCHES

"HAY HOLE"

RINGS TO SECURE SHEETS

9"×2" OAK PLANKING

BEAM   BEAM   BEAM   BEAM

IRON KNEES

3" THICK ELM BOTTOM

70'

OAK KNEES   ←— 9' APPROX —→

CABIN

←6' APPROX→

CABIN BLOCK

TOP PLANK

HOLD

STAY   STAND   STAY   STAY   STAND   STAY   STAND   STAY   BOX MAST

MAST   LOOBY

CRATCH

FORE DECK

HORSE DRAWN OR BUTTY BOAT

STOVE CHIMNEY

"ELUM"   WATER CAN   MOP

HATCH

HOLD   HATCH   HOLD

MAST

HATCH   FORE CABIN

THOS CLAYTON HORSE DRAWN TAR BOAT

[226]

INDEX OF PLACE NAMES

Names in italic are the dialect form which appear in the text